HEROES OF SCIENCE

WHO CHANGED THE WORLD

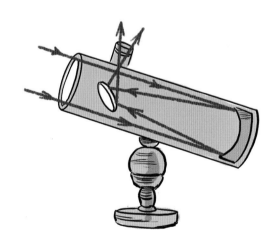

First edition for the United States and Canada published in 2019
by B.E.S. Publishing Co.

All inquiries should be addressed to:
B.E.S. Publishing Co.
250 Wireless Boulevard
Hauppauge, NY 11788
www.bes-publishing.com

ISBN: 978-1-4380-1200-1

Library of Congress Control No.: 2018959965

Conceived, designed, and produced by The Bright Press,
an imprint of The Quarto Group.
The Old Brewery, 6 Blundell Street,
London, N7 9BH, United Kingdom
T (0) 20 7700 6700 F (0) 20 7700 8066
www.QuartoKnows.com

Publisher: Mark Searle
Creative Director: James Evans
Managing Editor: Jacqui Sayers
Editor: Judith Chamberlain
Project Editor: Natalia Price-Cabrera
Art Director: Katherine Radcliffe
Design: Lyndsey Harwood and Geoff Borin

Date of Manufacture: December 2018
Manufactured by: Hung Hing Printing, Shenzhen, China

Printed in China

9 8 7 6 5 4 3 2 1

HEROES OF SCIENCE
WHO CHANGED THE WORLD

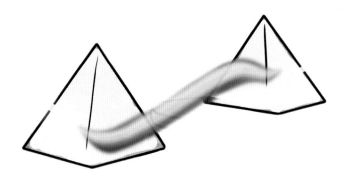

ILLUSTRATED BY DAVE SHEPHARD
CONSULTANT EDITOR EMILY SOHN

PUBLISHING

CONTENTS

ERATOSTHENES............................8
Greek (276–194BCE)

Eratosthenes was a great thinker and the first to estimate the size and tilt of the Earth. He realized that the Earth spins and he mapped out the equator and poles. Eratosthenes also helped put Earth into perspective within the scope of the universe.

NICOLAUS COPERNICUS...............20
Polish (1473–1543)

In Nicolaus' time, it was common knowledge that the Earth was the center of the solar system and that the sun and other planets moved around it. Nicolaus had a different explanation: the sun was at the center of it all. Only the moon orbited the Earth. His ideas were controversial but ultimately changed the way astronomers looked at the movement of objects in the sky.

ISAAC NEWTON 32
British (1643–1727)

Isaac made many contributions to the scientific revolution of his time. He realized that white light is made up of all the colors of the rainbow. And he used his understanding of light to make telescopes more powerful. In these ways and many others, he offered people new concepts for seeing the world.

EDWARD JENNER 44
British (1749–1823)

Edward created the world's first vaccine for a virus called smallpox. Before he did his research on viruses, smallpox killed many people. His work paved the way for the creation of many more vaccines. In 1980, thanks to Edward's early work, the world was declared free of smallpox.

CHARLES DARWIN 56
British (1809–1882)

During a five-year expedition, Charles spent more than a month on the Galapagos Islands. While there, he saw an amazing variety of life and developed new ideas about how animals survive and adapt. His theory, called evolution by natural selection, was a new way to explain life on Earth.

LOUIS PASTEUR 68
French (1822–1895)

Bacteria cause illnesses: this was one of Louis's major discoveries. He also figured out that bacteria can spoil beer, wine, and milk. His interest in germs helped him develop vaccines for some diseases, including tuberculosis and rabies. He also figured out that heat can kill bacteria in liquids: a process now known as pasteurization.

ALBERT EINSTEIN 80
German–American (1879–1955)

Often described as a genius, Albert made major breakthroughs in physics. Through thought experiments, he offered a new way of thinking about space, time, and space-time. One of his most important papers produced the famous equation $E = MC^2$. This equation led to major advances in understanding and using nuclear energy.

MARIE CURIE 92
Polish–French (1867–1934)

Marie won two Nobel Prizes for her work on radioactivity and her discovery of two new elements: radium and polonium. Her research led to powerful X-ray machines that could look inside the human body. The work may have contributed to her death, but it transformed the ability of doctors to diagnose and treat cancer.

WATSON, CRICK & FRANKLIN 104

American, British & British (1928–present, 1916–2004 & 1920–1958)

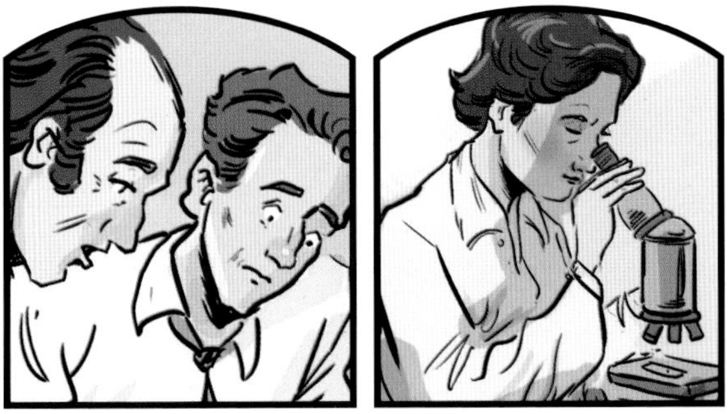

DNA is like the instruction manual for life, directing the creation of proteins that make us who we are. These three researchers figured out that DNA is shaped like a double helix, or a twisted ladder. Understanding its structure led to discoveries about how DNA works and how it sometimes makes mistakes—research that continues today.

VERA RUBIN 116

American (1928–2016)

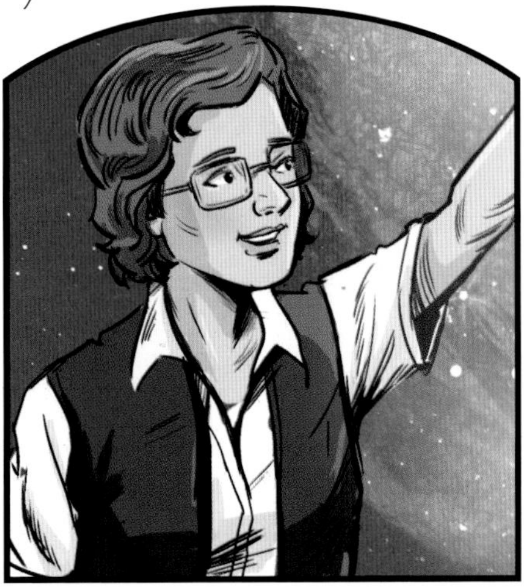

By carefully observing the movement of stars and galaxies in the night sky, Vera found evidence for an invisible force at work in the universe. Called dark matter, she reasoned that it makes up the majority of matter around us. Her work suggests that the remaining deepest mysteries of the universe lie not in, but between the stars.

ERATOSTHENES
(276–194 BCE)
THE WORLD MEASURER

ERATOSTHENES WAS CHIEF LIBRARIAN AT THE LIBRARY OF ALEXANDRIA IN EGYPT MORE THAN 2,000 YEARS AGO. THE LIBRARY CONTAINED OVER HALF A MILLION SCROLLS. EVERYTHING THAT HAD BEEN DISCOVERED BY THE GREEKS WAS AT HIS FINGERTIPS.

HE WAS PARTICULARLY INTERESTED IN THE STUDY OF THE EARTH. HE USED THE WORD "GEOGRAPHY" TO DESCRIBE THIS INTEREST. IN GREEK, "GEO" MEANS "EARTH," AND "GRAPHY" ORIGINALLY MEANT "PROCESS OF WRITING" AND WAS LATER USED TO MEAN "FIELD OF STUDY." IT IS NOT KNOWN FOR SURE WHETHER HE COINED THIS WORD OR ADOPTED IT.

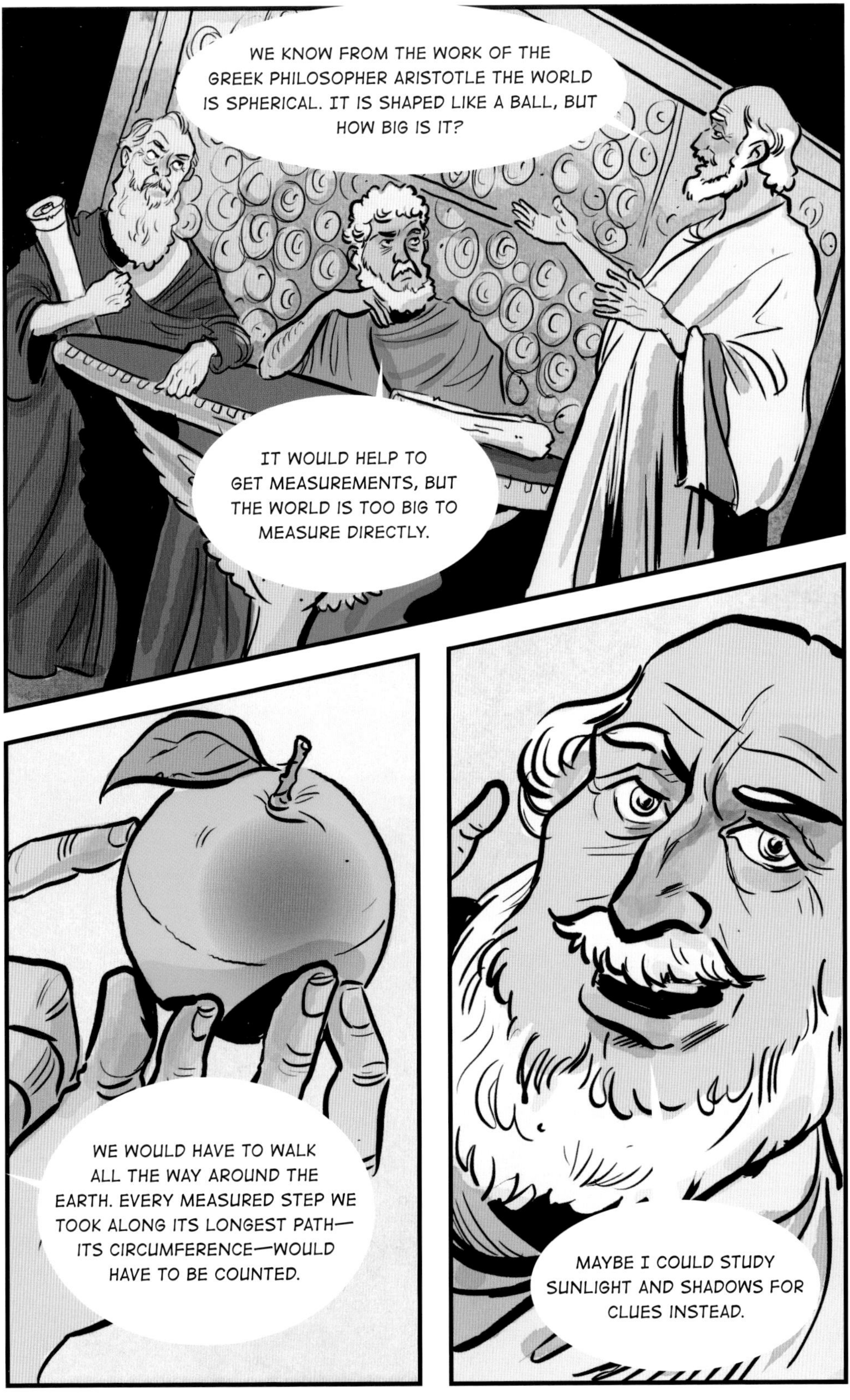
WE KNOW FROM THE WORK OF THE GREEK PHILOSOPHER ARISTOTLE THE WORLD IS SPHERICAL. IT IS SHAPED LIKE A BALL, BUT HOW BIG IS IT?
IT WOULD HELP TO GET MEASUREMENTS, BUT THE WORLD IS TOO BIG TO MEASURE DIRECTLY.
WE WOULD HAVE TO WALK ALL THE WAY AROUND THE EARTH. EVERY MEASURED STEP WE TOOK ALONG ITS LONGEST PATH—ITS CIRCUMFERENCE—WOULD HAVE TO BE COUNTED.
MAYBE I COULD STUDY SUNLIGHT AND SHADOWS FOR CLUES INSTEAD.

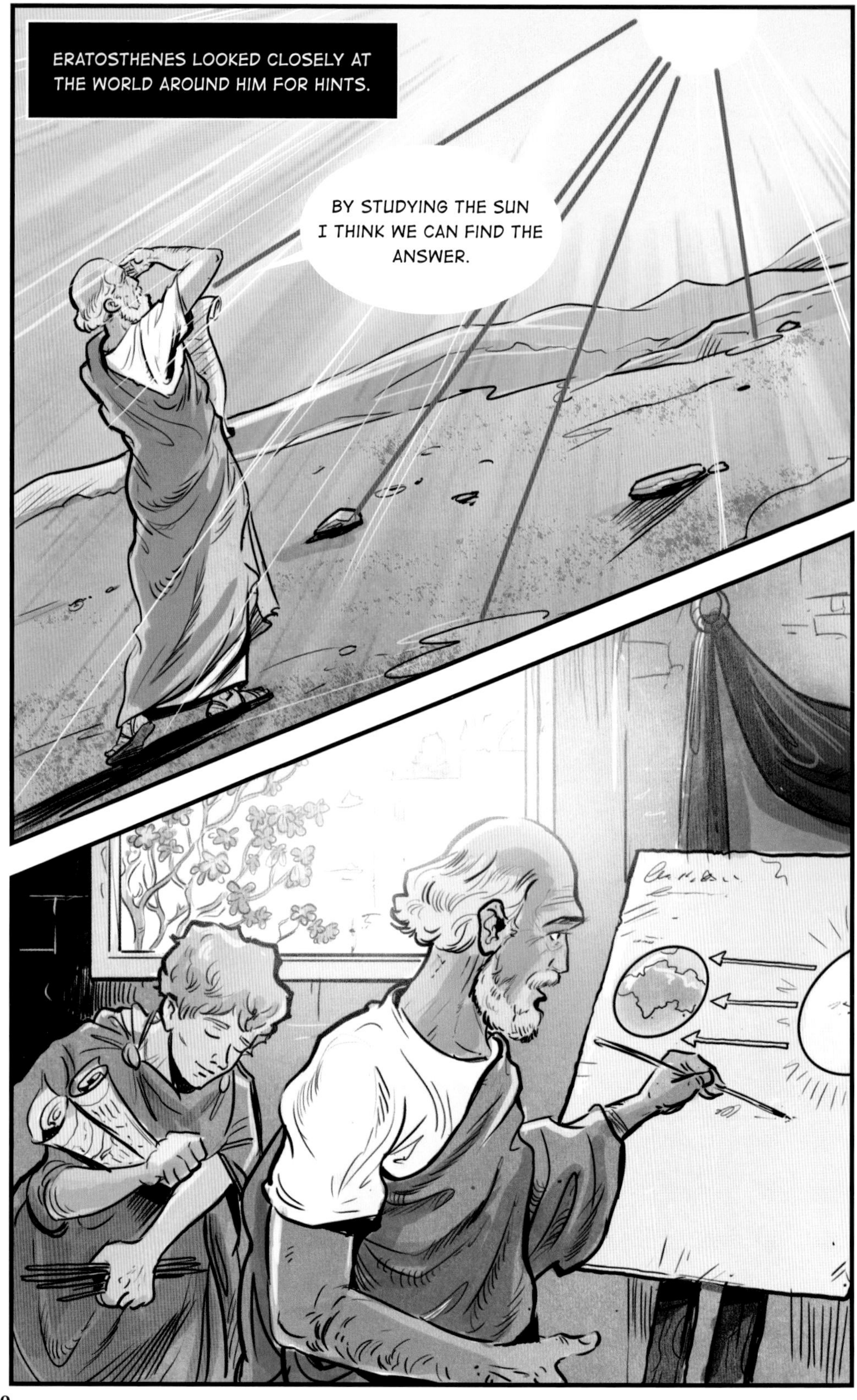
ERATOSTHENES LOOKED CLOSELY AT THE WORLD AROUND HIM FOR HINTS.
BY STUDYING THE SUN I THINK WE CAN FIND THE ANSWER.

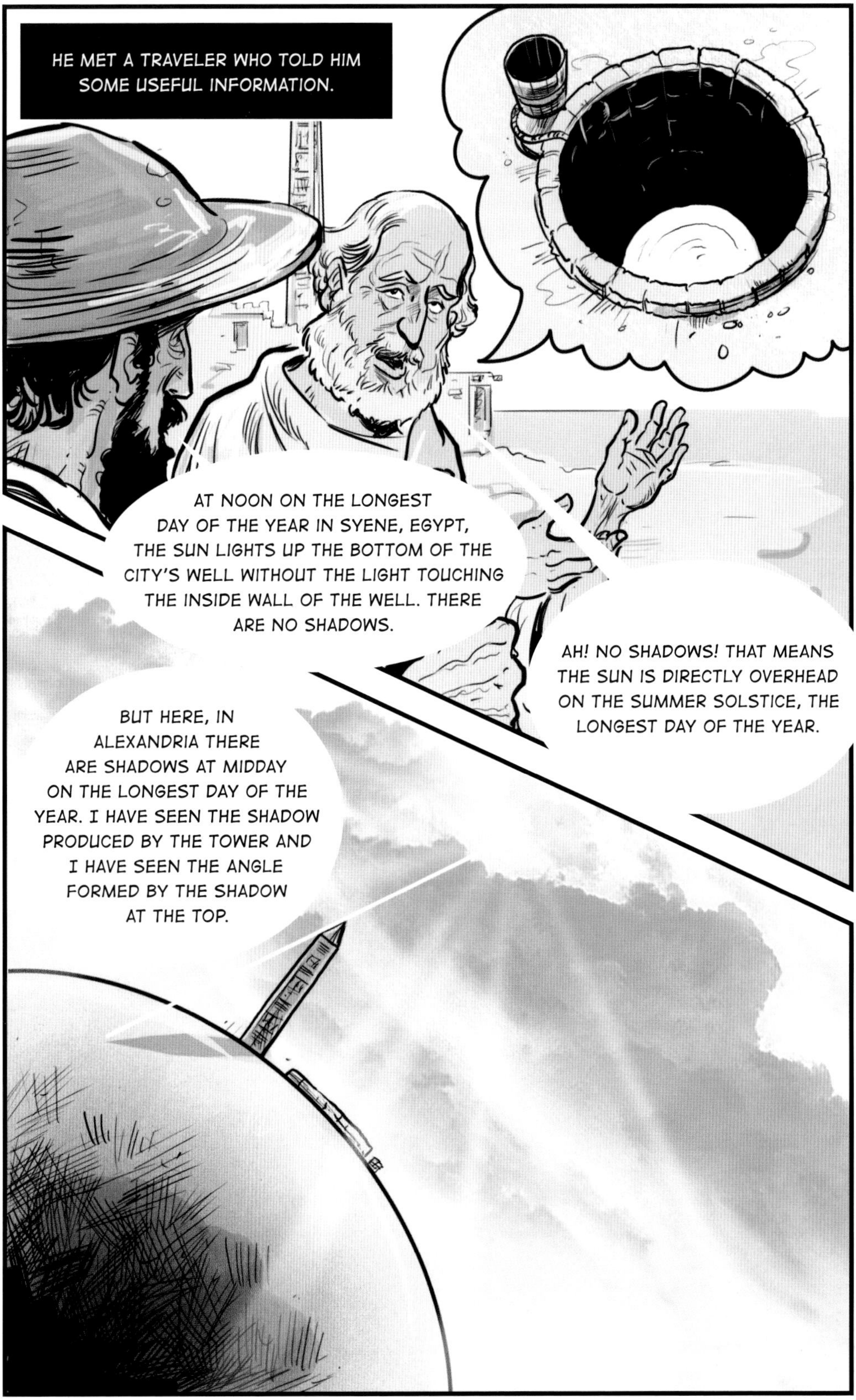
HE MET A TRAVELER WHO TOLD HIM SOME USEFUL INFORMATION.
AT NOON ON THE LONGEST DAY OF THE YEAR IN SYENE, EGYPT, THE SUN LIGHTS UP THE BOTTOM OF THE CITY'S WELL WITHOUT THE LIGHT TOUCHING THE INSIDE WALL OF THE WELL. THERE ARE NO SHADOWS.
AH! NO SHADOWS! THAT MEANS THE SUN IS DIRECTLY OVERHEAD ON THE SUMMER SOLSTICE, THE LONGEST DAY OF THE YEAR.
BUT HERE, IN ALEXANDRIA THERE ARE SHADOWS AT MIDDAY ON THE LONGEST DAY OF THE YEAR. I HAVE SEEN THE SHADOW PRODUCED BY THE TOWER AND I HAVE SEEN THE ANGLE FORMED BY THE SHADOW AT THE TOP.

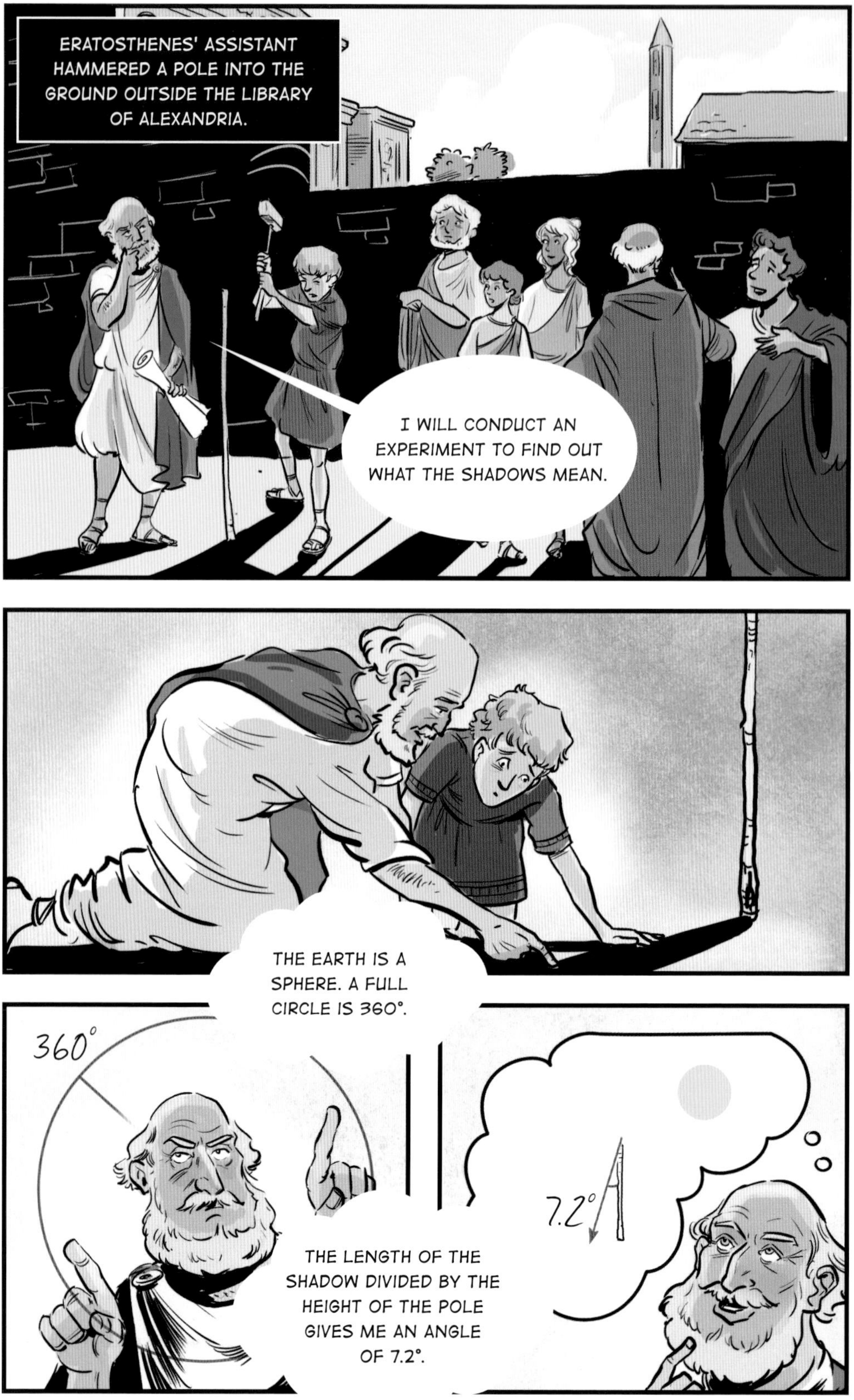
ERATOSTHENES' ASSISTANT HAMMERED A POLE INTO THE GROUND OUTSIDE THE LIBRARY OF ALEXANDRIA.
I WILL CONDUCT AN EXPERIMENT TO FIND OUT WHAT THE SHADOWS MEAN.
THE EARTH IS A SPHERE. A FULL CIRCLE IS 360°.
360°
THE LENGTH OF THE SHADOW DIVIDED BY THE HEIGHT OF THE POLE GIVES ME AN ANGLE OF 7.2°.
7.2°

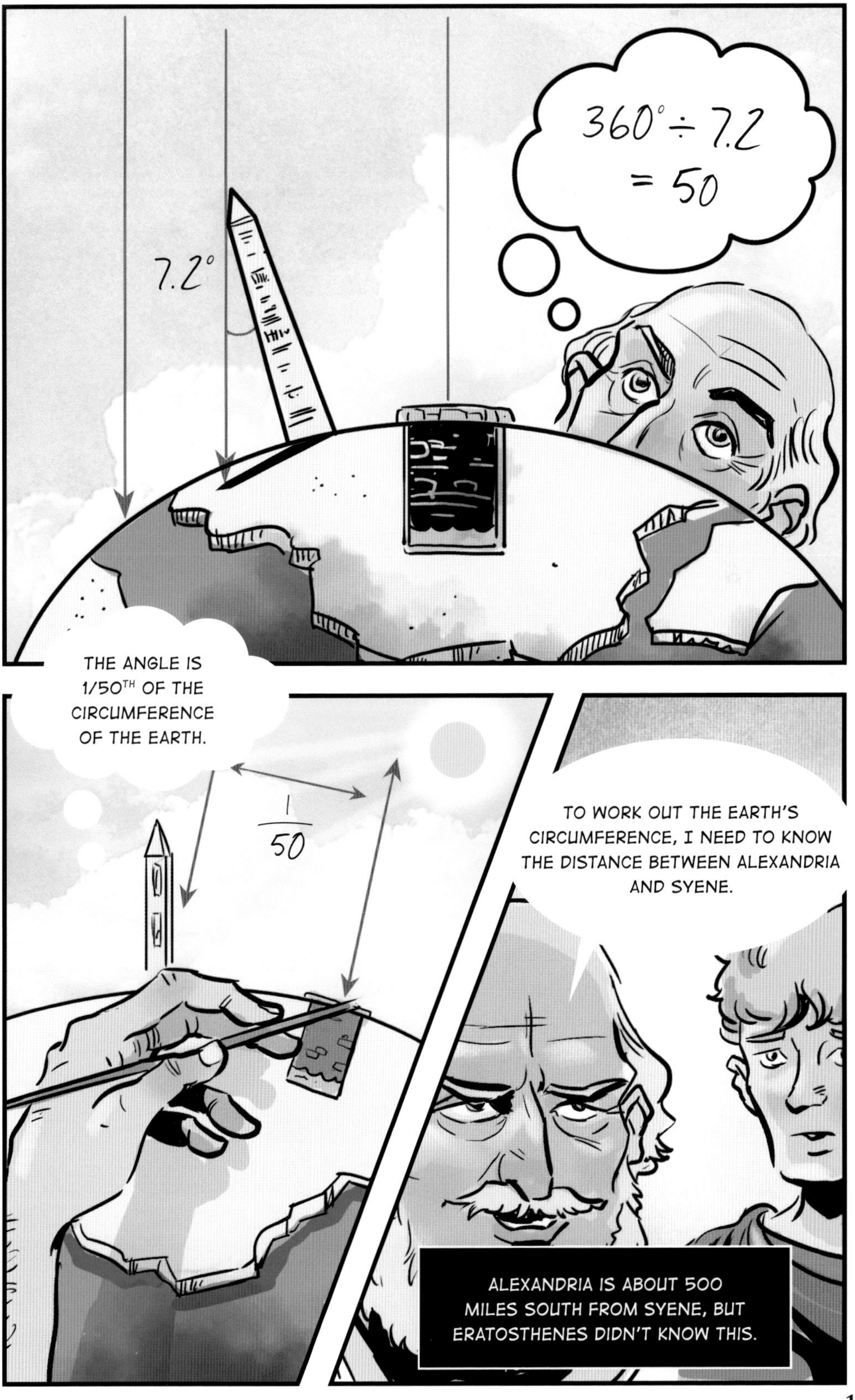
7.2°
360° ÷ 7.2
= 50
THE ANGLE IS 1/50TH OF THE CIRCUMFERENCE OF THE EARTH.
1/50
TO WORK OUT THE EARTH'S CIRCUMFERENCE, I NEED TO KNOW THE DISTANCE BETWEEN ALEXANDRIA AND SYENE.
ALEXANDRIA IS ABOUT 500 MILES SOUTH FROM SYENE, BUT ERATOSTHENES DIDN'T KNOW THIS.

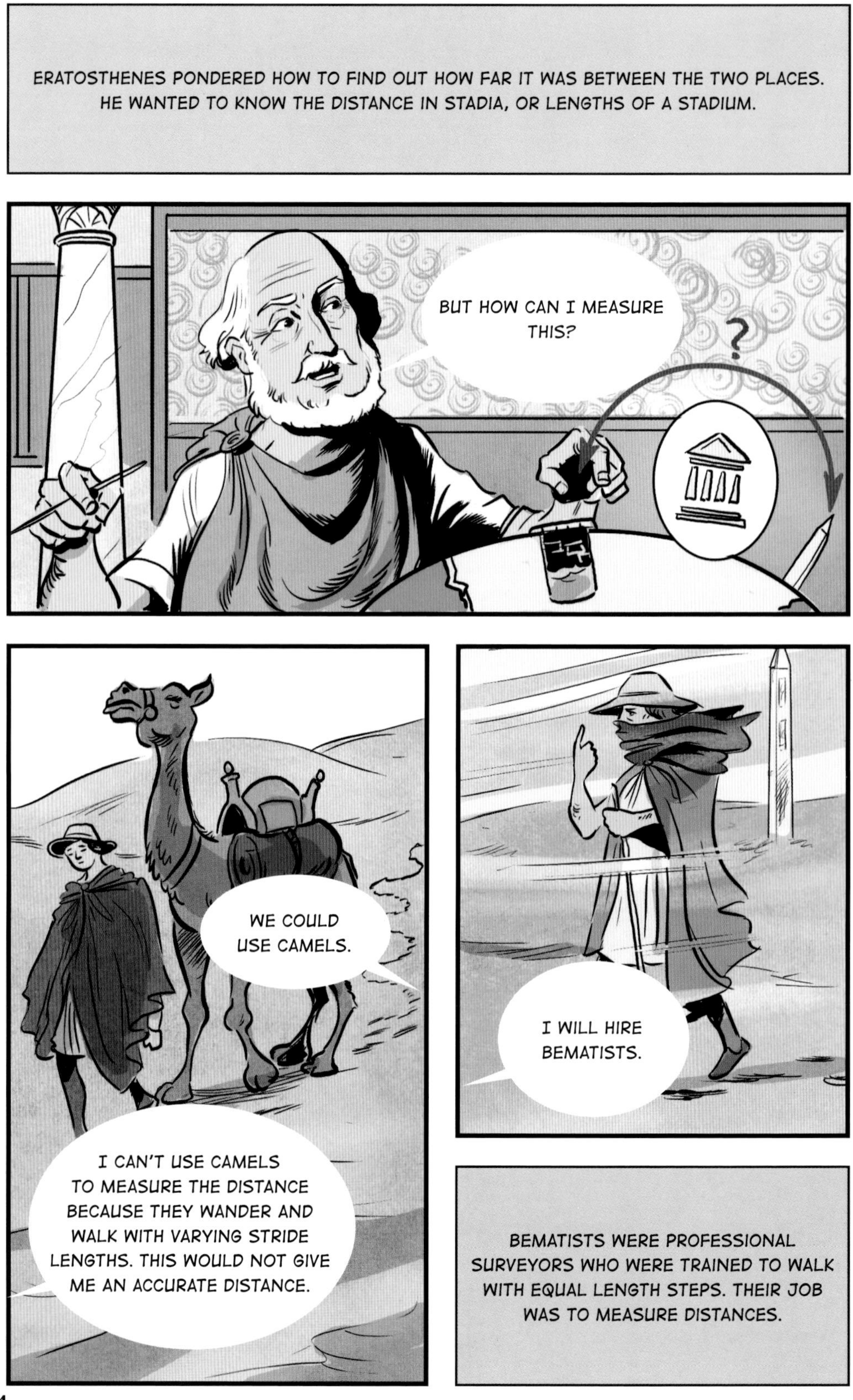
ERATOSTHENES PONDERED HOW TO FIND OUT HOW FAR IT WAS BETWEEN THE TWO PLACES. HE WANTED TO KNOW THE DISTANCE IN STADIA, OR LENGTHS OF A STADIUM.
BUT HOW CAN I MEASURE THIS?
?
WE COULD USE CAMELS.
I CAN'T USE CAMELS TO MEASURE THE DISTANCE BECAUSE THEY WANDER AND WALK WITH VARYING STRIDE LENGTHS. THIS WOULD NOT GIVE ME AN ACCURATE DISTANCE.
I WILL HIRE BEMATISTS.
BEMATISTS WERE PROFESSIONAL SURVEYORS WHO WERE TRAINED TO WALK WITH EQUAL LENGTH STEPS. THEIR JOB WAS TO MEASURE DISTANCES.

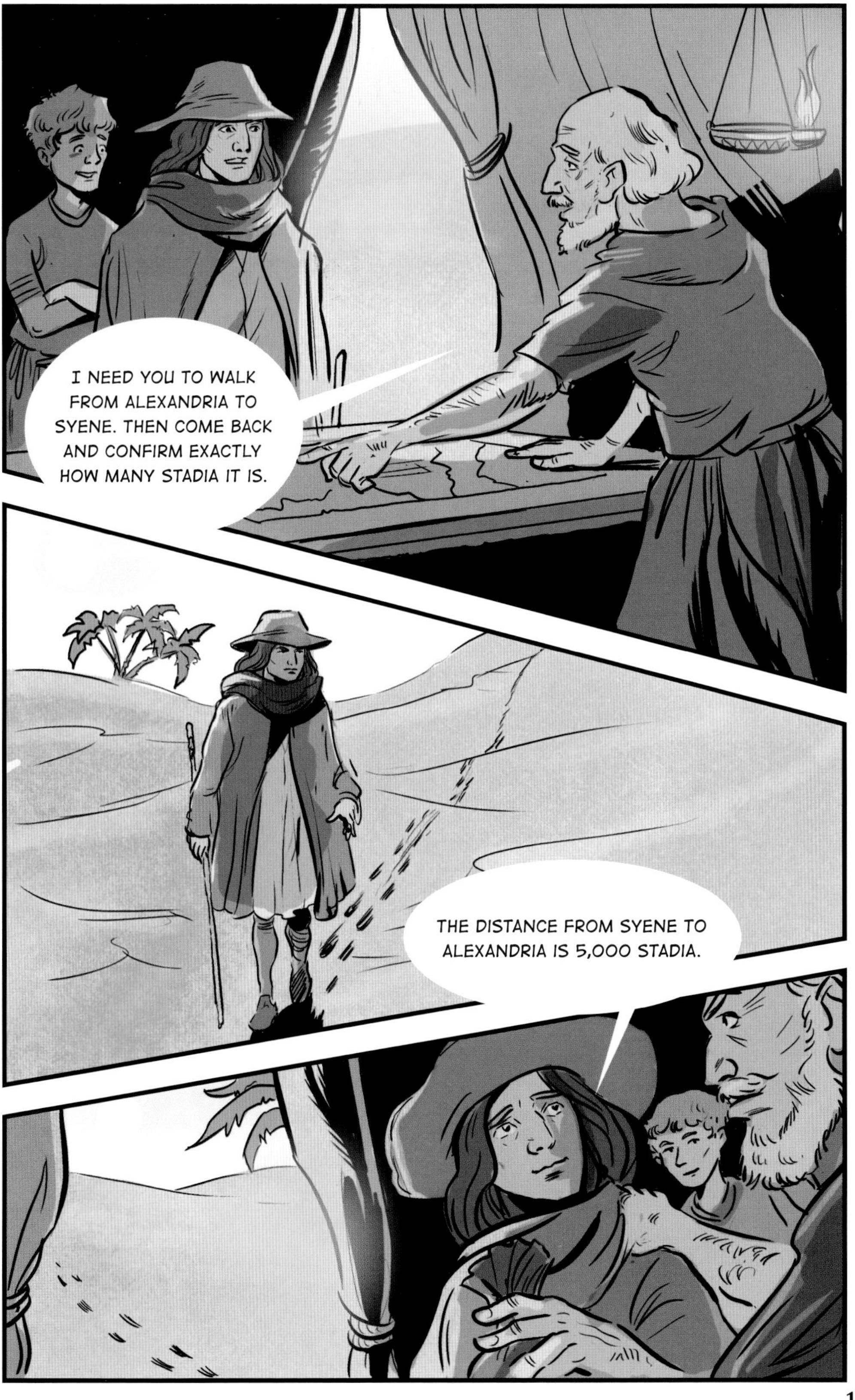
I NEED YOU TO WALK FROM ALEXANDRIA TO SYENE. THEN COME BACK AND CONFIRM EXACTLY HOW MANY STADIA IT IS.
THE DISTANCE FROM SYENE TO ALEXANDRIA IS 5,000 STADIA.

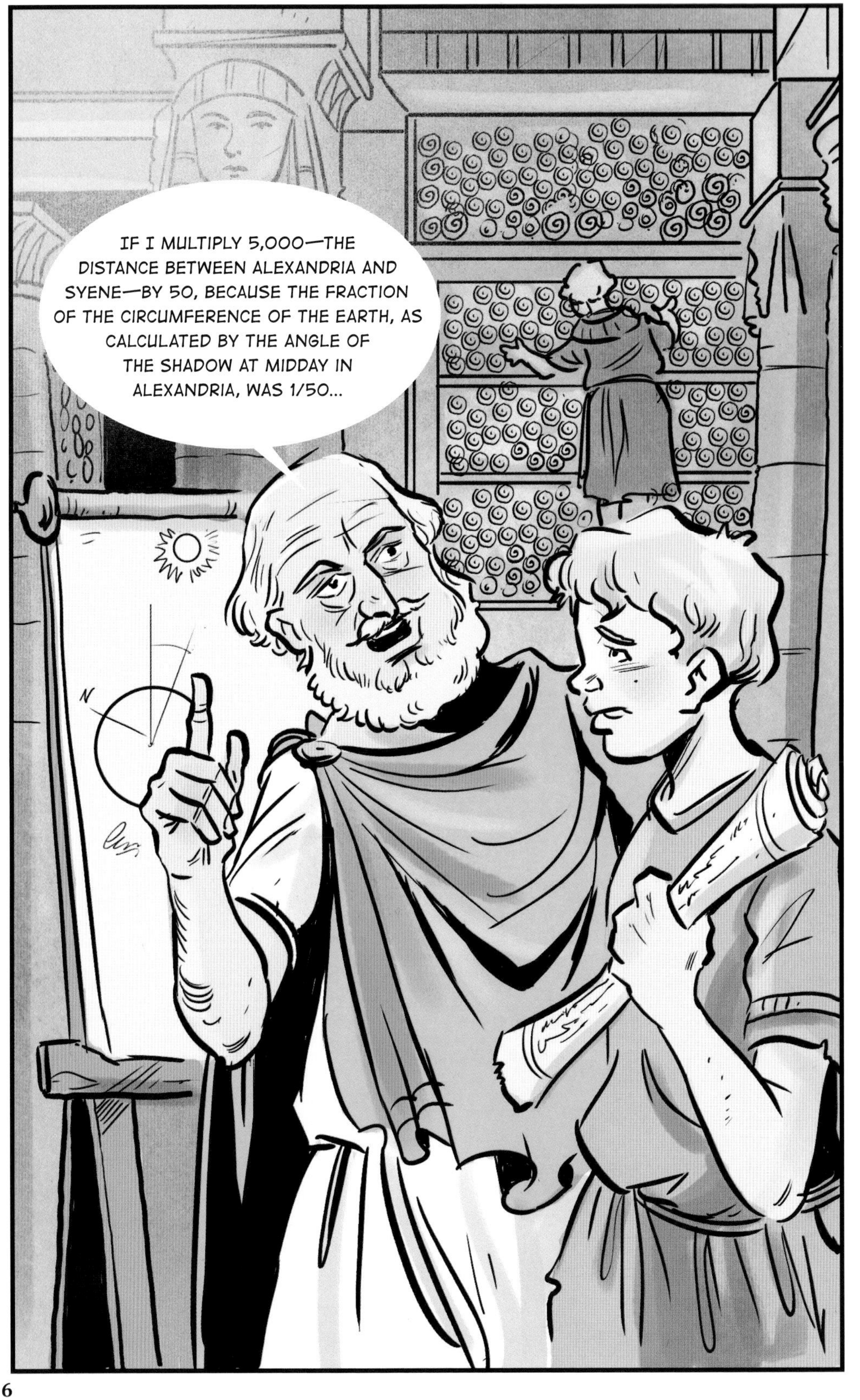
IF I MULTIPLY 5,000—THE DISTANCE BETWEEN ALEXANDRIA AND SYENE—BY 50, BECAUSE THE FRACTION OF THE CIRCUMFERENCE OF THE EARTH, AS CALCULATED BY THE ANGLE OF THE SHADOW AT MIDDAY IN ALEXANDRIA, WAS 1/50...
N

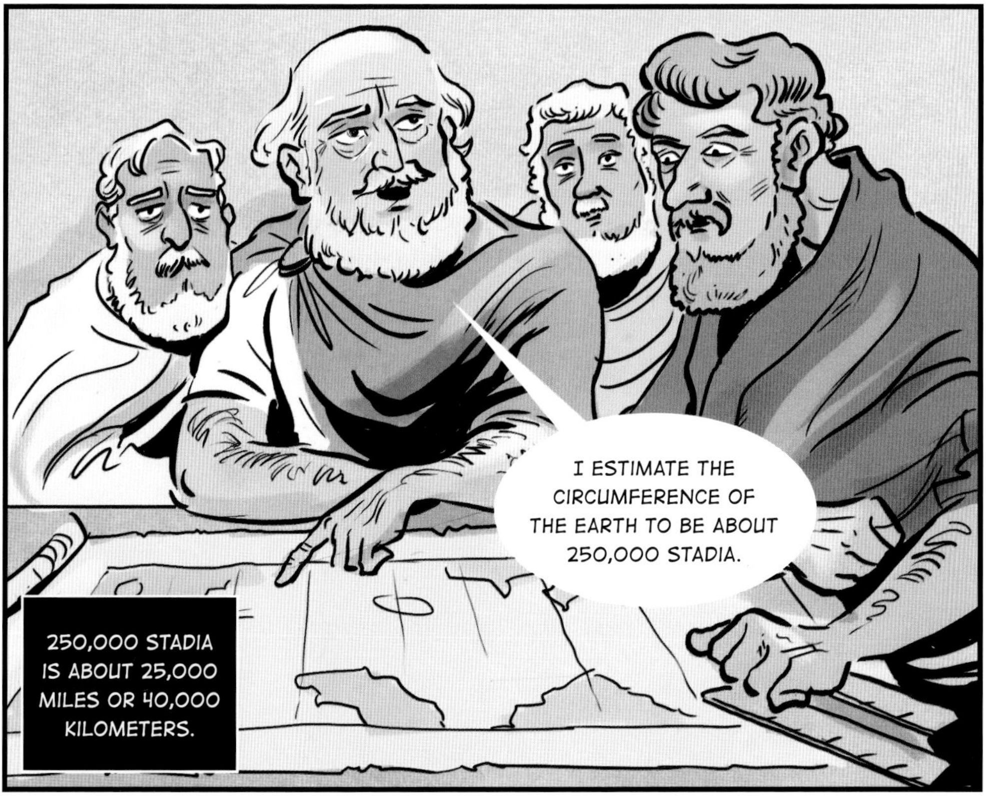
I ESTIMATE THE CIRCUMFERENCE OF THE EARTH TO BE ABOUT 250,000 STADIA.
250,000 STADIA IS ABOUT 25,000 MILES OR 40,000 KILOMETERS.

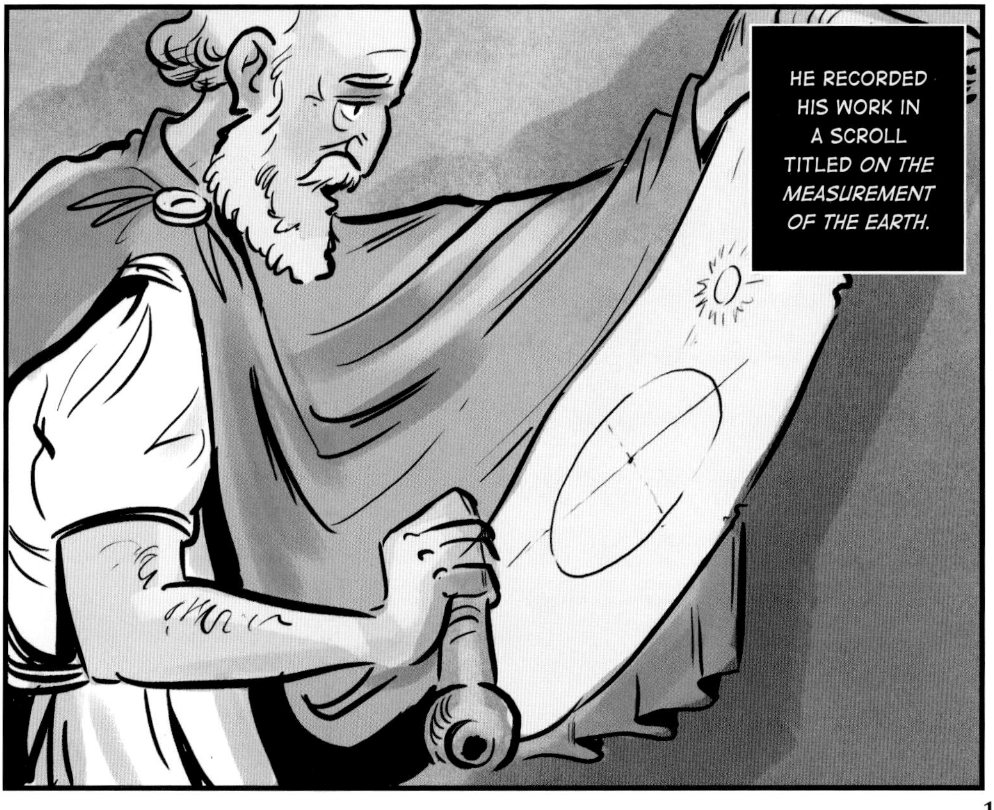
HE RECORDED HIS WORK IN A SCROLL TITLED *ON THE MEASUREMENT OF THE EARTH.*

ERATOSTHENES ALSO NOTICED THE STARS ROTATED ONCE A DAY AROUND THE EARTH. HE WAS ONE OF THE FIRST PEOPLE TO REALIZE THE EARTH WAS TILTED ON ITS AXIS. THE AXIS IS AN IMAGINARY LINE FROM THE NORTH POLE TO THE SOUTH POLE THROUGH THE CENTER OF THE EARTH. THE EARTH ROTATES AROUND IT. HE CALCULATED THE TILT OF THE EARTH'S AXIS TO WITHIN A DEGREE.

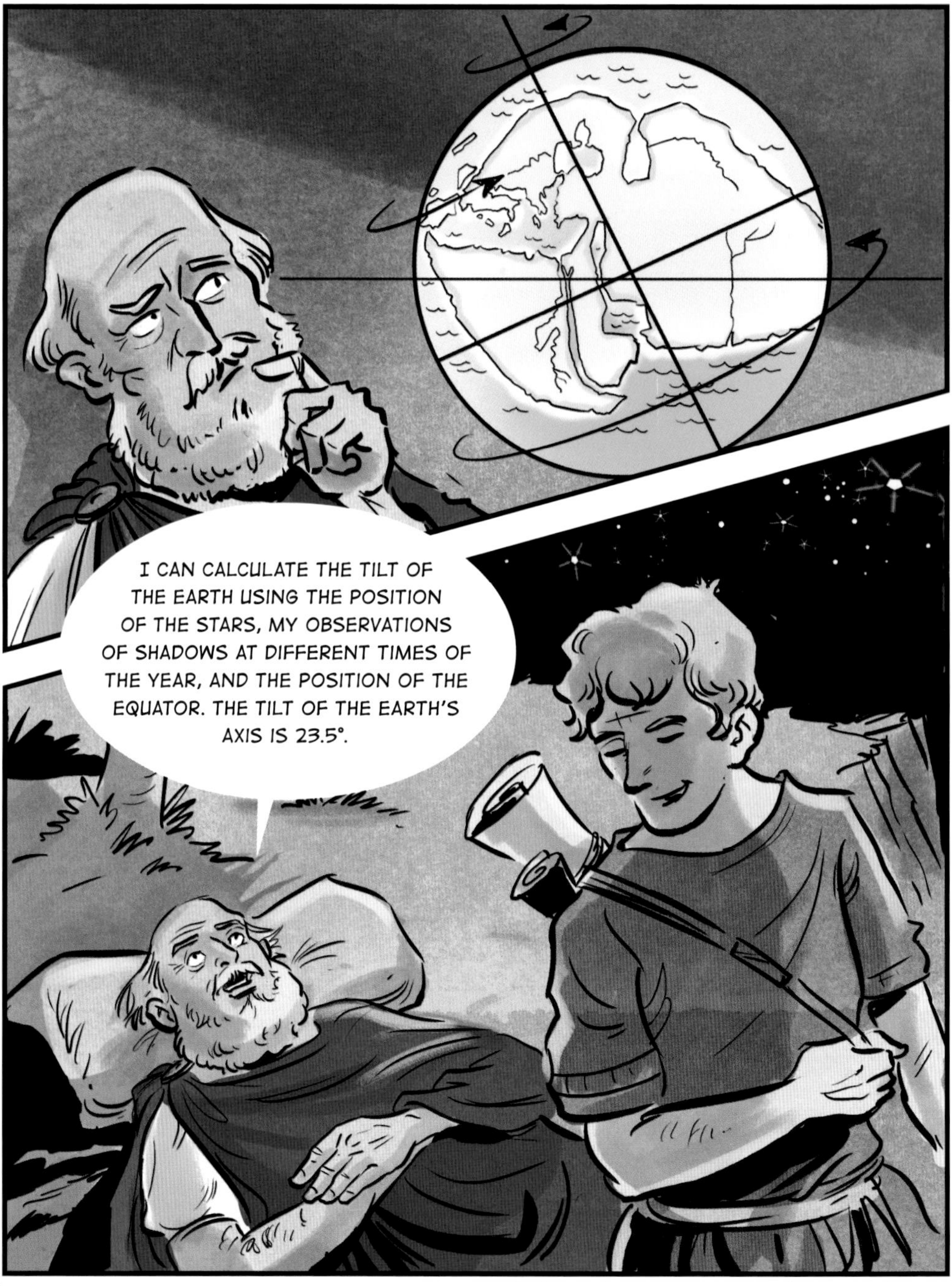
I CAN CALCULATE THE TILT OF THE EARTH USING THE POSITION OF THE STARS, MY OBSERVATIONS OF SHADOWS AT DIFFERENT TIMES OF THE YEAR, AND THE POSITION OF THE EQUATOR. THE TILT OF THE EARTH'S AXIS IS 23.5°.

HE ALSO PRODUCED THE FIRST MAP OF THE WORLD WHICH USED LINES THAT CROSSED EACH OTHER, SIMILAR TO MODERN-DAY LINES OF LONGITUDE AND LATITUDE.

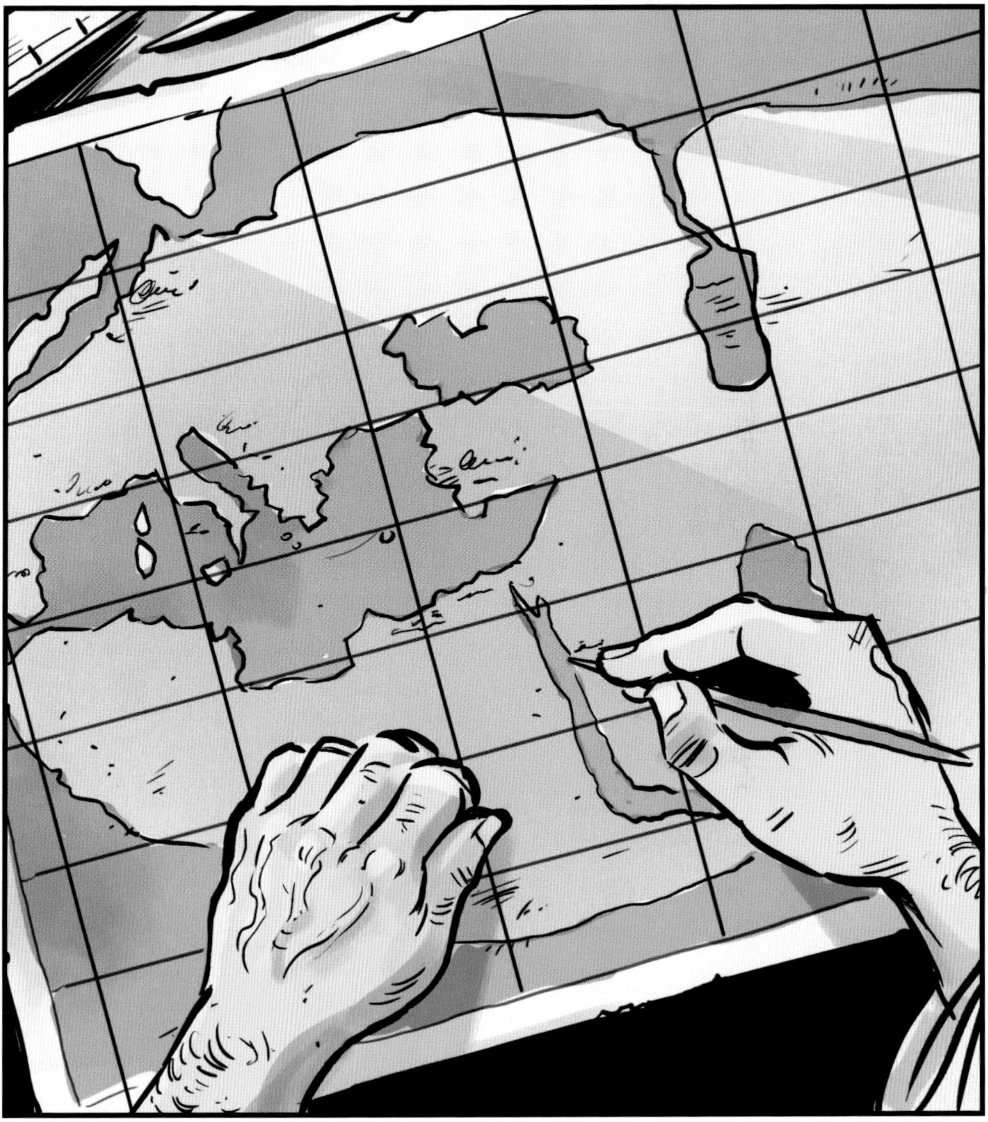

HE MARKED THE EQUATOR AND THOUGHT ABOUT THE SIZE OF POLAR ZONES AND HOW FAR THEY WERE FROM THE TROPICS. ERATOSTHENES WAS THE FIRST PERSON TO OFFER A SENSE OF SIZE AND SCALE FOR THE EARTH.

NICOLAUS COPERNICUS
(1473–1543)
INSTIGATOR OF A SCIENTIFIC REVOLUTION

NICOLAUS COPERNICUS WENT TO THE UNIVERSITY OF BOLOGNA IN ITALY TO STUDY RELIGION. WHILE HE WAS THERE, HE BECAME INTERESTED IN ASTRONOMY AND THE STUDY OF THE STARS. HE ALSO MET THE PRINCIPAL ASTRONOMER OF THE UNIVERSITY, DOMENICO MARIA NOVARA. THEY DISCUSSED THEIR IDEAS AND OBSERVATIONS ABOUT THE SUN AND PLANETS.

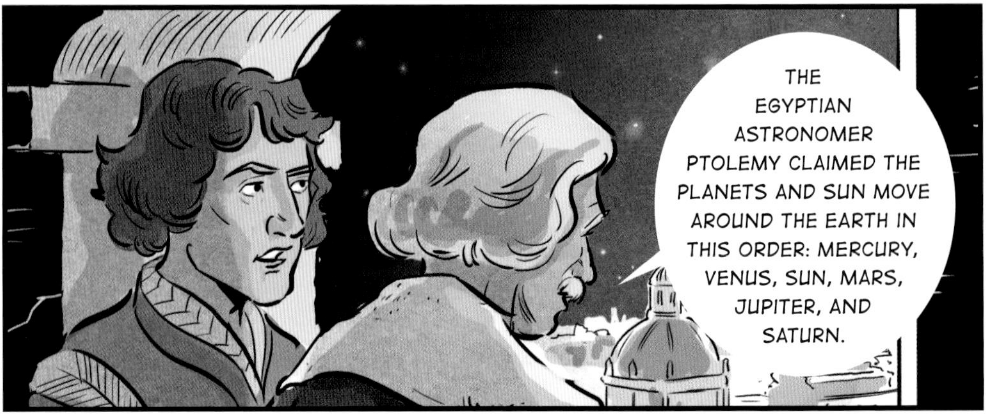
THE EGYPTIAN ASTRONOMER PTOLEMY CLAIMED THE PLANETS AND SUN MOVE AROUND THE EARTH IN THIS ORDER: MERCURY, VENUS, SUN, MARS, JUPITER, AND SATURN.

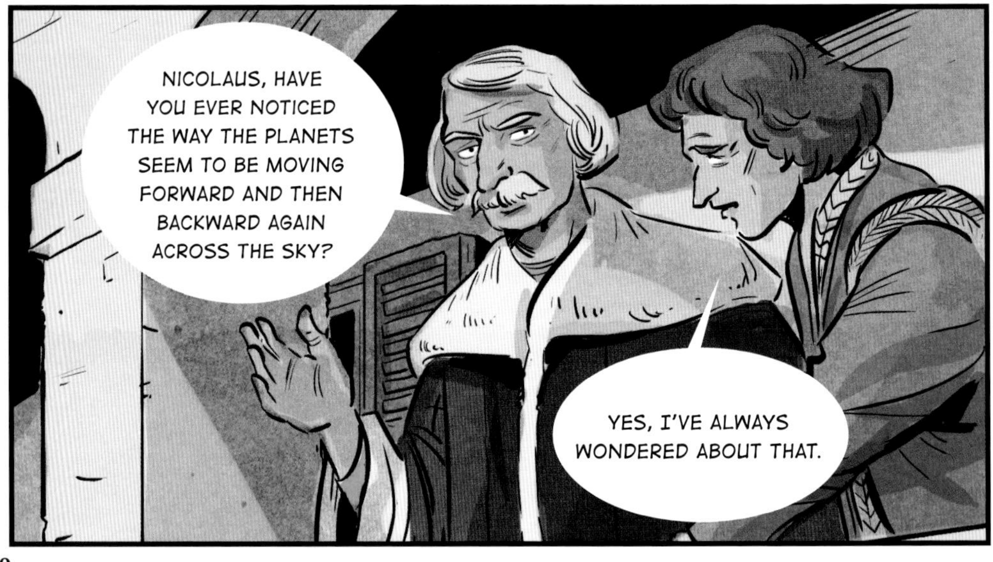
NICOLAUS, HAVE YOU EVER NOTICED THE WAY THE PLANETS SEEM TO BE MOVING FORWARD AND THEN BACKWARD AGAIN ACROSS THE SKY?
YES, I'VE ALWAYS WONDERED ABOUT THAT.

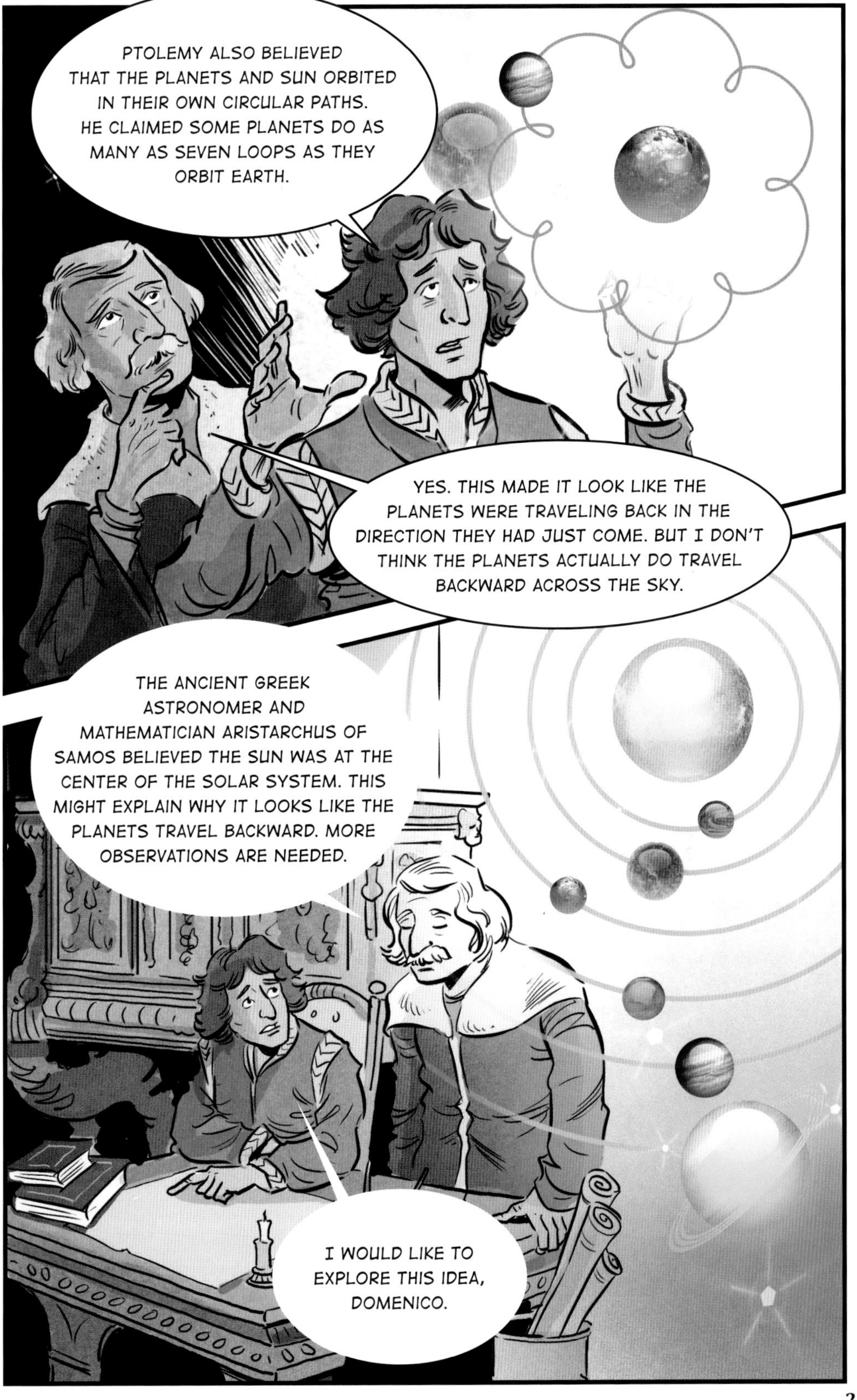
PTOLEMY ALSO BELIEVED THAT THE PLANETS AND SUN ORBITED IN THEIR OWN CIRCULAR PATHS. HE CLAIMED SOME PLANETS DO AS MANY AS SEVEN LOOPS AS THEY ORBIT EARTH.
YES. THIS MADE IT LOOK LIKE THE PLANETS WERE TRAVELING BACK IN THE DIRECTION THEY HAD JUST COME. BUT I DON'T THINK THE PLANETS ACTUALLY DO TRAVEL BACKWARD ACROSS THE SKY.
THE ANCIENT GREEK ASTRONOMER AND MATHEMATICIAN ARISTARCHUS OF SAMOS BELIEVED THE SUN WAS AT THE CENTER OF THE SOLAR SYSTEM. THIS MIGHT EXPLAIN WHY IT LOOKS LIKE THE PLANETS TRAVEL BACKWARD. MORE OBSERVATIONS ARE NEEDED.
I WOULD LIKE TO EXPLORE THIS IDEA, DOMENICO.

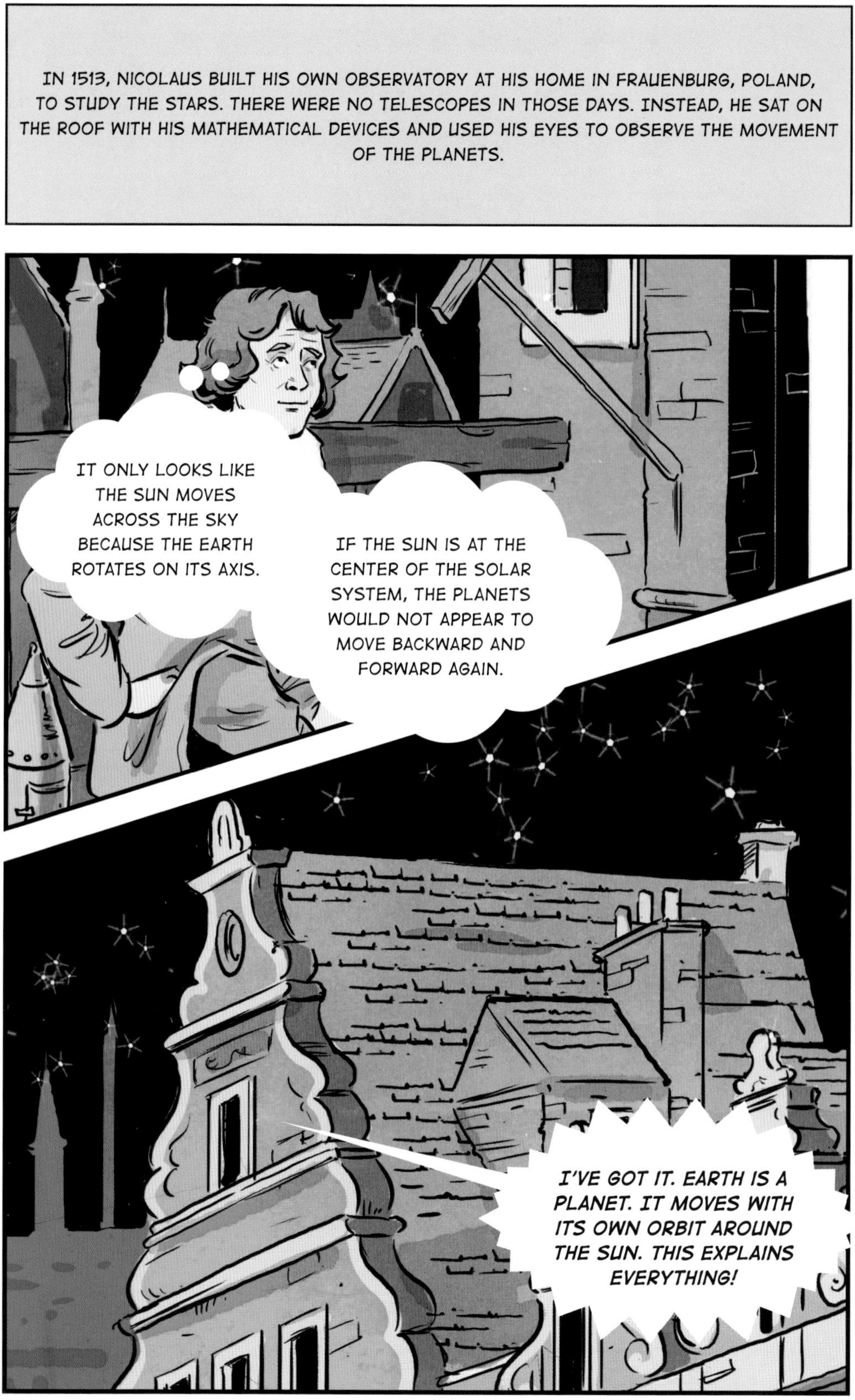
IN 1513, NICOLAUS BUILT HIS OWN OBSERVATORY AT HIS HOME IN FRAUENBURG, POLAND, TO STUDY THE STARS. THERE WERE NO TELESCOPES IN THOSE DAYS. INSTEAD, HE SAT ON THE ROOF WITH HIS MATHEMATICAL DEVICES AND USED HIS EYES TO OBSERVE THE MOVEMENT OF THE PLANETS.
IT ONLY LOOKS LIKE THE SUN MOVES ACROSS THE SKY BECAUSE THE EARTH ROTATES ON ITS AXIS.
IF THE SUN IS AT THE CENTER OF THE SOLAR SYSTEM, THE PLANETS WOULD NOT APPEAR TO MOVE BACKWARD AND FORWARD AGAIN.
I'VE GOT IT. EARTH IS A PLANET. IT MOVES WITH ITS OWN ORBIT AROUND THE SUN. THIS EXPLAINS EVERYTHING!

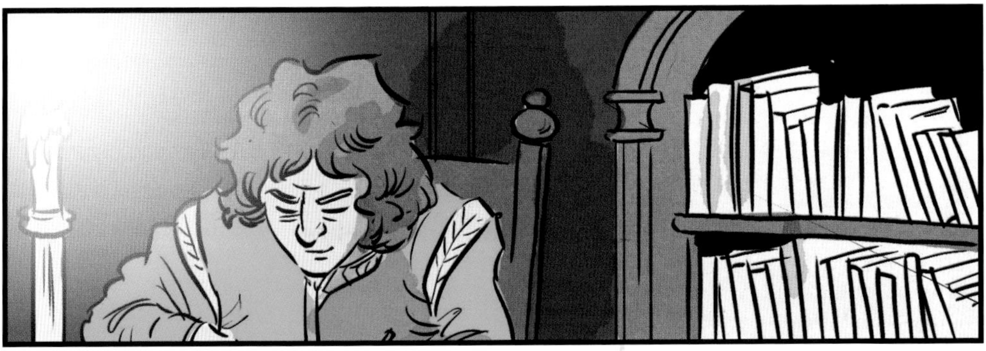

NICOLAUS DECIDED TO WRITE DOWN HIS IDEAS. IN 1514, HE COMPLETED HIS HANDWRITTEN 40-PAGE BOOKLET CALLED *LITTLE COMMENTARY.* IT OUTLINED A NEW THEORY ABOUT THE MOVEMENT OF THE PLANETS AND EARTH AROUND THE SUN. NICOLAUS DISTRIBUTED THE BOOKLET TO HIS FRIENDS AND EXPLAINED HIS IDEAS TO THEM.

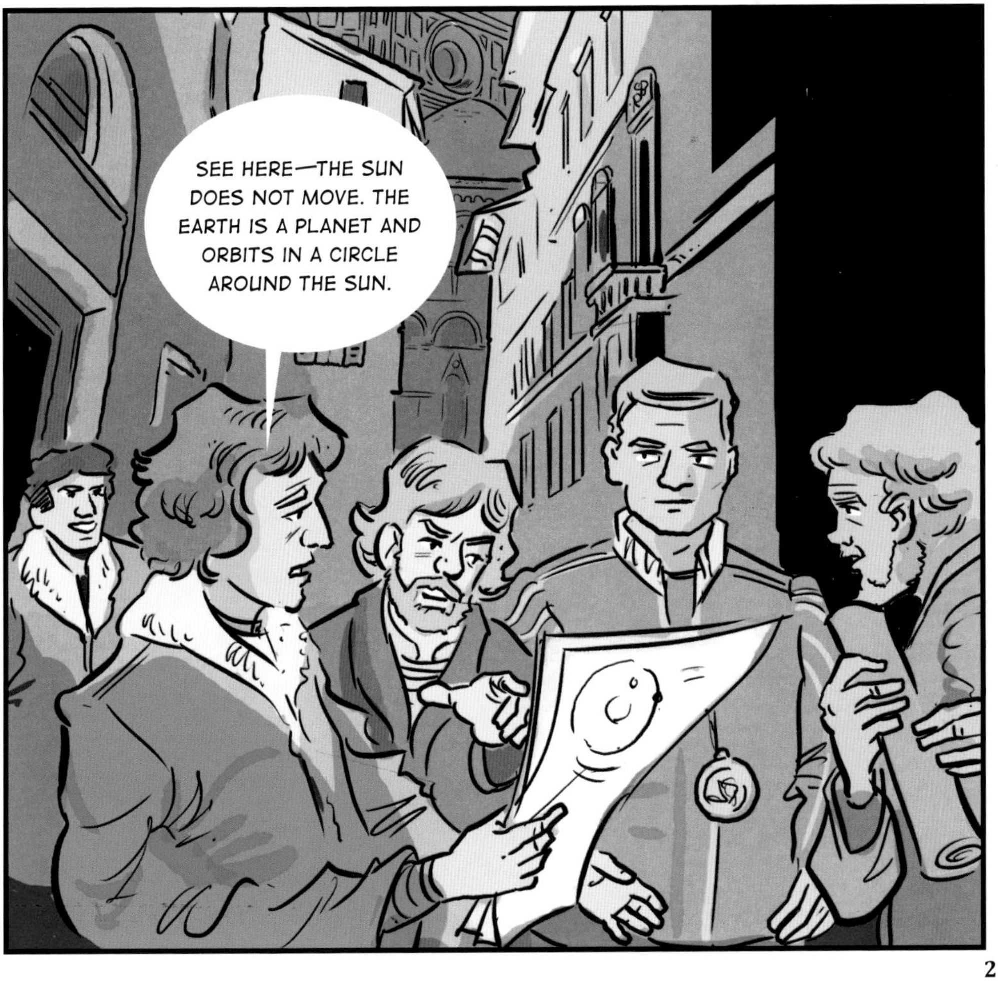
SEE HERE—THE SUN DOES NOT MOVE. THE EARTH IS A PLANET AND ORBITS IN A CIRCLE AROUND THE SUN.

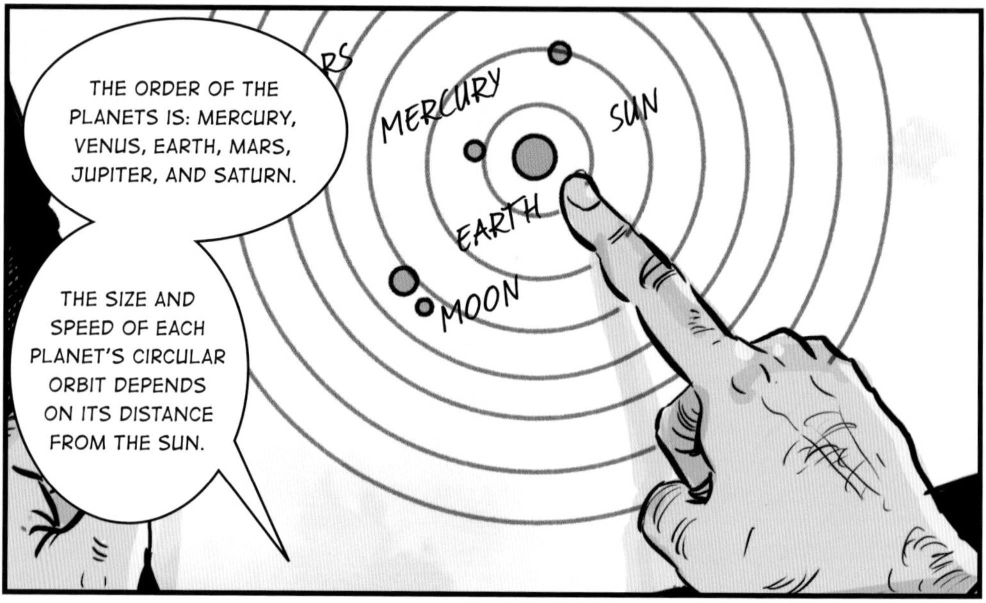
THE ORDER OF THE PLANETS IS: MERCURY, VENUS, EARTH, MARS, JUPITER, AND SATURN.
THE SIZE AND SPEED OF EACH PLANET'S CIRCULAR ORBIT DEPENDS ON ITS DISTANCE FROM THE SUN.
MERCURY
SUN
EARTH
MOON

THIS IS NICOLAUS' HELIOCENTRIC THEORY OF THE SOLAR SYSTEM. SCIENTISTS ONLY KNEW OF SIX PLANETS AT THIS TIME. HE WORKED OUT THE ORDER OF THE PLANETS BY WATCHING THEIR MOVEMENTS AND CALCULATING THEIR ORBITS.

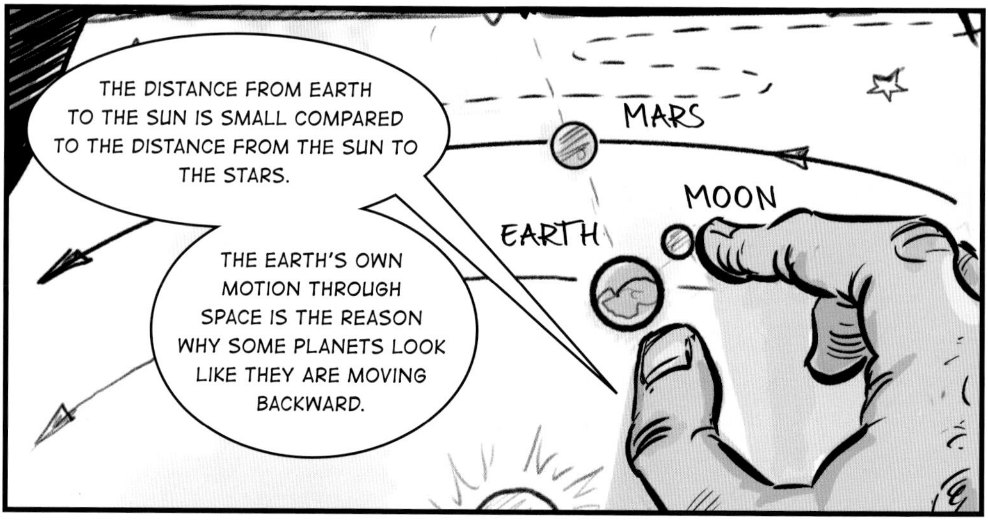
THE DISTANCE FROM EARTH TO THE SUN IS SMALL COMPARED TO THE DISTANCE FROM THE SUN TO THE STARS.
THE EARTH'S OWN MOTION THROUGH SPACE IS THE REASON WHY SOME PLANETS LOOK LIKE THEY ARE MOVING BACKWARD.
MARS
MOON
EARTH

BY TRACKING MARS' MOVEMENTS ACROSS THE NIGHT SKY, NICOLAUS FOUND EARTH HAS A SMALLER ORBIT THAN MARS. WHEN EARTH PASSES BY MARS, THE PLANET MARS APPEARS TO GO BACKWARD. WHEN EARTH FINISHES PASSING BY, MARS APPEARS TO MOVE FORWARD AGAIN.

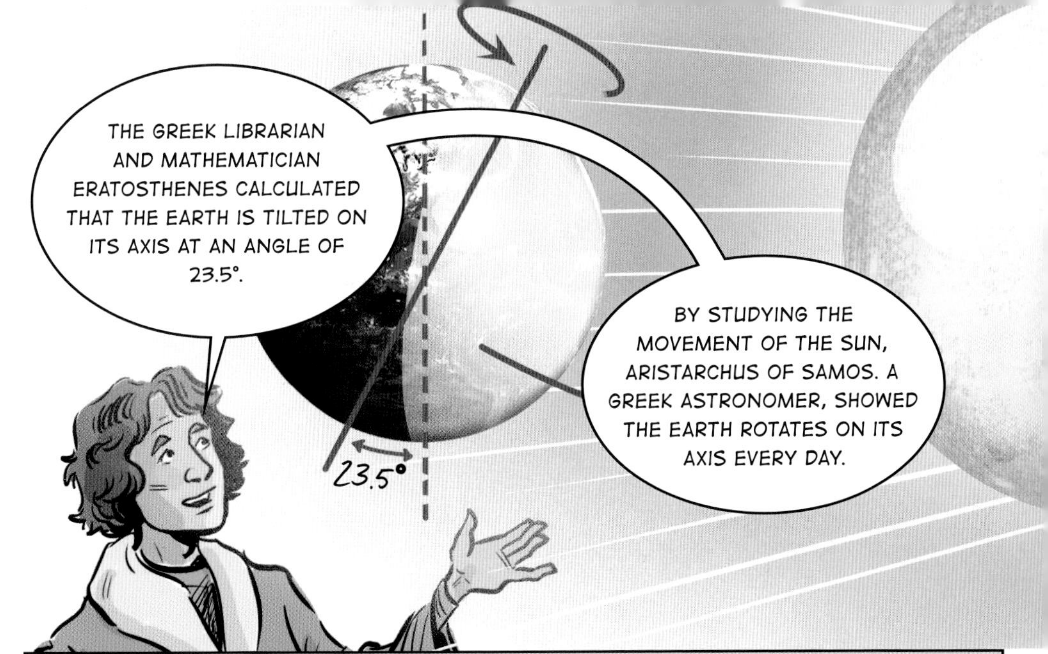
THE GREEK LIBRARIAN AND MATHEMATICIAN ERATOSTHENES CALCULATED THAT THE EARTH IS TILTED ON ITS AXIS AT AN ANGLE OF 23.5°.
BY STUDYING THE MOVEMENT OF THE SUN, ARISTARCHUS OF SAMOS. A GREEK ASTRONOMER, SHOWED THE EARTH ROTATES ON ITS AXIS EVERY DAY.
23.5°

NICOLAUS' OBSERVATIONS OF THE CONSTELLATIONS AND HIS KNOWLEDGE OF OTHER ASTRONOMICAL FINDINGS HELPED HIM TO CALCULATE THAT EARTH ROTATES DAILY ON ITS AXIS. THIS EXPLAINED WHY THE STARS LOOKED LIKE THEY WERE MOVING.

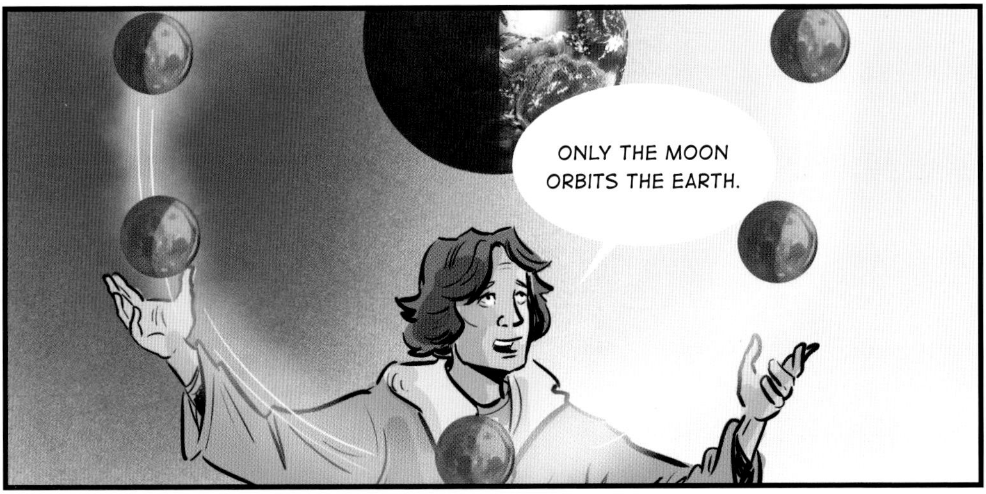
ONLY THE MOON ORBITS THE EARTH.

BY WATCHING THE PHASES OF THE MOON AND WITNESSING A LUNAR ECLIPSE IN ROME IN 1500, NICOLAUS WAS ABLE TO FIGURE OUT THAT THE MOON ORBITED EARTH. A LUNAR ECLIPSE IS WHERE THE MOON SEEMS TO DISAPPEAR AND REAPPEAR AGAIN AS IT PASSES BETWEEN THE EARTH AND SUN.

THE EARTH ORBITS COUNTERCLOCKWISE AROUND THE SUN. THE SEASONS ARE CREATED BY EARTH'S TILT ON ITS AXIS.

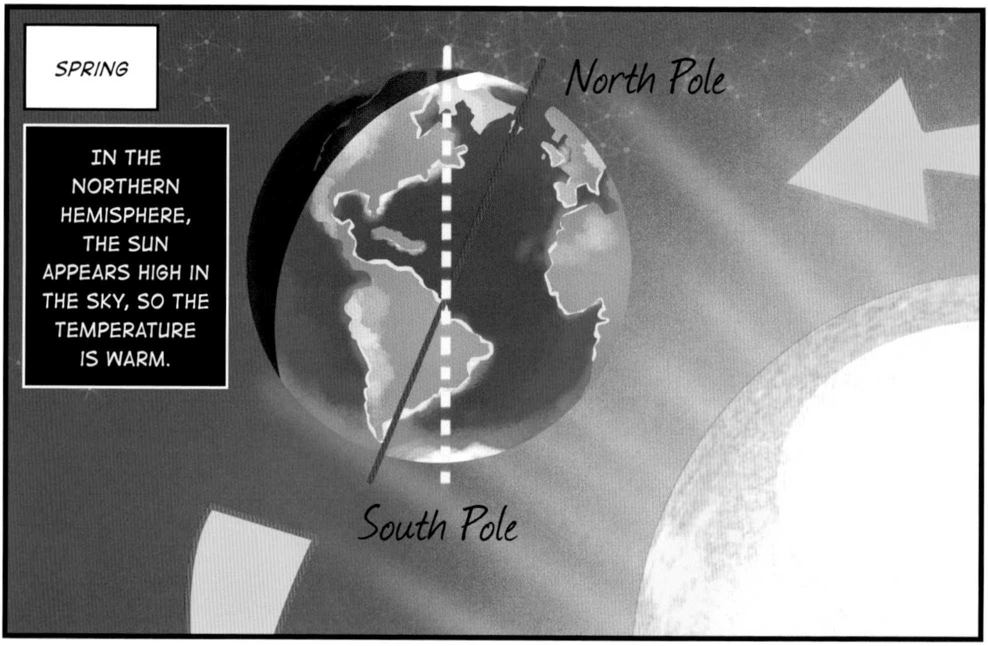
SPRING
IN THE NORTHERN HEMISPHERE, THE SUN APPEARS HIGH IN THE SKY, SO THE TEMPERATURE IS WARM.
North Pole
South Pole

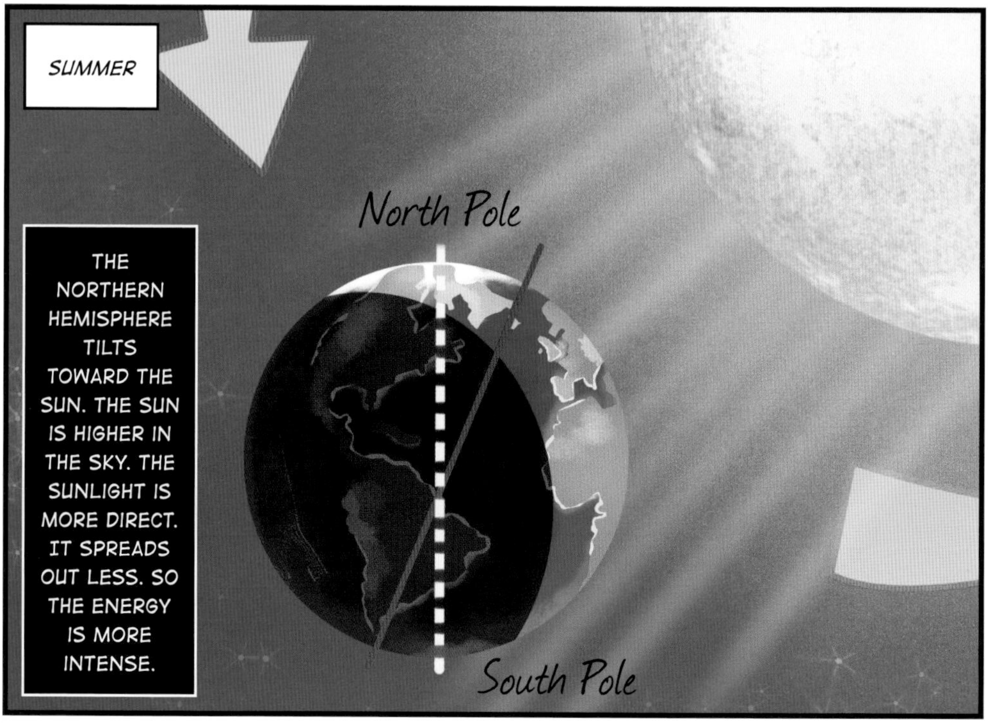
SUMMER
North Pole
THE NORTHERN HEMISPHERE TILTS TOWARD THE SUN. THE SUN IS HIGHER IN THE SKY. THE SUNLIGHT IS MORE DIRECT. IT SPREADS OUT LESS. SO THE ENERGY IS MORE INTENSE.
South Pole

THE NORTH POLE ALWAYS POINTS IN THE SAME DIRECTION. THE SUNLIGHT'S ANGLE AFFECTS ITS INTENSITY AND THE LENGTH OF THE DAY DURING EACH OF THE SEASONS.

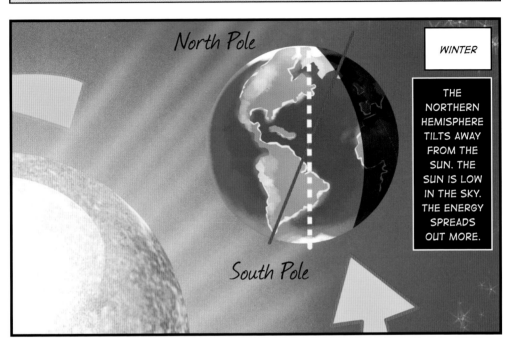

North Pole

South Pole

WINTER

THE NORTHERN HEMISPHERE TILTS AWAY FROM THE SUN. THE SUN IS LOW IN THE SKY. THE ENERGY SPREADS OUT MORE.

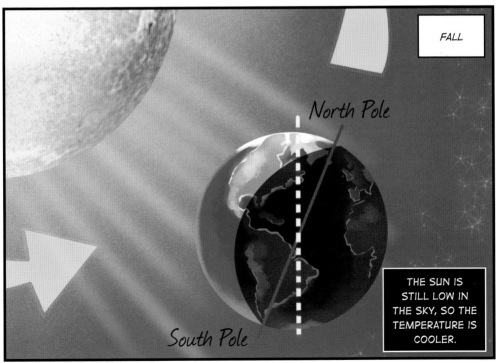

FALL

North Pole

South Pole

THE SUN IS STILL LOW IN THE SKY, SO THE TEMPERATURE IS COOLER.

NICOLAUS' FRIENDS WARNED HIM THAT THE CHURCH MIGHT NOT BE HAPPY WITH HIS THEORIES.

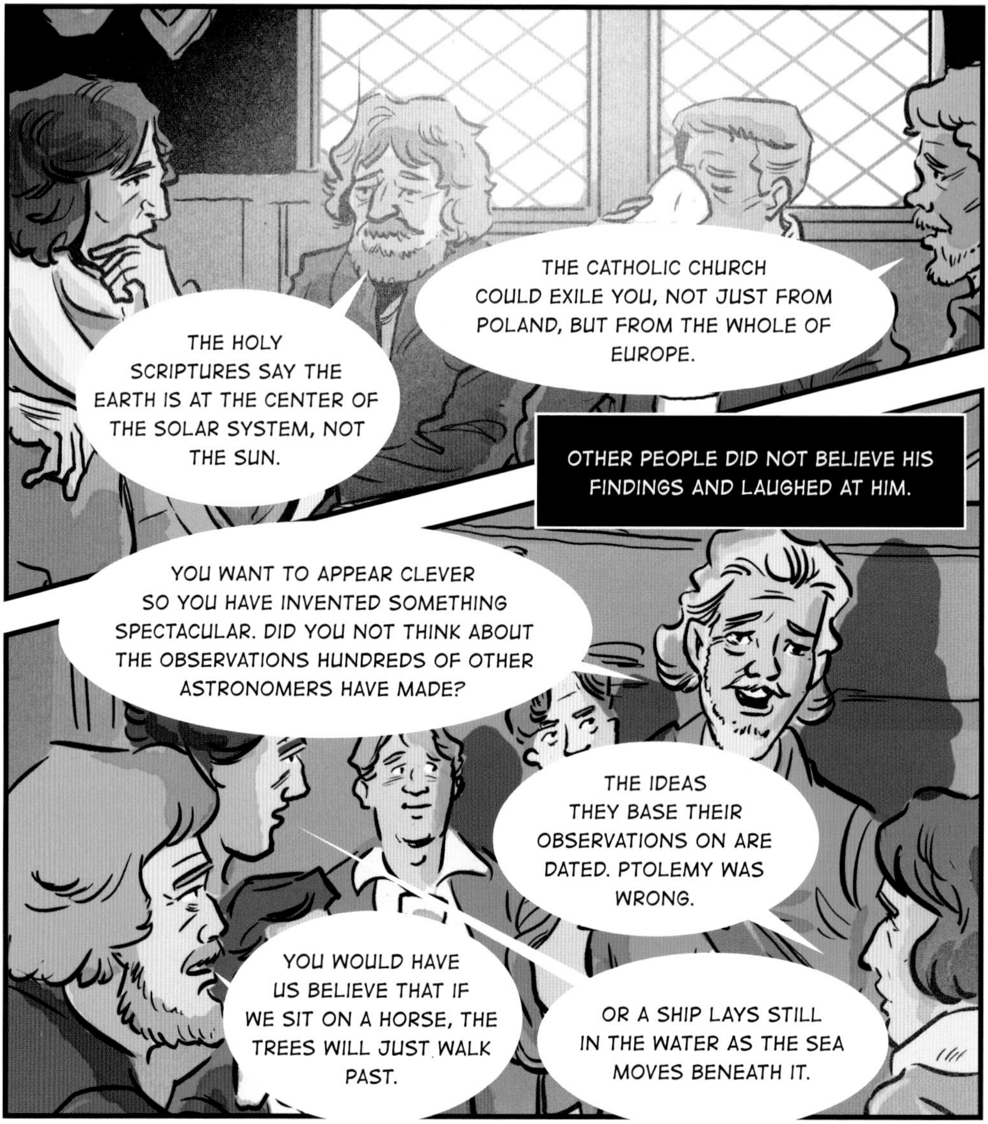
THE HOLY SCRIPTURES SAY THE EARTH IS AT THE CENTER OF THE SOLAR SYSTEM, NOT THE SUN.
THE CATHOLIC CHURCH COULD EXILE YOU, NOT JUST FROM POLAND, BUT FROM THE WHOLE OF EUROPE.
OTHER PEOPLE DID NOT BELIEVE HIS FINDINGS AND LAUGHED AT HIM.
YOU WANT TO APPEAR CLEVER SO YOU HAVE INVENTED SOMETHING SPECTACULAR. DID YOU NOT THINK ABOUT THE OBSERVATIONS HUNDREDS OF OTHER ASTRONOMERS HAVE MADE?
THE IDEAS THEY BASE THEIR OBSERVATIONS ON ARE DATED. PTOLEMY WAS WRONG.
YOU WOULD HAVE US BELIEVE THAT IF WE SIT ON A HORSE, THE TREES WILL JUST WALK PAST.
OR A SHIP LAYS STILL IN THE WATER AS THE SEA MOVES BENEATH IT.

TWENTY-FIVE YEARS LATER, NICOLAUS HAD STILL NOT PUBLISHED HIS IDEAS. NOT ONLY WAS HE WORRIED ABOUT THE REACTION OF THE CHURCH, HE WAS ALSO WORRIED HIS IDEAS WOULD NOT BE ACCEPTED BY OTHER ASTRONOMERS.

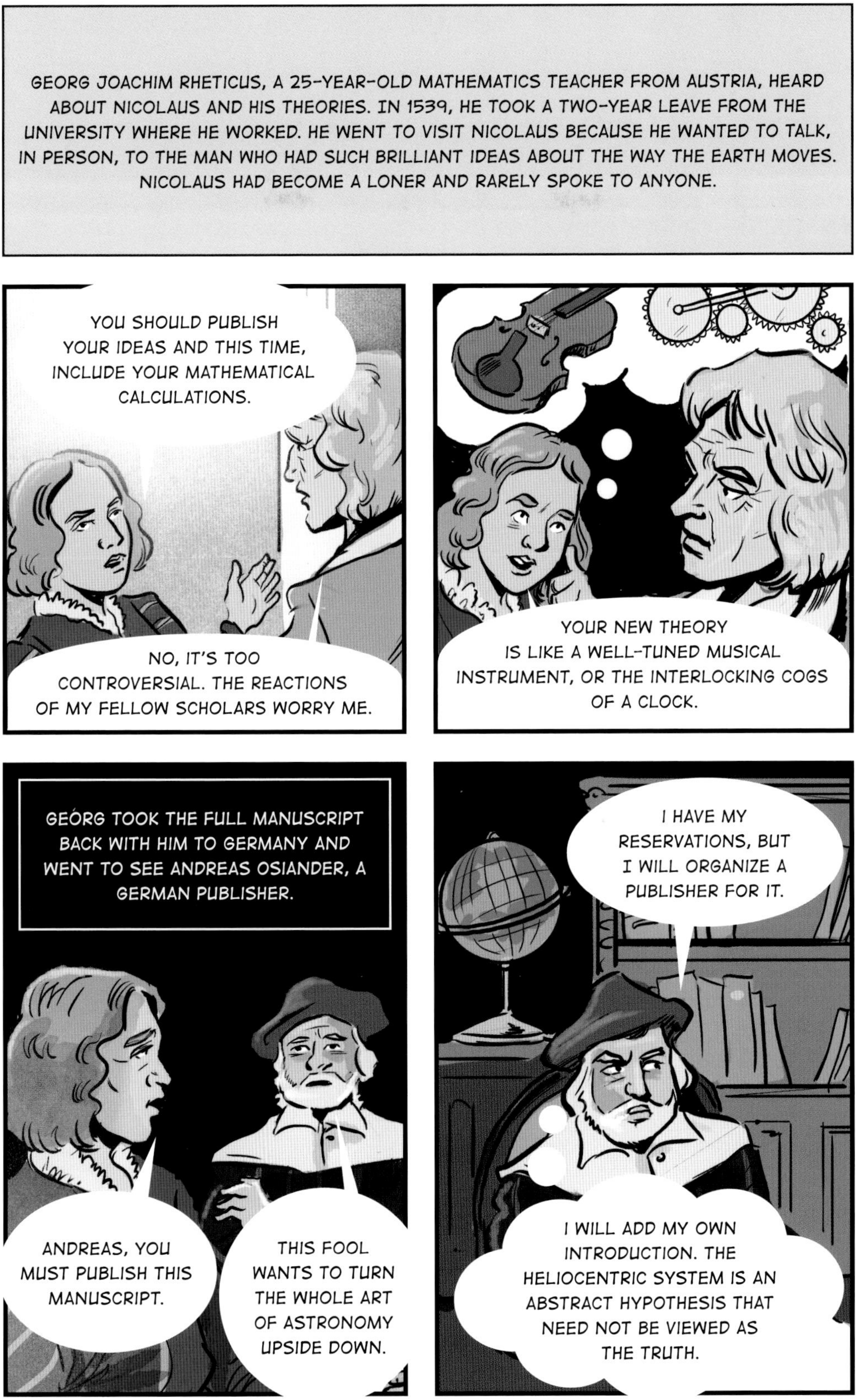
GEORG JOACHIM RHETICUS, A 25-YEAR-OLD MATHEMATICS TEACHER FROM AUSTRIA, HEARD ABOUT NICOLAUS AND HIS THEORIES. IN 1539, HE TOOK A TWO-YEAR LEAVE FROM THE UNIVERSITY WHERE HE WORKED. HE WENT TO VISIT NICOLAUS BECAUSE HE WANTED TO TALK, IN PERSON, TO THE MAN WHO HAD SUCH BRILLIANT IDEAS ABOUT THE WAY THE EARTH MOVES. NICOLAUS HAD BECOME A LONER AND RARELY SPOKE TO ANYONE.
YOU SHOULD PUBLISH YOUR IDEAS AND THIS TIME, INCLUDE YOUR MATHEMATICAL CALCULATIONS.
NO, IT'S TOO CONTROVERSIAL. THE REACTIONS OF MY FELLOW SCHOLARS WORRY ME.
YOUR NEW THEORY IS LIKE A WELL-TUNED MUSICAL INSTRUMENT, OR THE INTERLOCKING COGS OF A CLOCK.
GEORG TOOK THE FULL MANUSCRIPT BACK WITH HIM TO GERMANY AND WENT TO SEE ANDREAS OSIANDER, A GERMAN PUBLISHER.
ANDREAS, YOU MUST PUBLISH THIS MANUSCRIPT.
THIS FOOL WANTS TO TURN THE WHOLE ART OF ASTRONOMY UPSIDE DOWN.
I HAVE MY RESERVATIONS, BUT I WILL ORGANIZE A PUBLISHER FOR IT.
I WILL ADD MY OWN INTRODUCTION. THE HELIOCENTRIC SYSTEM IS AN ABSTRACT HYPOTHESIS THAT NEED NOT BE VIEWED AS THE TRUTH.

IN 1543, *ON THE REVOLUTIONS OF HEAVENLY SPHERES* WAS FINALLY IN PRINT.

GEORG TOOK A COPY OF THE BOOK TO NICOLAUS, WHO WAS DYING AFTER SUFFERING A STROKE.

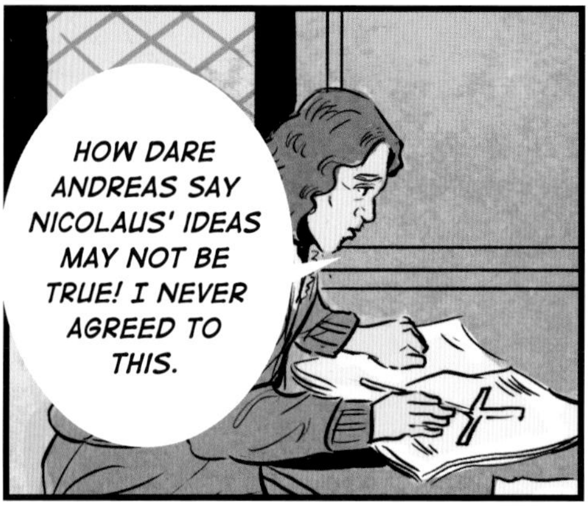
HOW DARE ANDREAS SAY NICOLAUS' IDEAS MAY NOT BE TRUE! I NEVER AGREED TO THIS.

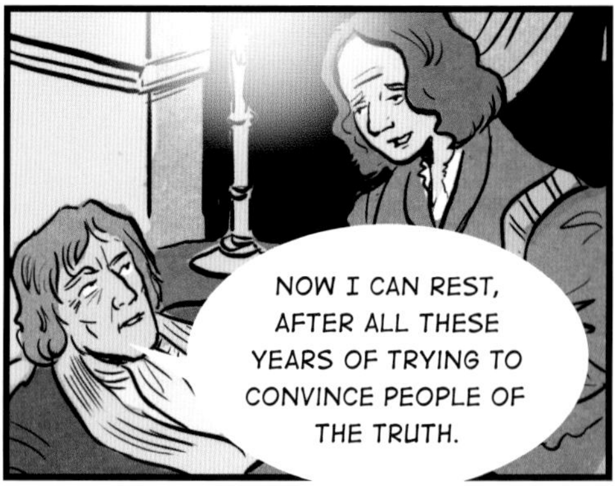
NOW I CAN REST, AFTER ALL THESE YEARS OF TRYING TO CONVINCE PEOPLE OF THE TRUTH.

NICOLAUS' MODEL CHANGED THE LAYOUT OF THE SOLAR SYSTEM. OTHER ASTRONOMERS WERE EXCITED BY HIS IDEAS AND INSPIRED TO CARRY OUT THEIR OWN INVESTIGATIONS.

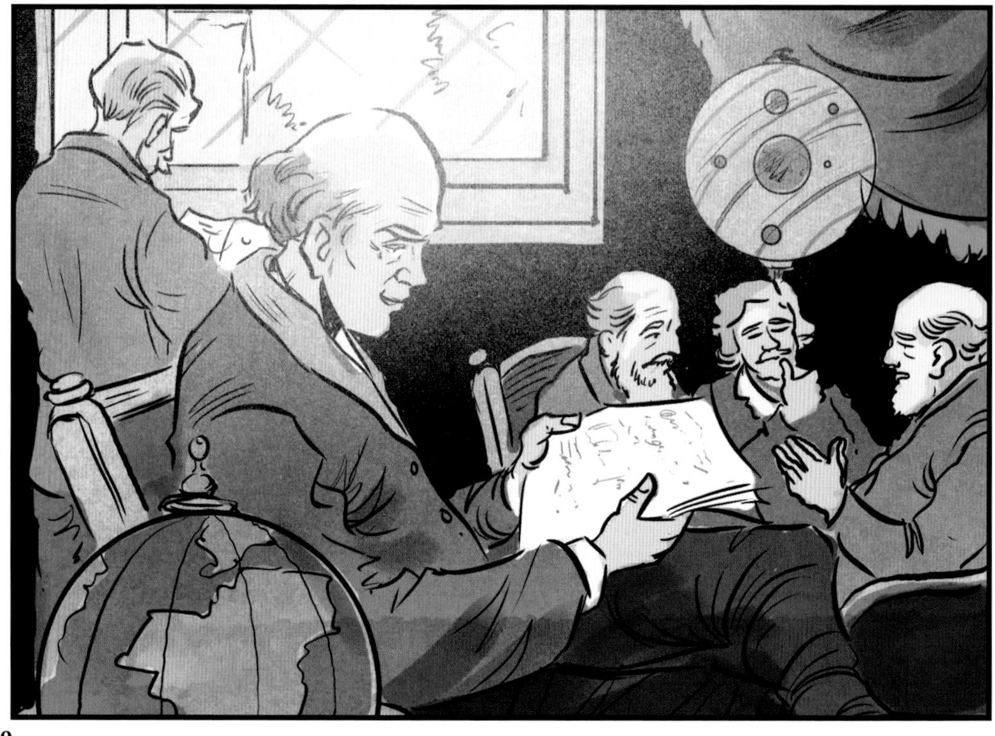

JOHANNES KEPLER WAS A GERMAN ASTRONOMER WHO AGREED WITH NICOLAUS ABOUT THE MOVEMENT OF EARTH. IN 1609, HE PROVED THAT THE SUN WAS THE CENTER OF THE SOLAR SYSTEM AND THAT THE PLANETS WERE IN THE ORDER NICOLAUS HAD PREDICTED. ONE DETAIL WAS DIFFERENT: NICOLAUS THOUGHT THE PLANETS MOVED IN CIRCLES AROUND THE SUN, BUT JOHANNES SHOWED THAT THEIR ORBITS WERE SHAPED LIKE ELLIPSES.

MANY YEARS LATER, GEORG WAS TALKING TO HIS FRIEND AND FELLOW MATHEMATICIAN AND ASTRONOMER, JOHANNES SCHÖNER.

ON THE REVOLUTION OF HEAVENLY SPHERES DID NOT CAUSE THE CONTROVERSY WITH THE CHURCH EVERYONE WAS EXPECTING.

IN HINDSIGHT, IT MAY HAVE BEEN ANDREAS' INTRODUCTION THAT PREVENTED THE BOOK FROM BEING BANNED.

HOWEVER, THE BOOK WAS BANNED BY A NEW POPE, PAUL V, IN 1616. IT WAS BROUGHT TO HIS ATTENTION AFTER THE ITALIAN ASTRONOMER GALILEO INVENTED THE TELESCOPE AND PUBLISHED HIS FINDINGS, WHICH SUPPORTED THE COPERNICAN THEORY. HIS IDEAS WOULD CREATE WAVES AMONG ASTRONOMERS FOR MANY YEARS TO COME.

ISAAC NEWTON
(1643–1727)
DISCOVERING RAINBOWS

ISAAC NEWTON WAS A DEEP THINKER WHO STRIVED TO DISCOVER MORE ABOUT HOW THE WORLD WORKED. HE DID NOT HAVE ANY FRIENDS AND PREFERRED TO BE ALONE. YET, HE LOVED SCHOOL, ESPECIALLY MATHEMATICS AND SCIENCE. HIS FATHER HAD DIED THREE MONTHS BEFORE HE WAS BORN SO HE LIVED WITH HIS GRANDMOTHER. HIS MOTHER HAD REMARRIED AND MOVED AWAY TO WOOLTHORPE, LINCOLNSHIRE IN ENGLAND. WHEN HE WAS 12 YEARS OLD, HIS MOTHER, NOW DIVORCED, TURNED UP AT ISAAC'S SCHOOL.

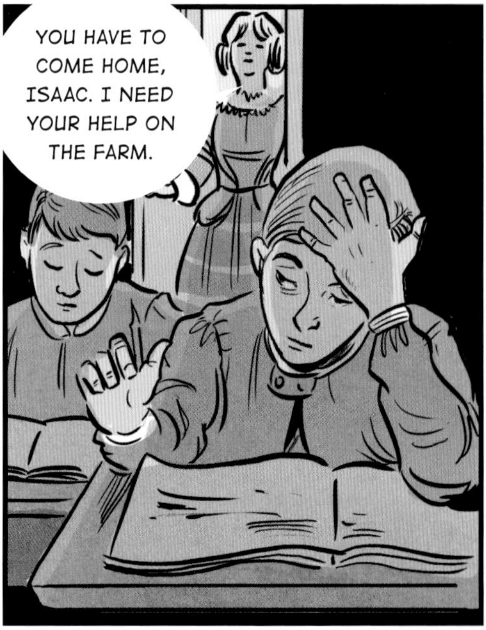
YOU HAVE TO COME HOME, ISAAC. I NEED YOUR HELP ON THE FARM.

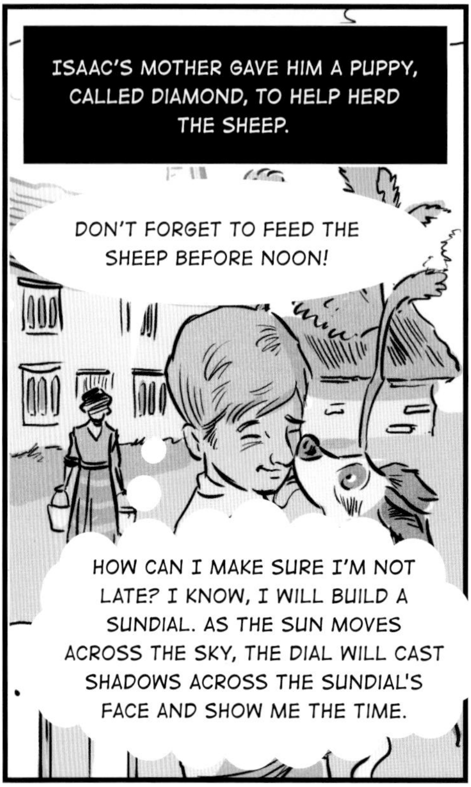
ISAAC'S MOTHER GAVE HIM A PUPPY, CALLED DIAMOND, TO HELP HERD THE SHEEP.
DON'T FORGET TO FEED THE SHEEP BEFORE NOON!
HOW CAN I MAKE SURE I'M NOT LATE? I KNOW, I WILL BUILD A SUNDIAL. AS THE SUN MOVES ACROSS THE SKY, THE DIAL WILL CAST SHADOWS ACROSS THE SUNDIAL'S FACE AND SHOW ME THE TIME.

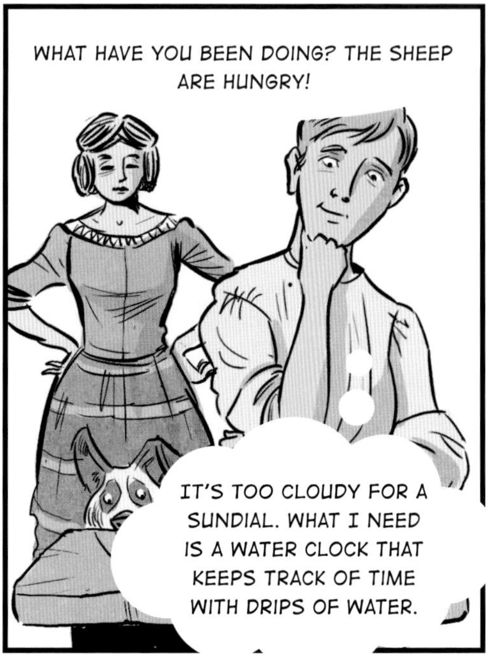
WHAT HAVE YOU BEEN DOING? THE SHEEP ARE HUNGRY!
IT'S TOO CLOUDY FOR A SUNDIAL. WHAT I NEED IS A WATER CLOCK THAT KEEPS TRACK OF TIME WITH DRIPS OF WATER.

ISAAC WENT TO CAMBRIDGE UNIVERSITY IN ENGLAND. HE WORKED AS A SERVANT TO PAY FOR HIS EDUCATION.

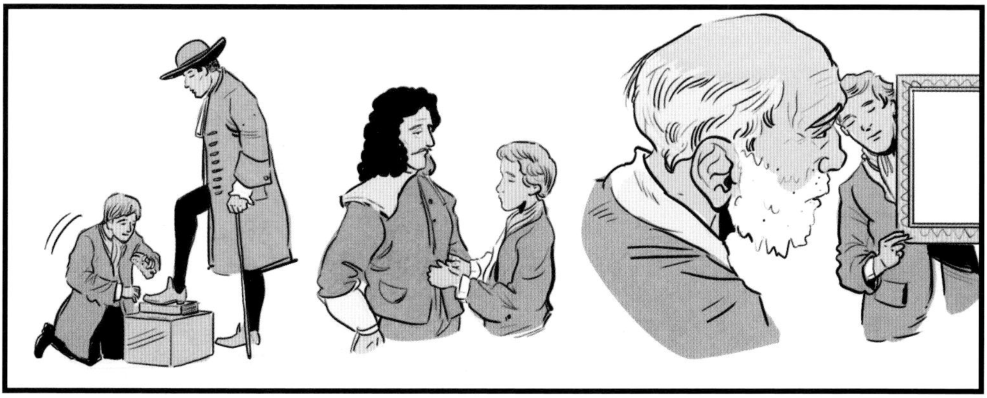

IN 1665, THE UNIVERSITY CLOSED FOR TWO YEARS BECAUSE OF THE PLAGUE. THIS TERRIBLE DISEASE KILLED A QUARTER OF LONDON'S POPULATION. ISAAC WENT HOME TO HIS MOTHER'S FARM IN WOOLTHORPE, LINCOLNSHIRE.

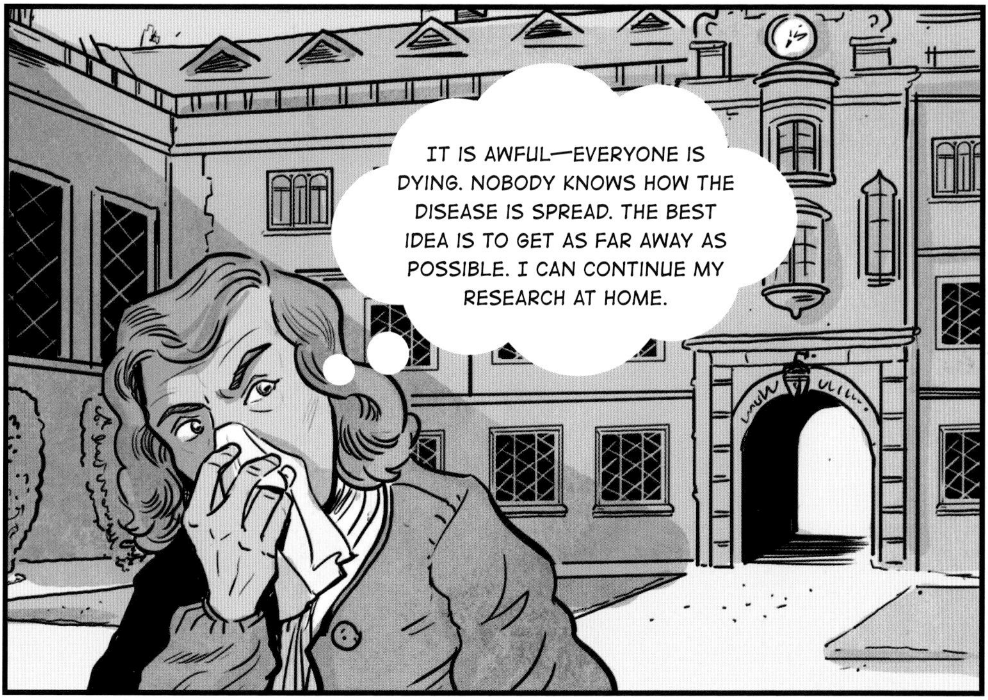
IT IS AWFUL—EVERYONE IS DYING. NOBODY KNOWS HOW THE DISEASE IS SPREAD. THE BEST IDEA IS TO GET AS FAR AWAY AS POSSIBLE. I CAN CONTINUE MY RESEARCH AT HOME.

AT A LOCAL MARKET, ISAAC FOUND A PIECE OF GLASS THAT HAD BEEN CUT AT PRECISE ANGLES. THIS IS CALLED A PRISM. WHEN HE EXAMINED IT IN SUNLIGHT, HE COULD SEE COLORS IN THE LIGHT AS IT EMERGED FROM THE PRISM.

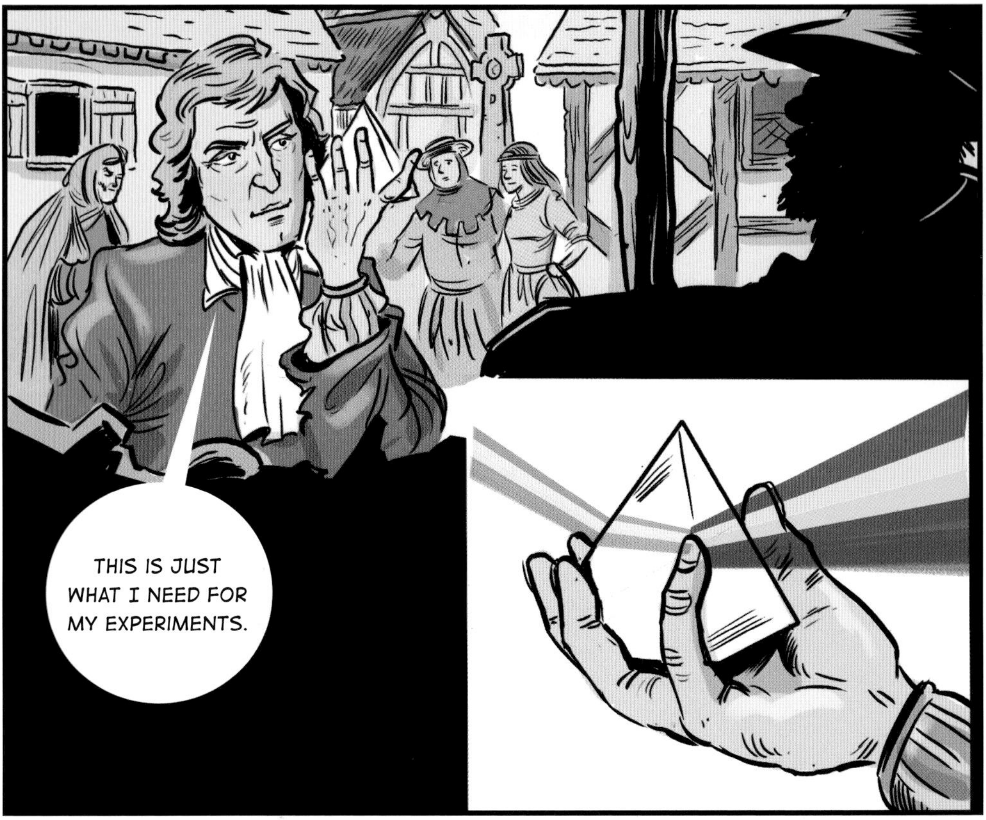
THIS IS JUST WHAT I NEED FOR MY EXPERIMENTS.

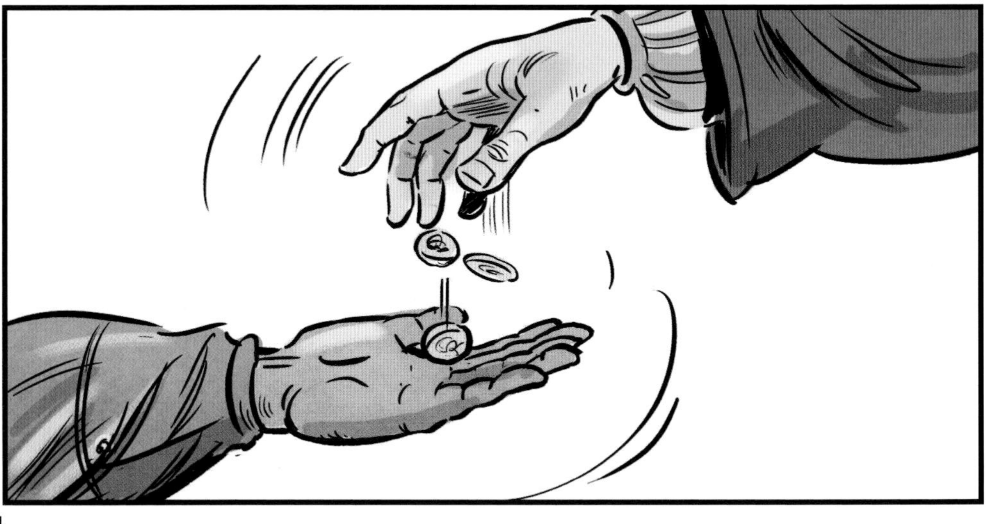

THE GREEK PHILOSOPHER ARISTOTLE HAD BELIEVED COLOR WAS SOMETHING TRANSMITTED FROM AN OBJECT TO THE EYE.

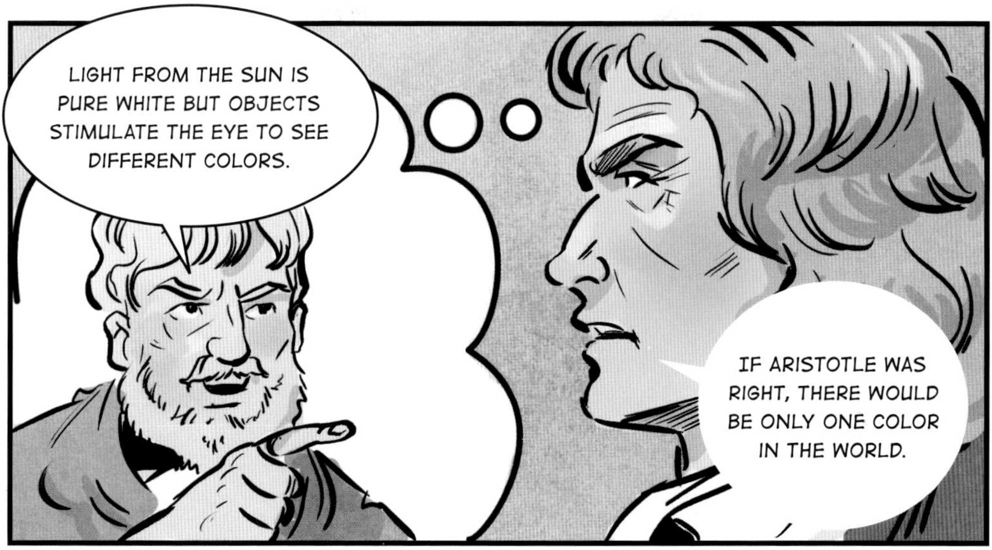
LIGHT FROM THE SUN IS PURE WHITE BUT OBJECTS STIMULATE THE EYE TO SEE DIFFERENT COLORS.
IF ARISTOTLE WAS RIGHT, THERE WOULD BE ONLY ONE COLOR IN THE WORLD.

FRENCH PHILOSOPHER AND MATHEMATICIAN RENE DESCARTES BELIEVED THERE WAS AN INVISIBLE MATERIAL, CALLED PLENUM, THAT FILLED THE UNIVERSE.

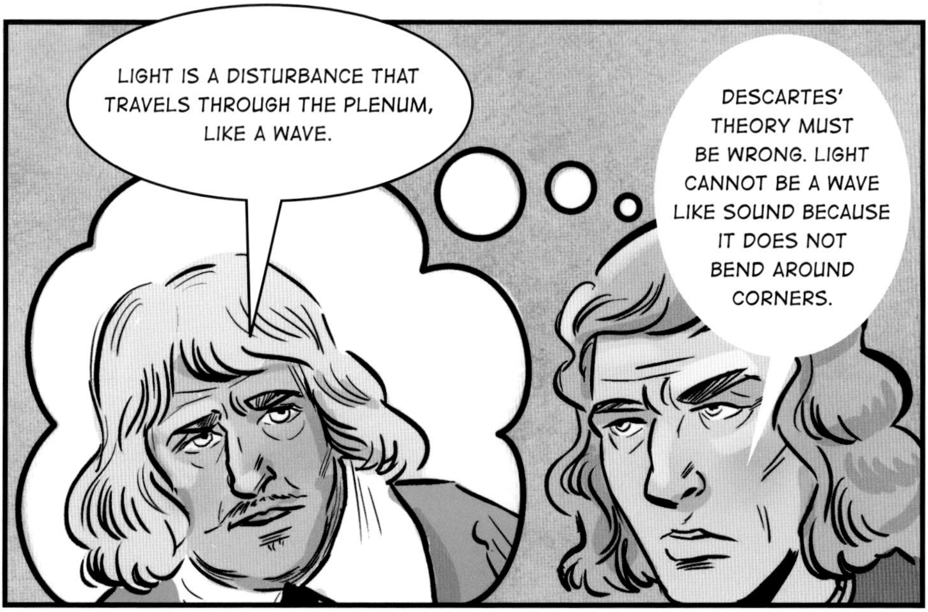
LIGHT IS A DISTURBANCE THAT TRAVELS THROUGH THE PLENUM, LIKE A WAVE.
DESCARTES' THEORY MUST BE WRONG. LIGHT CANNOT BE A WAVE LIKE SOUND BECAUSE IT DOES NOT BEND AROUND CORNERS.

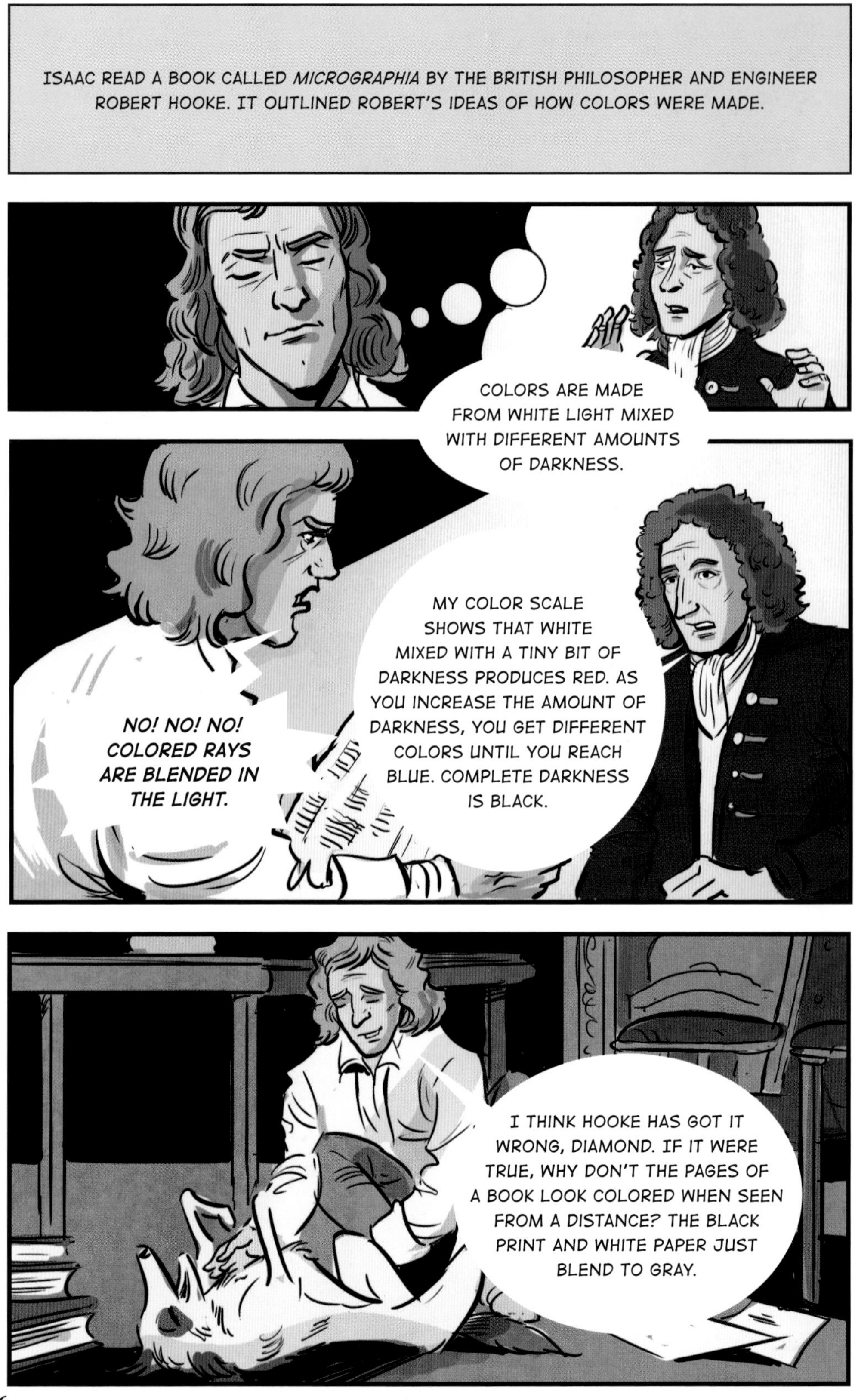
ISAAC READ A BOOK CALLED *MICROGRAPHIA* BY THE BRITISH PHILOSOPHER AND ENGINEER ROBERT HOOKE. IT OUTLINED ROBERT'S IDEAS OF HOW COLORS WERE MADE.
COLORS ARE MADE FROM WHITE LIGHT MIXED WITH DIFFERENT AMOUNTS OF DARKNESS.
MY COLOR SCALE SHOWS THAT WHITE MIXED WITH A TINY BIT OF DARKNESS PRODUCES RED. AS YOU INCREASE THE AMOUNT OF DARKNESS, YOU GET DIFFERENT COLORS UNTIL YOU REACH BLUE. COMPLETE DARKNESS IS BLACK.
NO! NO! NO! COLORED RAYS ARE BLENDED IN THE LIGHT.
I THINK HOOKE HAS GOT IT WRONG, DIAMOND. IF IT WERE TRUE, WHY DON'T THE PAGES OF A BOOK LOOK COLORED WHEN SEEN FROM A DISTANCE? THE BLACK PRINT AND WHITE PAPER JUST BLEND TO GRAY.

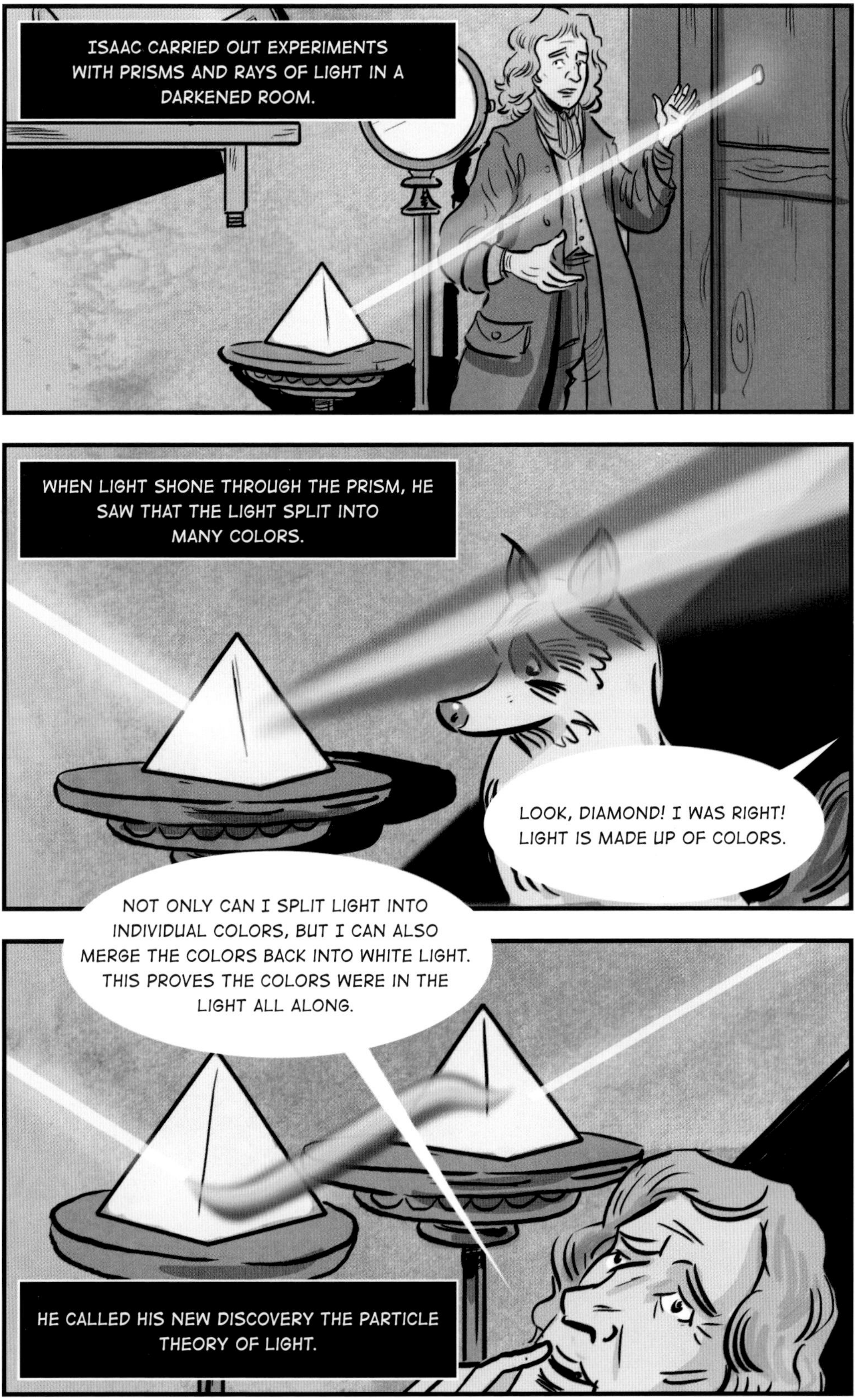
ISAAC CARRIED OUT EXPERIMENTS WITH PRISMS AND RAYS OF LIGHT IN A DARKENED ROOM.
WHEN LIGHT SHONE THROUGH THE PRISM, HE SAW THAT THE LIGHT SPLIT INTO MANY COLORS.
LOOK, DIAMOND! I WAS RIGHT! LIGHT IS MADE UP OF COLORS.
NOT ONLY CAN I SPLIT LIGHT INTO INDIVIDUAL COLORS, BUT I CAN ALSO MERGE THE COLORS BACK INTO WHITE LIGHT. THIS PROVES THE COLORS WERE IN THE LIGHT ALL ALONG.
HE CALLED HIS NEW DISCOVERY THE PARTICLE THEORY OF LIGHT.

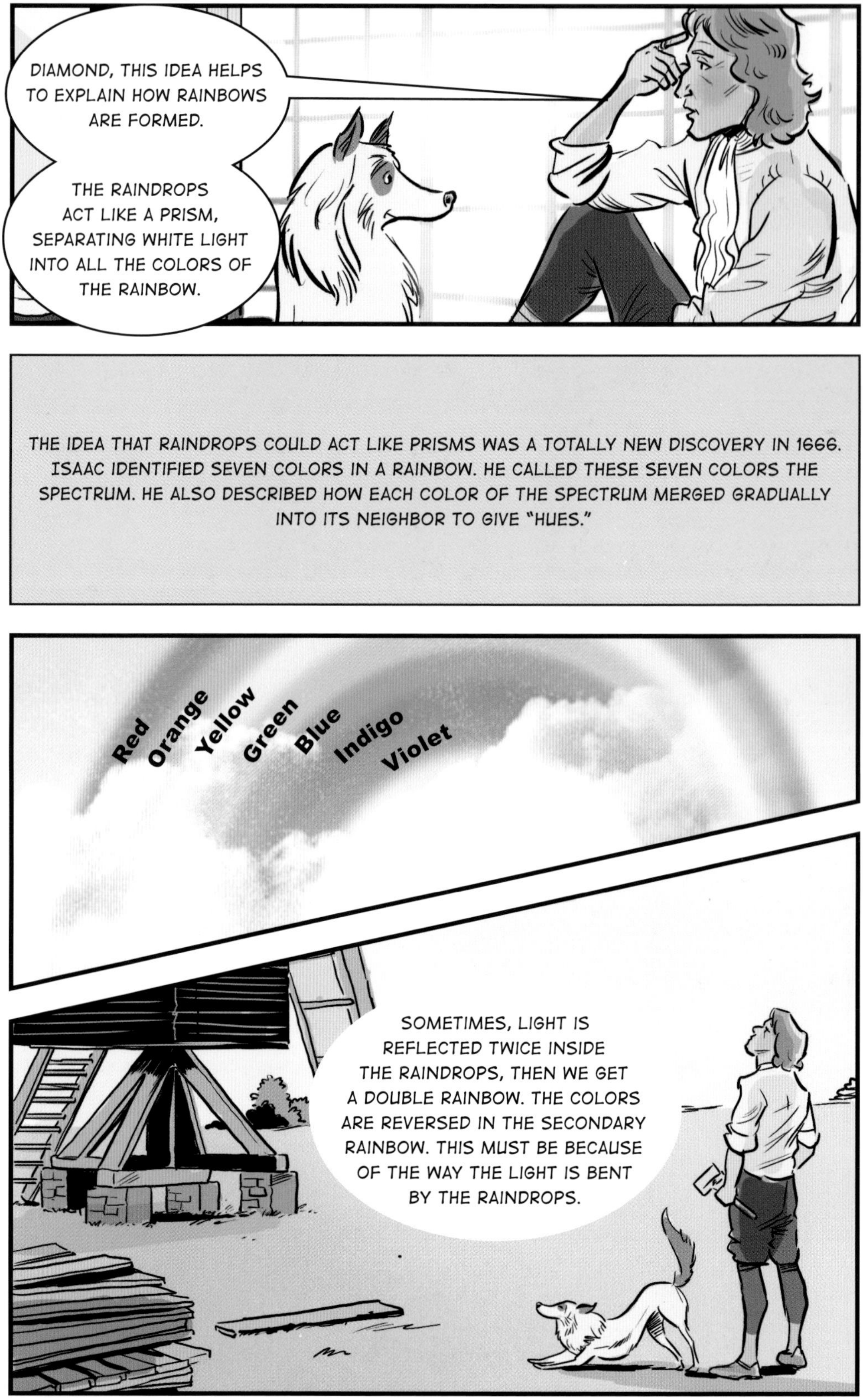
DIAMOND, THIS IDEA HELPS TO EXPLAIN HOW RAINBOWS ARE FORMED.
THE RAINDROPS ACT LIKE A PRISM, SEPARATING WHITE LIGHT INTO ALL THE COLORS OF THE RAINBOW.
THE IDEA THAT RAINDROPS COULD ACT LIKE PRISMS WAS A TOTALLY NEW DISCOVERY IN 1666. ISAAC IDENTIFIED SEVEN COLORS IN A RAINBOW. HE CALLED THESE SEVEN COLORS THE SPECTRUM. HE ALSO DESCRIBED HOW EACH COLOR OF THE SPECTRUM MERGED GRADUALLY INTO ITS NEIGHBOR TO GIVE "HUES."
Red
Orange
Yellow
Green
Blue
Indigo
Violet
SOMETIMES, LIGHT IS REFLECTED TWICE INSIDE THE RAINDROPS, THEN WE GET A DOUBLE RAINBOW. THE COLORS ARE REVERSED IN THE SECONDARY RAINBOW. THIS MUST BE BECAUSE OF THE WAY THE LIGHT IS BENT BY THE RAINDROPS.

HE NOTICED HIS TELESCOPE PRODUCED A RAINBOW EFFECT AROUND THE MOON. ISAAC BEGAN TO EXPERIMENT WITH GRINDING AND POLISHING MIRRORS AND LENSES. HE WANTED TO GET RID OF THIS RAINBOW EFFECT. IN 1668, ISAAC'S WORK WITH PRISMS, MIRRORS, AND LENSES HELPED HIM DESIGN A BETTER TELESCOPE USING CURVED MIRRORS INSTEAD OF LENSES. HE CALLED IT A REFLECTIVE TELESCOPE.

SUCCESS, DIAMOND! I NO LONGER HAVE A RAINBOW EFFECT AROUND OBJECTS. MY IMPROVED TELESCOPE ALSO HAS A HIGHER MAGNIFICATION.

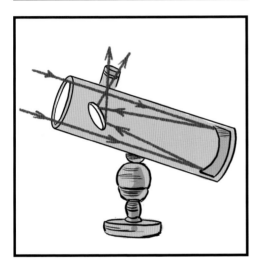

LIGHT FROM AN OBJECT ENTERS THE TELESCOPE TUBE AND BOUNCES OFF A CURVED MIRROR AT THE END OF THE TUBE. THIS IMAGE IS REFLECTED OFF A FLAT MIRROR AND THEN MAGNIFIED BY ANOTHER CURVED LENS IN THE EYE PIECE.

THE OLD TELESCOPE USES LENSES TO GATHER AND FOCUS LIGHT, WHILE MY REFLECTING TELESCOPE USES MIRRORS SO IT CAN SEE FURTHER AND CLEARER. THIS MEANS WE CAN OBSERVE FURTHER INTO SPACE THAN EVER BEFORE.

ISAAC SUBMITTED HIS DESIGN TO THE ROYAL SOCIETY. THEY ASKED HIM FOR A DEMONSTRATION OF THE TELESCOPE TO SEE FOR THEMSELVES IF THE REFLECTIVE TELESCOPE WAS BETTER THAN THE PREVIOUS DESIGN. THE ROYAL SOCIETY, A GROUP OF THE WORLD'S TOP SCIENTISTS, WAS SO IMPRESSED WITH ISAAC'S NEW TELESCOPE THEY ACCEPTED HIM AS A MEMBER.

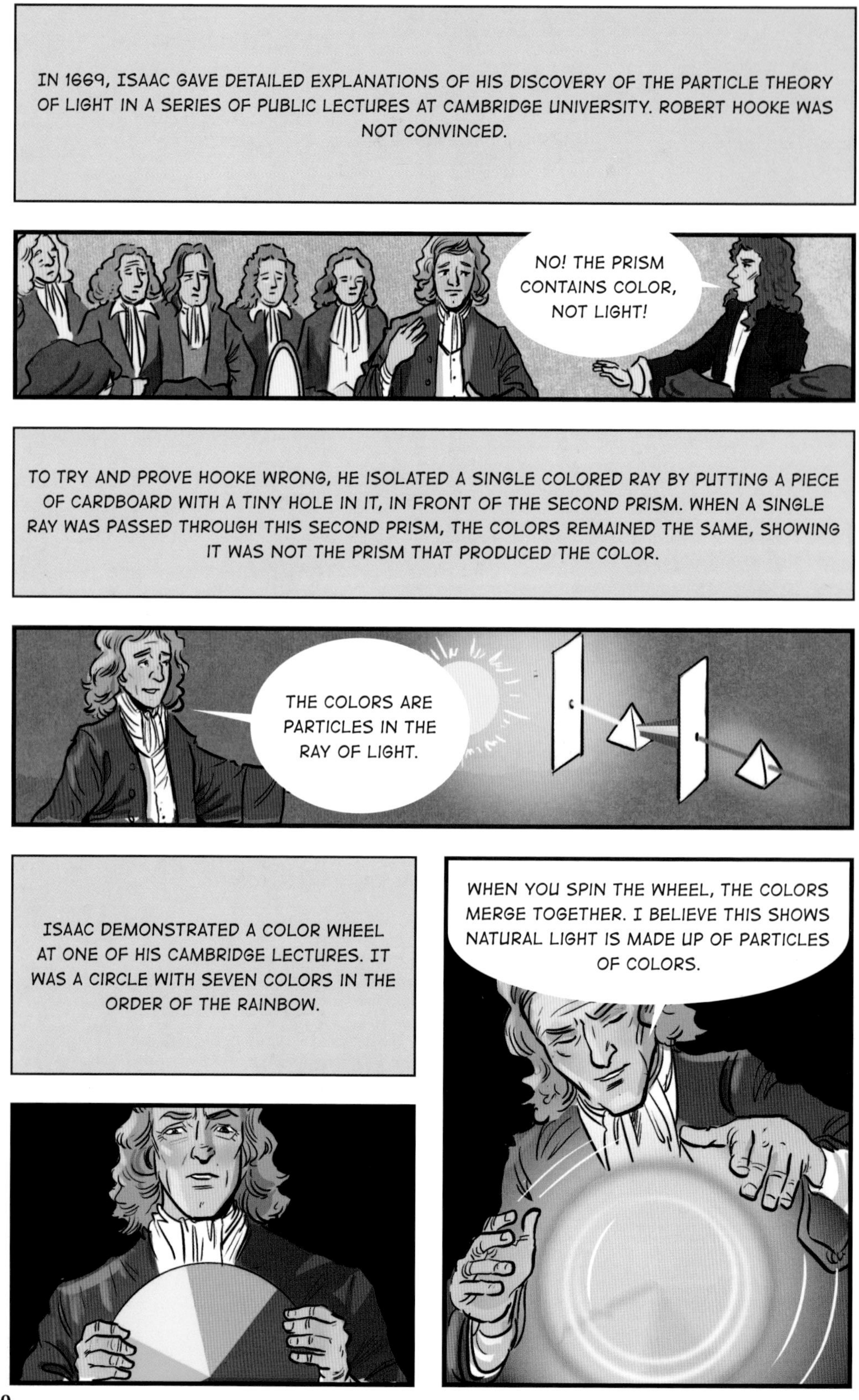
IN 1669, ISAAC GAVE DETAILED EXPLANATIONS OF HIS DISCOVERY OF THE PARTICLE THEORY OF LIGHT IN A SERIES OF PUBLIC LECTURES AT CAMBRIDGE UNIVERSITY. ROBERT HOOKE WAS NOT CONVINCED.
NO! THE PRISM CONTAINS COLOR, NOT LIGHT!
TO TRY AND PROVE HOOKE WRONG, HE ISOLATED A SINGLE COLORED RAY BY PUTTING A PIECE OF CARDBOARD WITH A TINY HOLE IN IT, IN FRONT OF THE SECOND PRISM. WHEN A SINGLE RAY WAS PASSED THROUGH THIS SECOND PRISM, THE COLORS REMAINED THE SAME, SHOWING IT WAS NOT THE PRISM THAT PRODUCED THE COLOR.
THE COLORS ARE PARTICLES IN THE RAY OF LIGHT.
ISAAC DEMONSTRATED A COLOR WHEEL AT ONE OF HIS CAMBRIDGE LECTURES. IT WAS A CIRCLE WITH SEVEN COLORS IN THE ORDER OF THE RAINBOW.
WHEN YOU SPIN THE WHEEL, THE COLORS MERGE TOGETHER. I BELIEVE THIS SHOWS NATURAL LIGHT IS MADE UP OF PARTICLES OF COLORS.

IN 1672, HE WROTE A LETTER TO THE ROYAL SOCIETY EXPLAINING HIS PARTICLE THEORY OF LIGHT AND HOW HE DID HIS EXPERIMENTS. HE CHALLENGED THE OTHER MEMBERS OF THE ROYAL SOCIETY TO PROVE HIM WRONG. SCIENTIFIC LETTERS TO THE ROYAL SOCIETY WERE PRINTED AND SENT OUT TO ALL MEMBERS. FRANCIS LINE, A MATHEMATICS PROFESSOR FROM LIEGE, BELGIUM, TOOK UP ISAAC'S CHALLENGE.

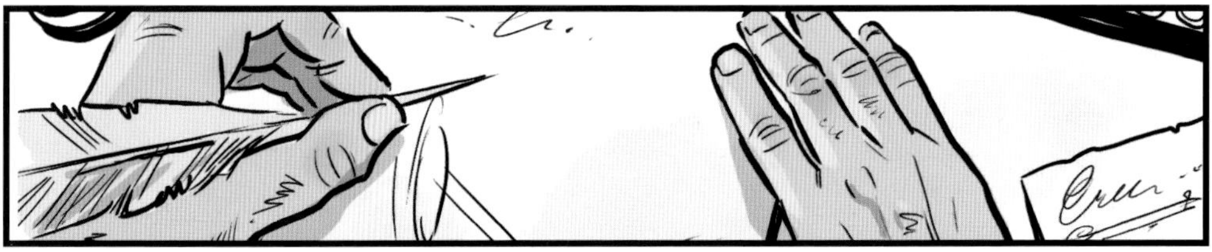

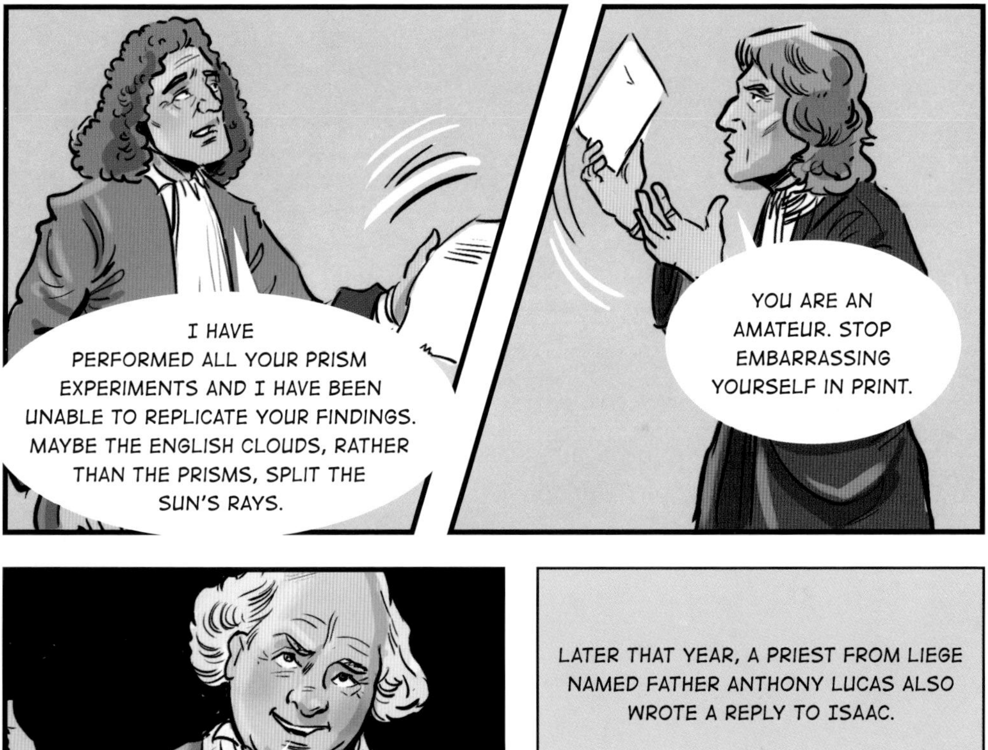
I HAVE PERFORMED ALL YOUR PRISM EXPERIMENTS AND I HAVE BEEN UNABLE TO REPLICATE YOUR FINDINGS. MAYBE THE ENGLISH CLOUDS, RATHER THAN THE PRISMS, SPLIT THE SUN'S RAYS.
YOU ARE AN AMATEUR. STOP EMBARRASSING YOURSELF IN PRINT.

LATER THAT YEAR, A PRIEST FROM LIEGE NAMED FATHER ANTHONY LUCAS ALSO WROTE A REPLY TO ISAAC.

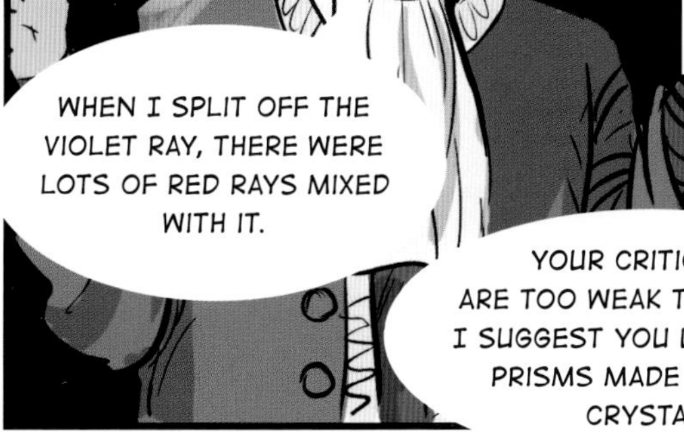
WHEN I SPLIT OFF THE VIOLET RAY, THERE WERE LOTS OF RED RAYS MIXED WITH IT.

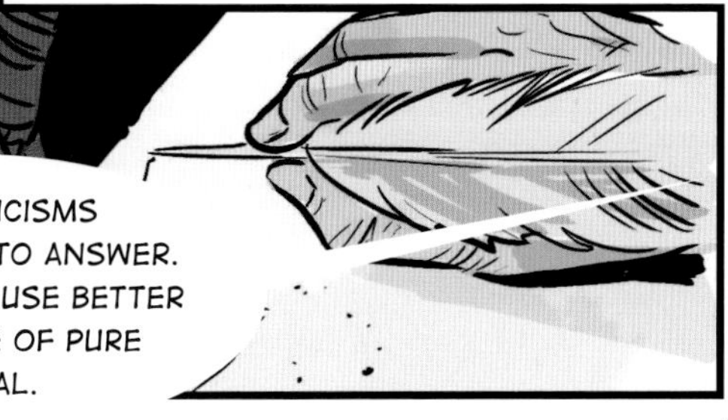
YOUR CRITICISMS ARE TOO WEAK TO ANSWER. I SUGGEST YOU USE BETTER PRISMS MADE OF PURE CRYSTAL.

ENCOURAGED BY THE CRITICISMS FROM OTHER MEMBERS OF THE ROYAL SOCIETY, ROBERT HOOKE CONTINUED A FIERCE BATTLE WITH ISAAC. IN 1675, HE PRESENTED HIS OWN THEORY TO THE ROYAL SOCIETY.

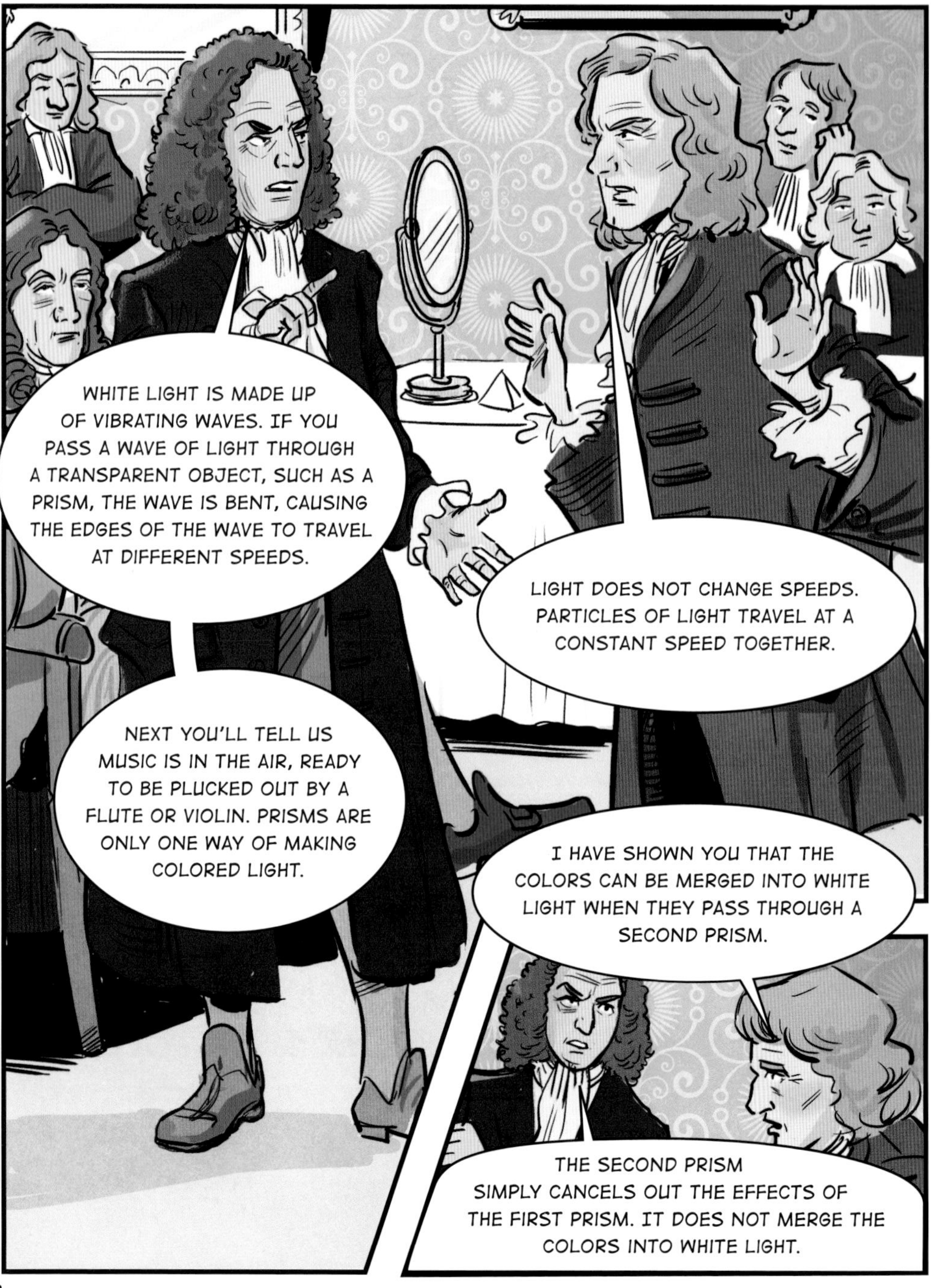
WHITE LIGHT IS MADE UP OF VIBRATING WAVES. IF YOU PASS A WAVE OF LIGHT THROUGH A TRANSPARENT OBJECT, SUCH AS A PRISM, THE WAVE IS BENT, CAUSING THE EDGES OF THE WAVE TO TRAVEL AT DIFFERENT SPEEDS.
LIGHT DOES NOT CHANGE SPEEDS. PARTICLES OF LIGHT TRAVEL AT A CONSTANT SPEED TOGETHER.
NEXT YOU'LL TELL US MUSIC IS IN THE AIR, READY TO BE PLUCKED OUT BY A FLUTE OR VIOLIN. PRISMS ARE ONLY ONE WAY OF MAKING COLORED LIGHT.
I HAVE SHOWN YOU THAT THE COLORS CAN BE MERGED INTO WHITE LIGHT WHEN THEY PASS THROUGH A SECOND PRISM.
THE SECOND PRISM SIMPLY CANCELS OUT THE EFFECTS OF THE FIRST PRISM. IT DOES NOT MERGE THE COLORS INTO WHITE LIGHT.

IN 1676, ÉDME MARIOTTE, AN EXPERIENCED INVESTIGATOR OF OPTICAL PHENOMENON IN PARIS, TRIED TO RECREATE ISAAC'S EXPERIMENTS. MARIOTTE FOUND THAT A PURE VIOLET RAY FROM THE FIRST PRISM HAD HINTS OF RED AND YELLOW AFTER IT WENT THROUGH THE SECOND PRISM. HIS RESULTS WERE PROBABLY CAUSED BY BUBBLES IN HIS PRISMS. ISAAC HAD GIVEN THE ROYAL SOCIETY A MANUSCRIPT FOR A BOOK THAT OUTLINED DETAILS OF HIS EXPERIMENTS. UPSET BY ALL THE CRITICISM, ISAAC WITHDREW HIS BOOK.

ROBERT HOOKE DIED IN 1703. WITHOUT OPPOSITION, ISAAC PUBLISHED HIS LIGHT PARTICLE THEORY IN 1704 IN A BOOK CALLED *OPTIK*. IT OUTLINED HIS THEORIES THAT LIGHT IS MADE UP OF A STREAM OF COLORED PARTICLES. ISAAC BECAME PRESIDENT OF THE ROYAL SOCIETY. AS PRESIDENT, HE WAS ABLE TO CHAMPION HIS LIGHT PARTICLE THEORY.

ISAAC'S DISCOVERY WAS IMPORTANT BECAUSE IT WAS A BIG STEP TOWARD UNDERSTANDING WHAT LIGHT IS AND HOW IT WORKS. IN 1705, QUEEN ANNE KNIGHTED ISAAC NEWTON FOR HIS CONTRIBUTIONS TO SCIENCE. HE BECAME KNOWN AS SIR ISAAC NEWTON.

EDWARD JENNER
(1749–1823)
THE MAN WHO SAVED LIVES

WHEN EDWARD JENNER WAS EIGHT YEARS OLD, HE WAS INOCULATED FOR SMALLPOX. THE GOAL WAS TO PREVENT HIM FROM EVER GETTING SMALLPOX BY TEACHING HIS BODY TO FIGHT OFF A SMALL AMOUNT OF THE DISEASE. DOCTORS SQUEEZED SOME PUS OUT OF A SMALLPOX SPOT AND RUBBED IT INTO A CUT MADE ON SOMEONE'S ARM. IT WAS A DANGEROUS PROCEDURE AS PEOPLE COULD GET THE DISEASE AND DIE. THE INOCULATION CAUSED EDWARD RECURRING HEALTH PROBLEMS THROUGHOUT HIS LIFE.

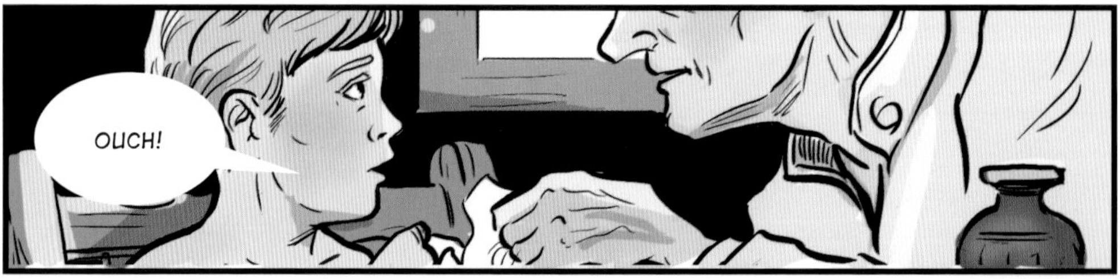
OUCH!

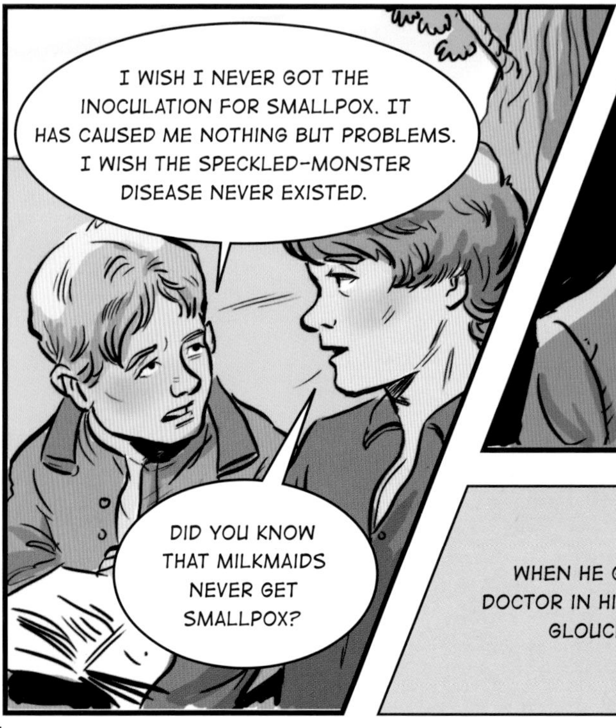
I WISH I NEVER GOT THE INOCULATION FOR SMALLPOX. IT HAS CAUSED ME NOTHING BUT PROBLEMS. I WISH THE SPECKLED-MONSTER DISEASE NEVER EXISTED.
DID YOU KNOW THAT MILKMAIDS NEVER GET SMALLPOX?

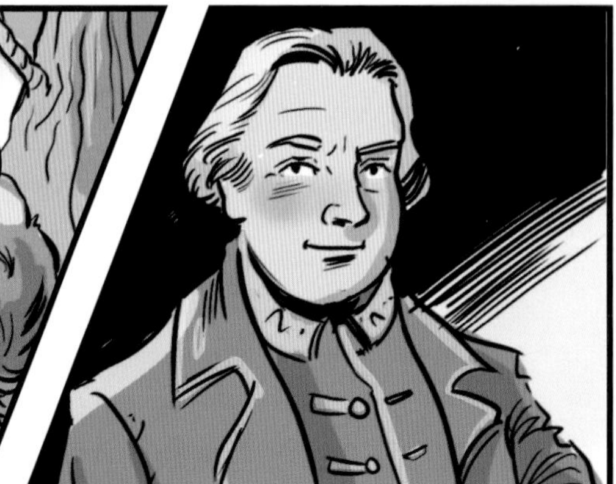

WHEN HE GREW UP, EDWARD BECAME A DOCTOR IN HIS HOMETOWN OF BERKELEY IN GLOUCESTERSHIRE, ENGLAND.

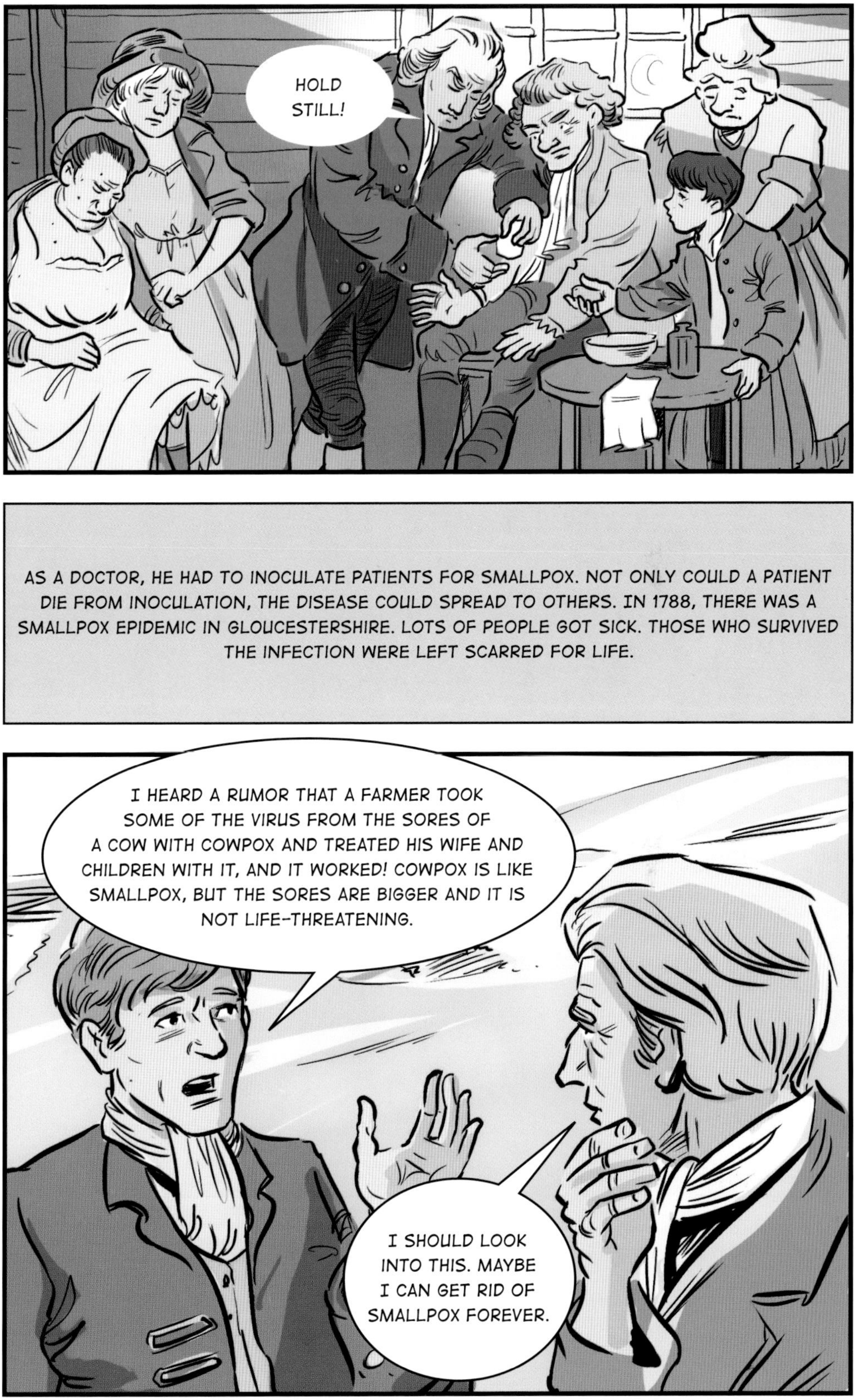
HOLD STILL!
AS A DOCTOR, HE HAD TO INOCULATE PATIENTS FOR SMALLPOX. NOT ONLY COULD A PATIENT DIE FROM INOCULATION, THE DISEASE COULD SPREAD TO OTHERS. IN 1788, THERE WAS A SMALLPOX EPIDEMIC IN GLOUCESTERSHIRE. LOTS OF PEOPLE GOT SICK. THOSE WHO SURVIVED THE INFECTION WERE LEFT SCARRED FOR LIFE.
I HEARD A RUMOR THAT A FARMER TOOK SOME OF THE VIRUS FROM THE SORES OF A COW WITH COWPOX AND TREATED HIS WIFE AND CHILDREN WITH IT, AND IT WORKED! COWPOX IS LIKE SMALLPOX, BUT THE SORES ARE BIGGER AND IT IS NOT LIFE-THREATENING.
I SHOULD LOOK INTO THIS. MAYBE I CAN GET RID OF SMALLPOX FOREVER.

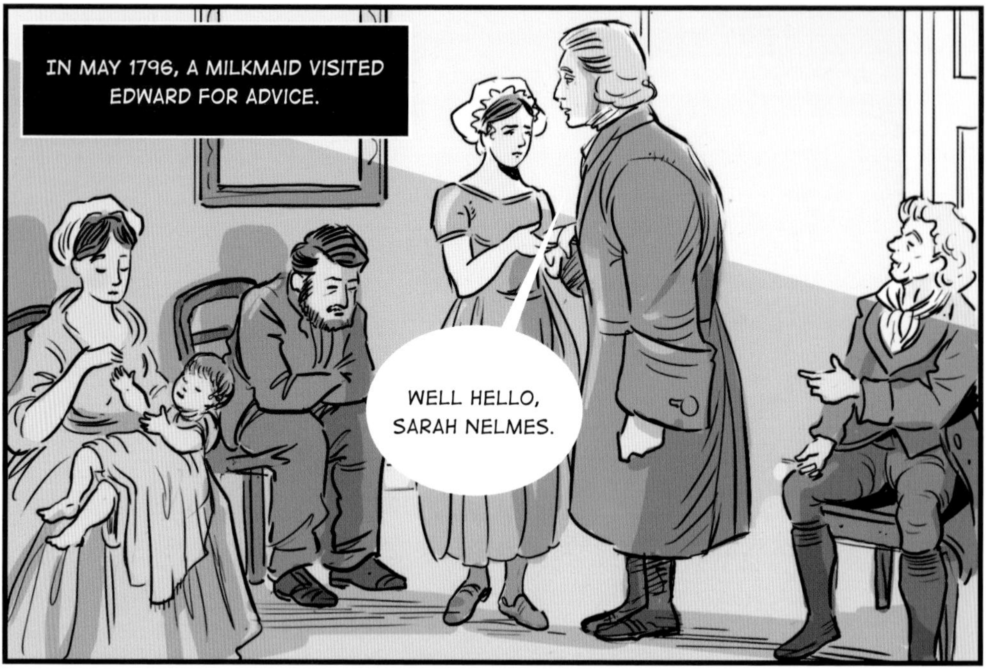
IN MAY 1796, A MILKMAID VISITED EDWARD FOR ADVICE.
WELL HELLO, SARAH NELMES.

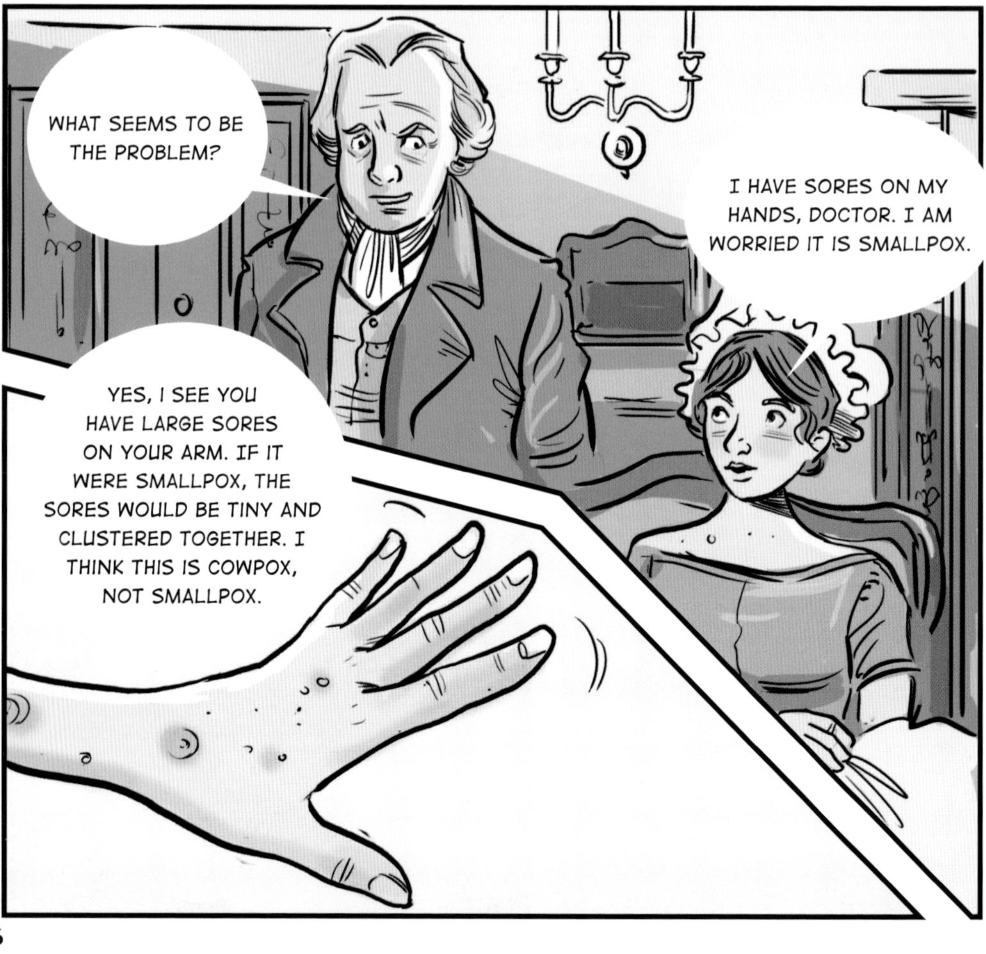
WHAT SEEMS TO BE THE PROBLEM?
I HAVE SORES ON MY HANDS, DOCTOR. I AM WORRIED IT IS SMALLPOX.
YES, I SEE YOU HAVE LARGE SORES ON YOUR ARM. IF IT WERE SMALLPOX, THE SORES WOULD BE TINY AND CLUSTERED TOGETHER. I THINK THIS IS COWPOX, NOT SMALLPOX.

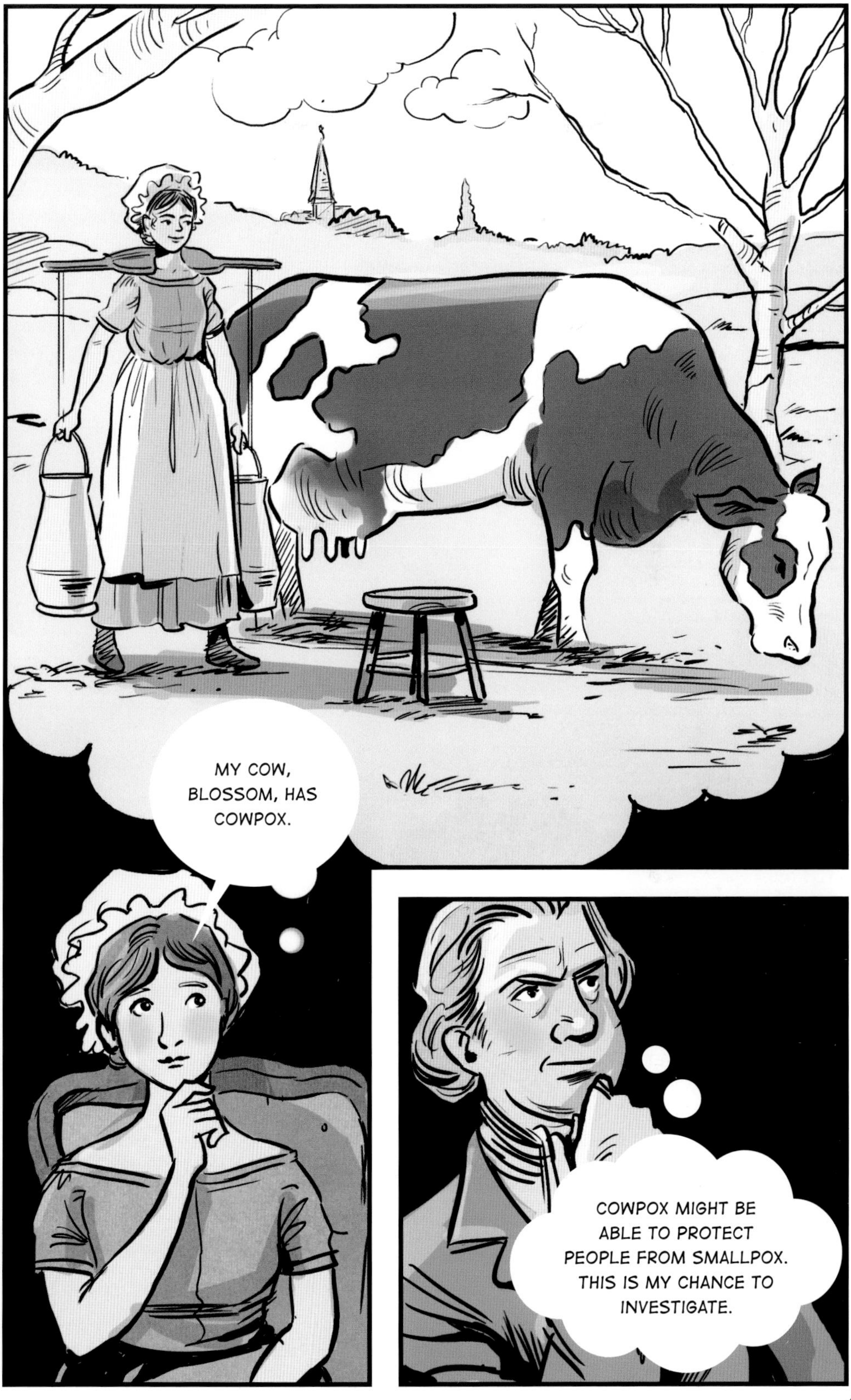
MY COW, BLOSSOM, HAS COWPOX.
COWPOX MIGHT BE ABLE TO PROTECT PEOPLE FROM SMALLPOX. THIS IS MY CHANCE TO INVESTIGATE.

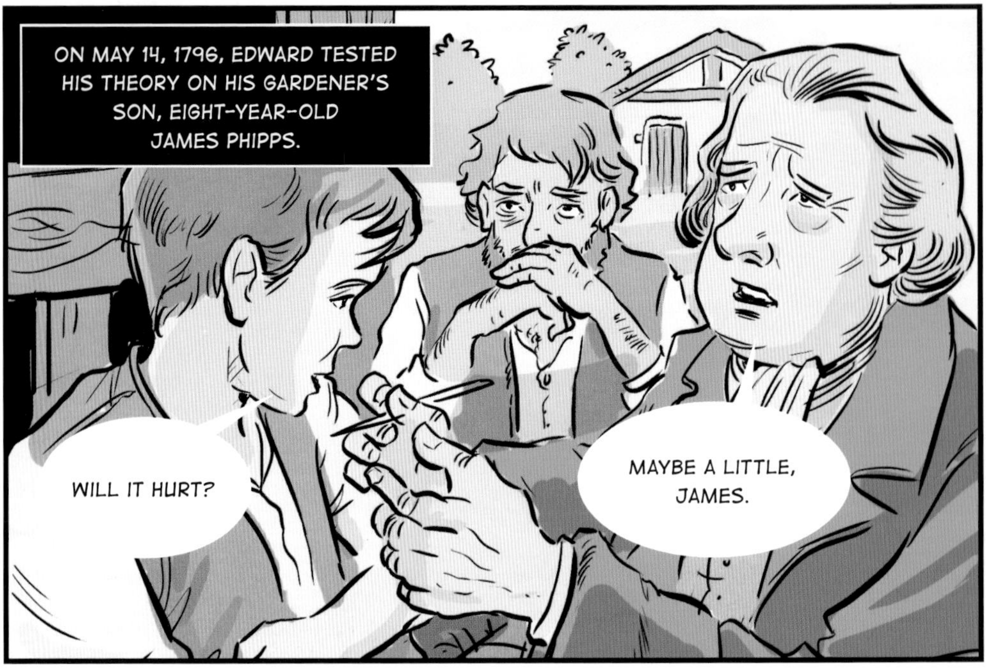
ON MAY 14, 1796, EDWARD TESTED HIS THEORY ON HIS GARDENER'S SON, EIGHT-YEAR-OLD JAMES PHIPPS.
WILL IT HURT?
MAYBE A LITTLE, JAMES.

EDWARD CUT JAMES' ARM AND ADDED SOME FLUID FROM THE SORES ON SARAH'S HAND. A FEW DAYS LATER, JAMES GOT COWPOX. THAT PROVED THE DISEASE COULD BE PASSED FROM PERSON TO PERSON AND NOT JUST FROM COWS TO PEOPLE.

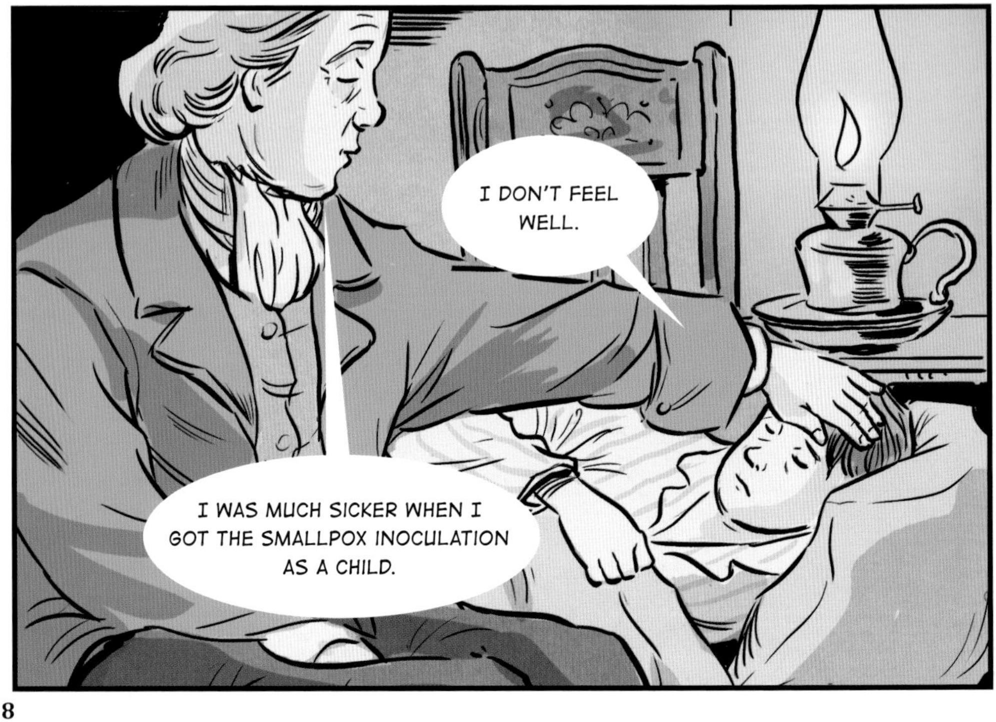
I DON'T FEEL WELL.
I WAS MUCH SICKER WHEN I GOT THE SMALLPOX INOCULATION AS A CHILD.

ON JULY 1, 1796, EDWARD TRIED TO INFECT JAMES WITH SMALLPOX. HE MADE A SMALL CUT ON JAMES' ARM AND RUBBED LIVE SMALLPOX INTO IT.

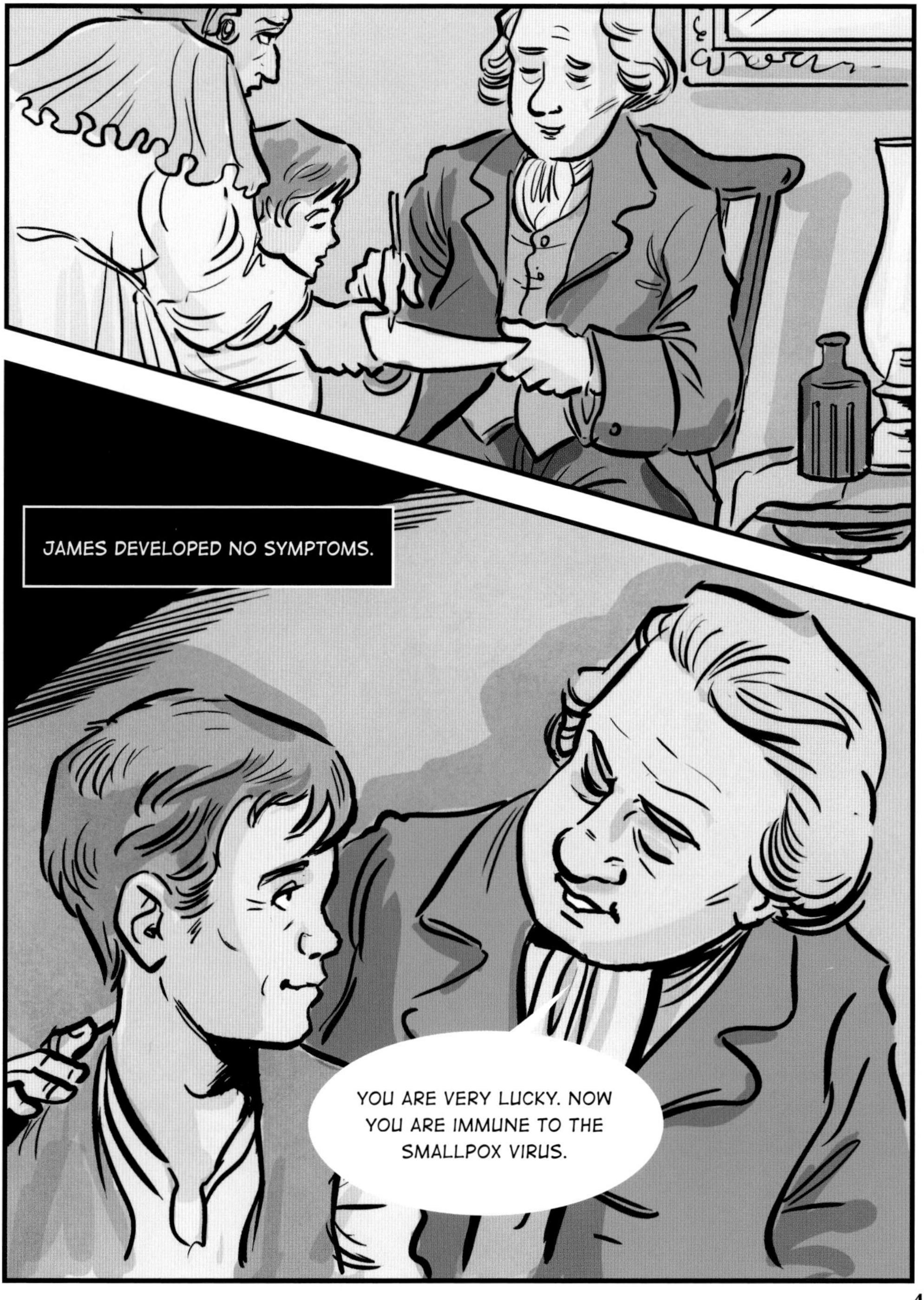
JAMES DEVELOPED NO SYMPTOMS.
YOU ARE VERY LUCKY. NOW YOU ARE IMMUNE TO THE SMALLPOX VIRUS.

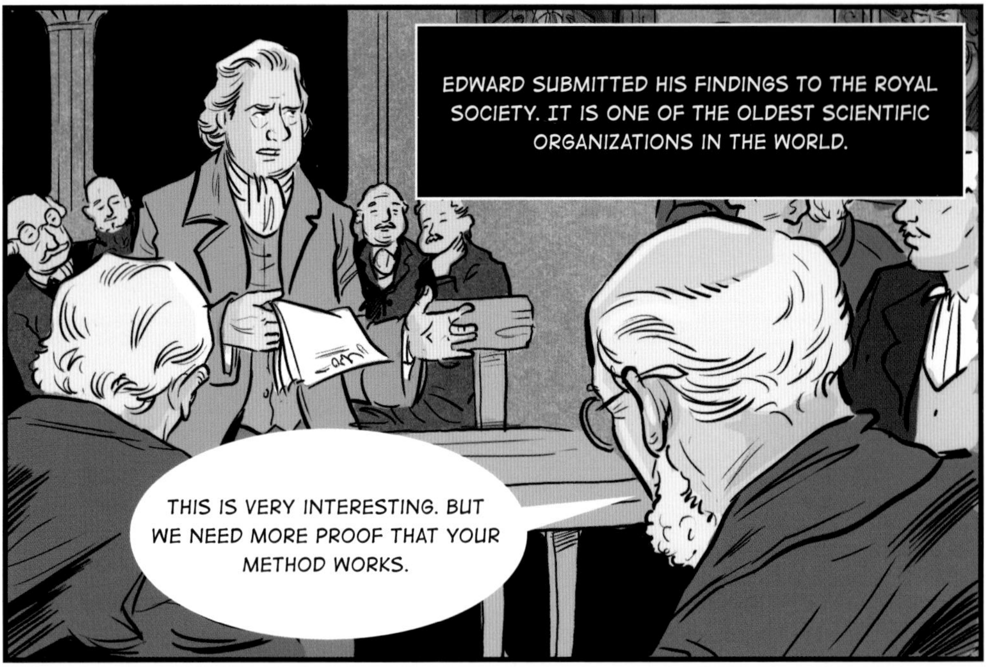
EDWARD SUBMITTED HIS FINDINGS TO THE ROYAL SOCIETY. IT IS ONE OF THE OLDEST SCIENTIFIC ORGANIZATIONS IN THE WORLD.
THIS IS VERY INTERESTING. BUT WE NEED MORE PROOF THAT YOUR METHOD WORKS.

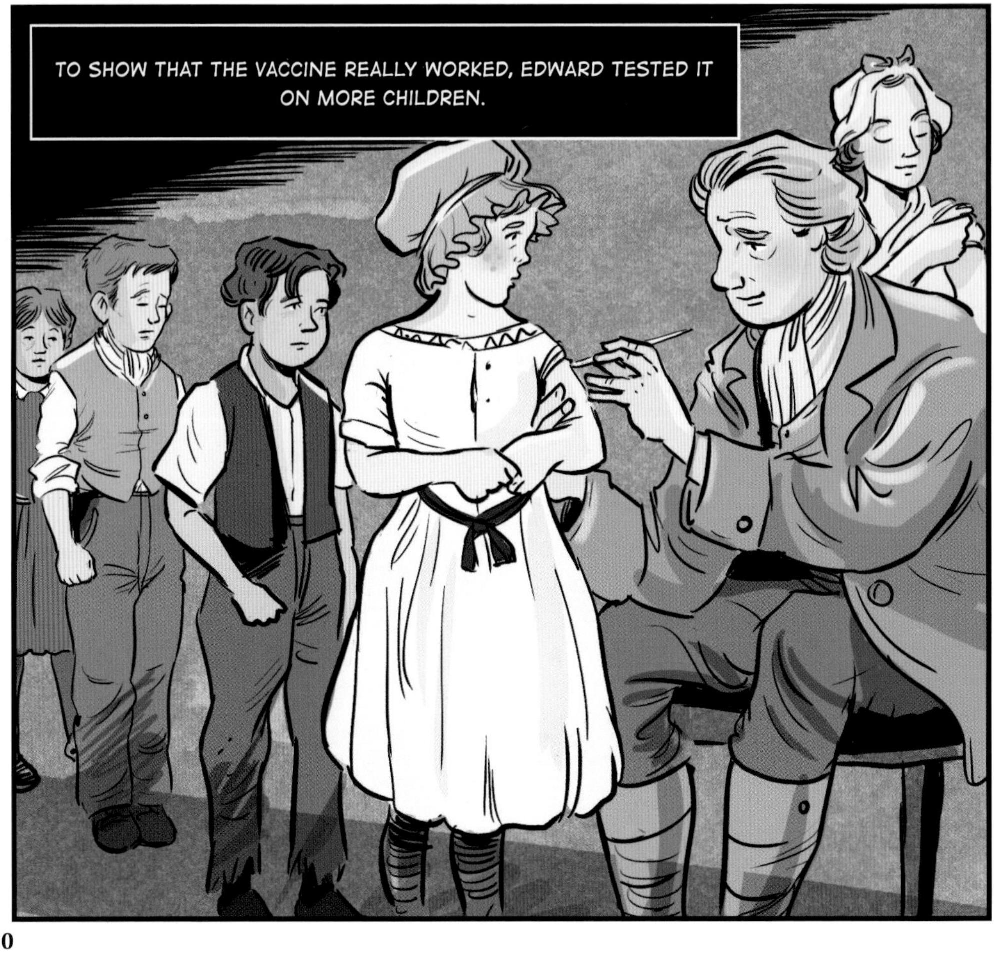
TO SHOW THAT THE VACCINE REALLY WORKED, EDWARD TESTED IT ON MORE CHILDREN.

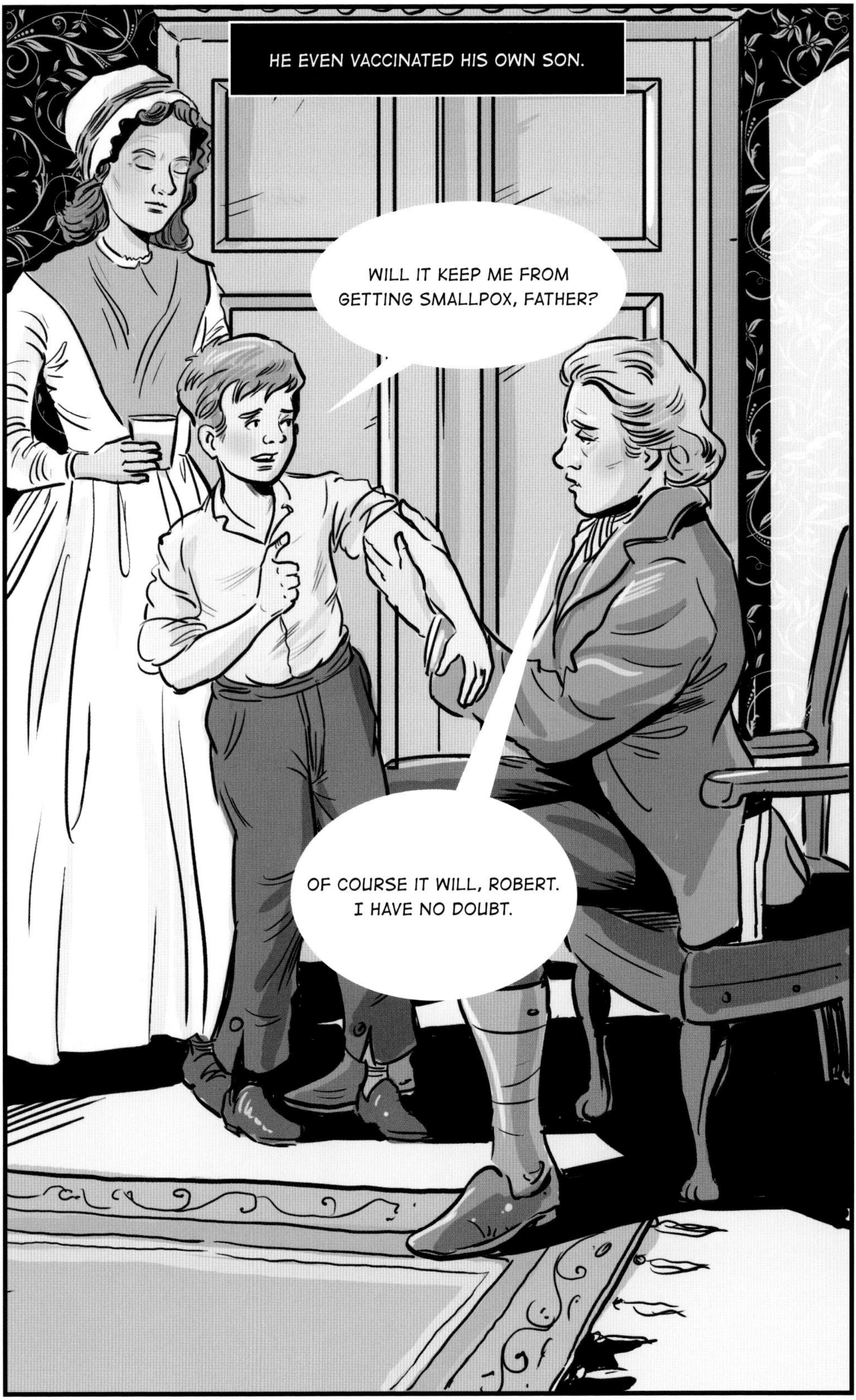
HE EVEN VACCINATED HIS OWN SON.
WILL IT KEEP ME FROM GETTING SMALLPOX, FATHER?
OF COURSE IT WILL, ROBERT. I HAVE NO DOUBT.

EDWARD WENT TO LONDON TO FIND MORE VOLUNTEERS TO TRY HIS NEW VACCINE. THREE MONTHS LATER, HE HAD NOT FOUND ANY. MANY PEOPLE LAUGHED AT HIM AND REFUSED TO BE TREATED WITH MEDICINE FROM COWS.

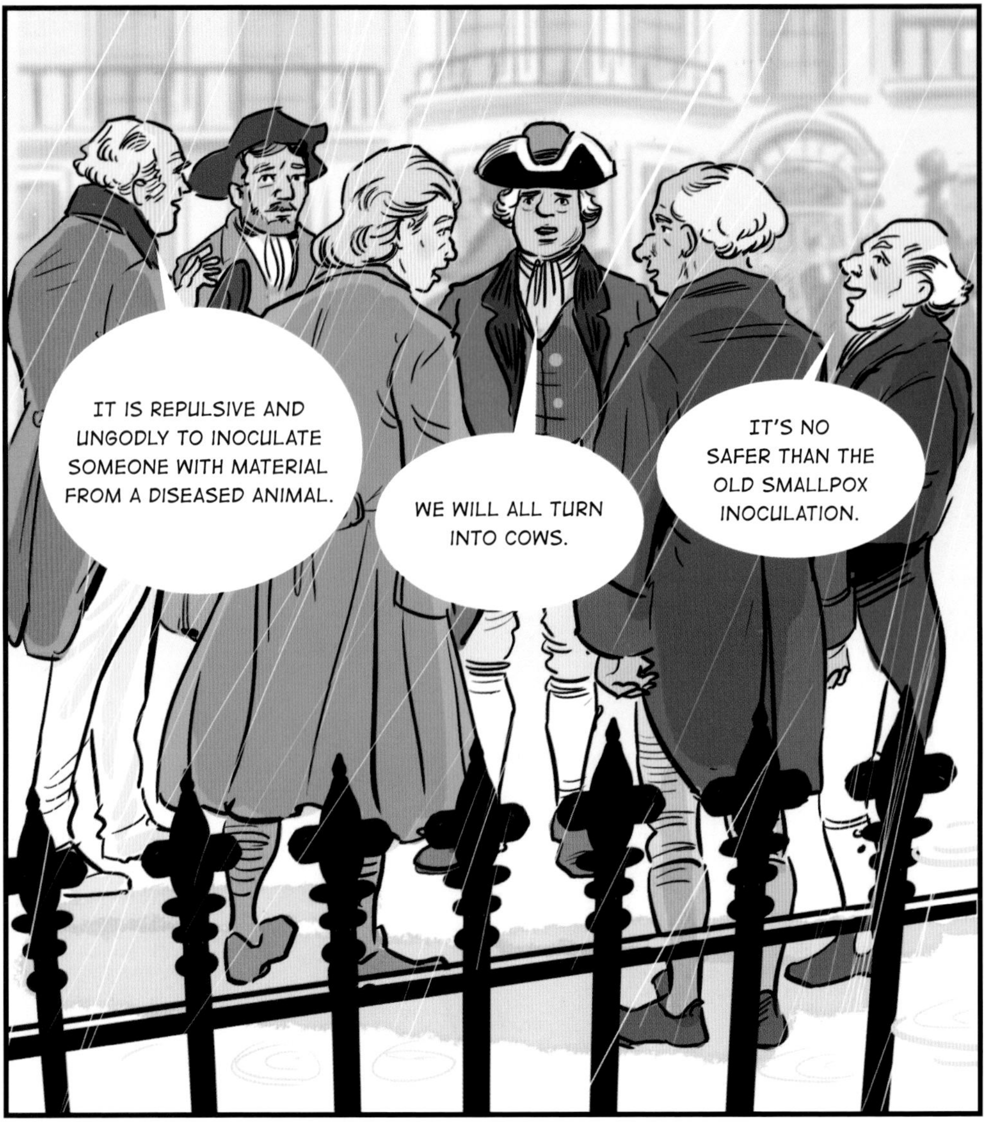
IT IS REPULSIVE AND UNGODLY TO INOCULATE SOMEONE WITH MATERIAL FROM A DISEASED ANIMAL.
WE WILL ALL TURN INTO COWS.
IT'S NO SAFER THAN THE OLD SMALLPOX INOCULATION.

DESPITE THEIR RESISTANCE, HE CONTINUED TO PROMOTE THE SMALLPOX VACCINE. THIS WAS THE FIRST VACCINE EVER MADE.

EDWARD DISCOVERED HE COULD DRY OUT THE VACCINE. HE SENT SAMPLES OF THE VACCINE FREE TO ANYONE WHO ASKED FOR IT AROUND THE WORLD.

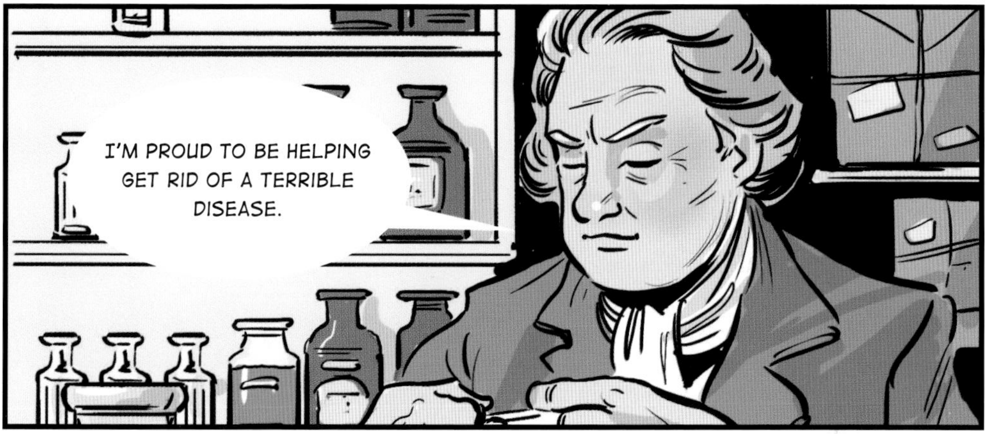
I'M PROUD TO BE HELPING GET RID OF A TERRIBLE DISEASE.

HE GAVE SOME OF THE VACCINE TO HIS FRIEND, DOCTOR HENRY CLINE. HENRY TRIED IT OUT ON SOME OF HIS PATIENTS. HE WAS SO IMPRESSED, HE RECOMMENDED THE VACCINATION TO ALL OF HIS PATIENTS.

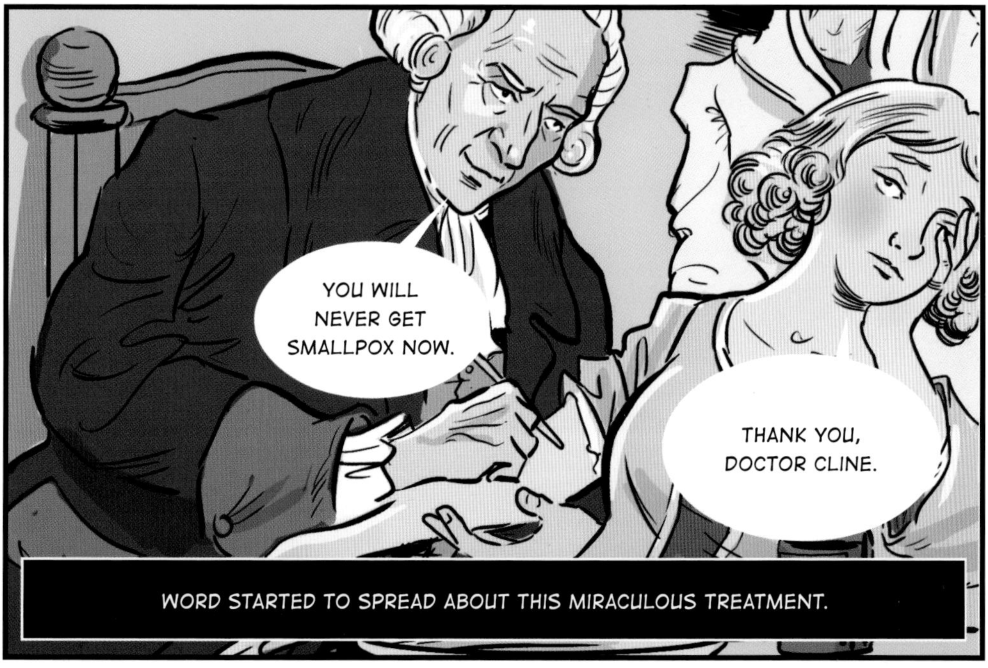
YOU WILL NEVER GET SMALLPOX NOW.
THANK YOU, DOCTOR CLINE.
WORD STARTED TO SPREAD ABOUT THIS MIRACULOUS TREATMENT.

EDWARD CONTINUED HIS WORK OF VACCINATING PEOPLE TO PREVENT THEM FROM CATCHING SMALLPOX. HE EVEN BUILT A ONE-ROOM HUT IN HIS GARDEN THAT HE CALLED THE *TEMPLE OF VACCINA*. THERE, HE PROVIDED FREE VACCINES TO POOR PEOPLE. HE NEVER SOUGHT TO BECOME RICH AND FAMOUS, HE JUST WANTED TO STOP THE SPREAD OF A HORRIBLE DISEASE.

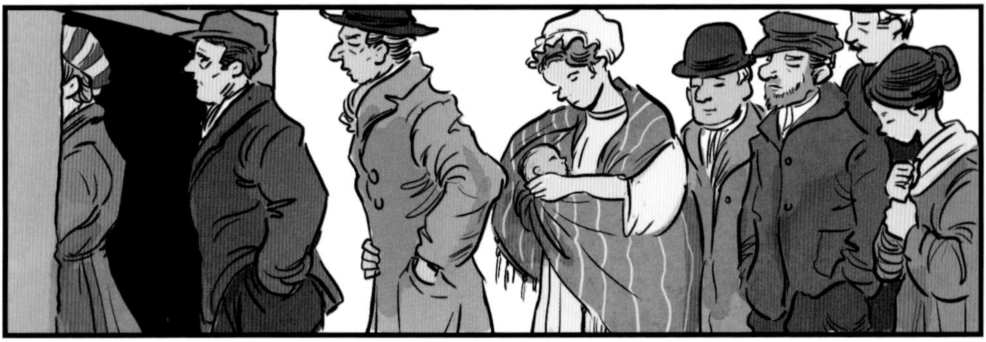

IN RECOGNITION OF HIS RELENTLESS WORK ON THE SMALLPOX VACCINE, EDWARD WAS MADE PHYSICIAN EXTRAORDINAIRE TO KING GEORGE IV IN 1821. THE KING ADVISED HIS SISTER-IN-LAW, THE DUCHESS OF KENT, TO HAVE HER DAUGHTER VACCINATED.

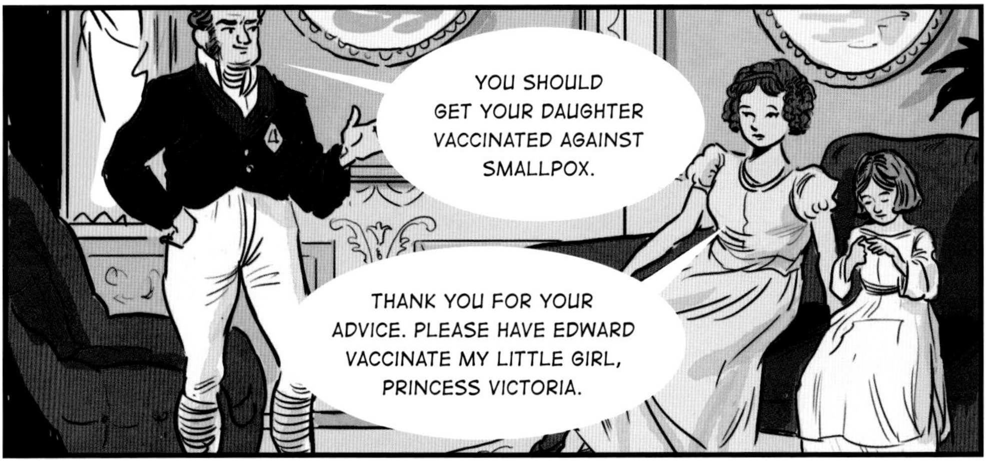
YOU SHOULD GET YOUR DAUGHTER VACCINATED AGAINST SMALLPOX.
THANK YOU FOR YOUR ADVICE. PLEASE HAVE EDWARD VACCINATE MY LITTLE GIRL, PRINCESS VICTORIA.

IT WASN'T UNTIL AFTER JENNER'S DEATH IN 1823 THAT PEOPLE RECOGNIZED THE IMPORTANCE OF HIS WORK. THIS WAS THE WORLD'S FIRST VACCINE AND IT PAVED THE WAY FOR MANY OTHER VACCINES FOR VARIOUS DISEASES.

BUT PEOPLE ALL OVER THE WORLD WERE STILL DYING OF SMALLPOX. IN 1966, THE WORLD HEALTH ORGANIZATION CAMPAIGNED FOR WORLDWIDE VACCINATION AGAINST SMALLPOX. THE DIRECTOR AT THE TIME WAS DOCTOR DONALD A. HENDERSON.

WE MUST VACCINATE EVERYONE. IT IS THE ONLY WAY TO GET RID OF SMALLPOX COMPLETELY.

IN 1980, DONALD ANNOUNCED THAT SMALLPOX HAD FINALLY BEEN ERADICATED AROUND THE WORLD.

SMALLPOX IS DEAD.

EDWARD JENNER HAD PIONEERED THE MODERN SCIENCE OF VIROLOGY, WHICH IS THE STUDY OF VIRUSES. HIS WORK IN THE FIELD OF IMMUNOLOGY HAS SAVED MORE LIVES THAN THE WORK OF ANY OTHER HUMAN ON EARTH.

CHARLES DARWIN
(1809–1882)
ORIGIN OF SPECIES

AS A BOY, CHARLES DARWIN LOVED FISHING, TRACKING ANIMALS, AND READING ABOUT NATURE.

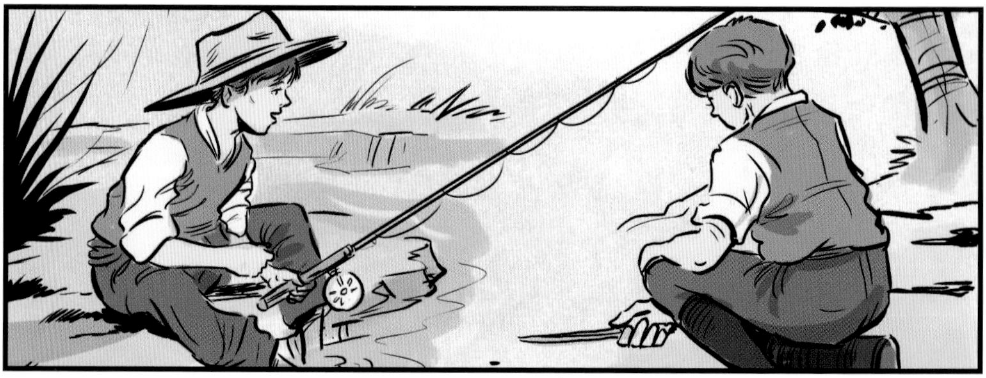

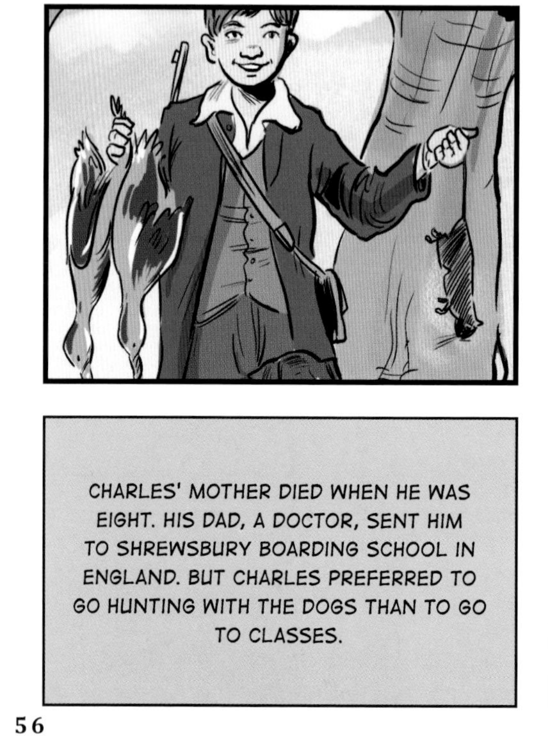

CHARLES' MOTHER DIED WHEN HE WAS EIGHT. HIS DAD, A DOCTOR, SENT HIM TO SHREWSBURY BOARDING SCHOOL IN ENGLAND. BUT CHARLES PREFERRED TO GO HUNTING WITH THE DOGS THAN TO GO TO CLASSES.

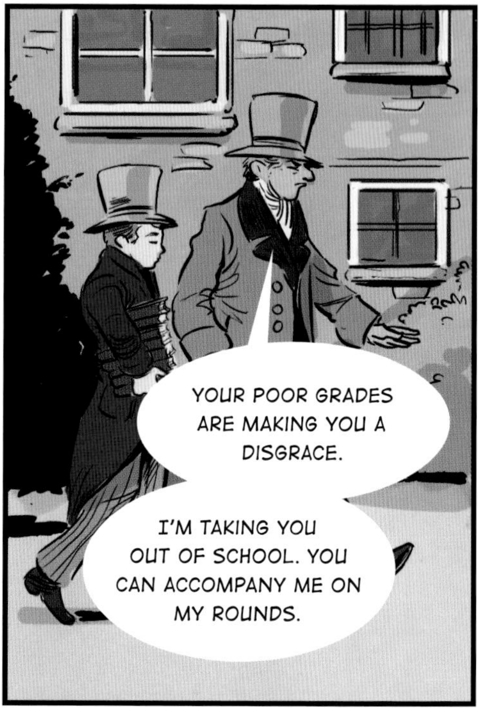
YOUR POOR GRADES ARE MAKING YOU A DISGRACE.
I'M TAKING YOU OUT OF SCHOOL. YOU CAN ACCOMPANY ME ON MY ROUNDS.

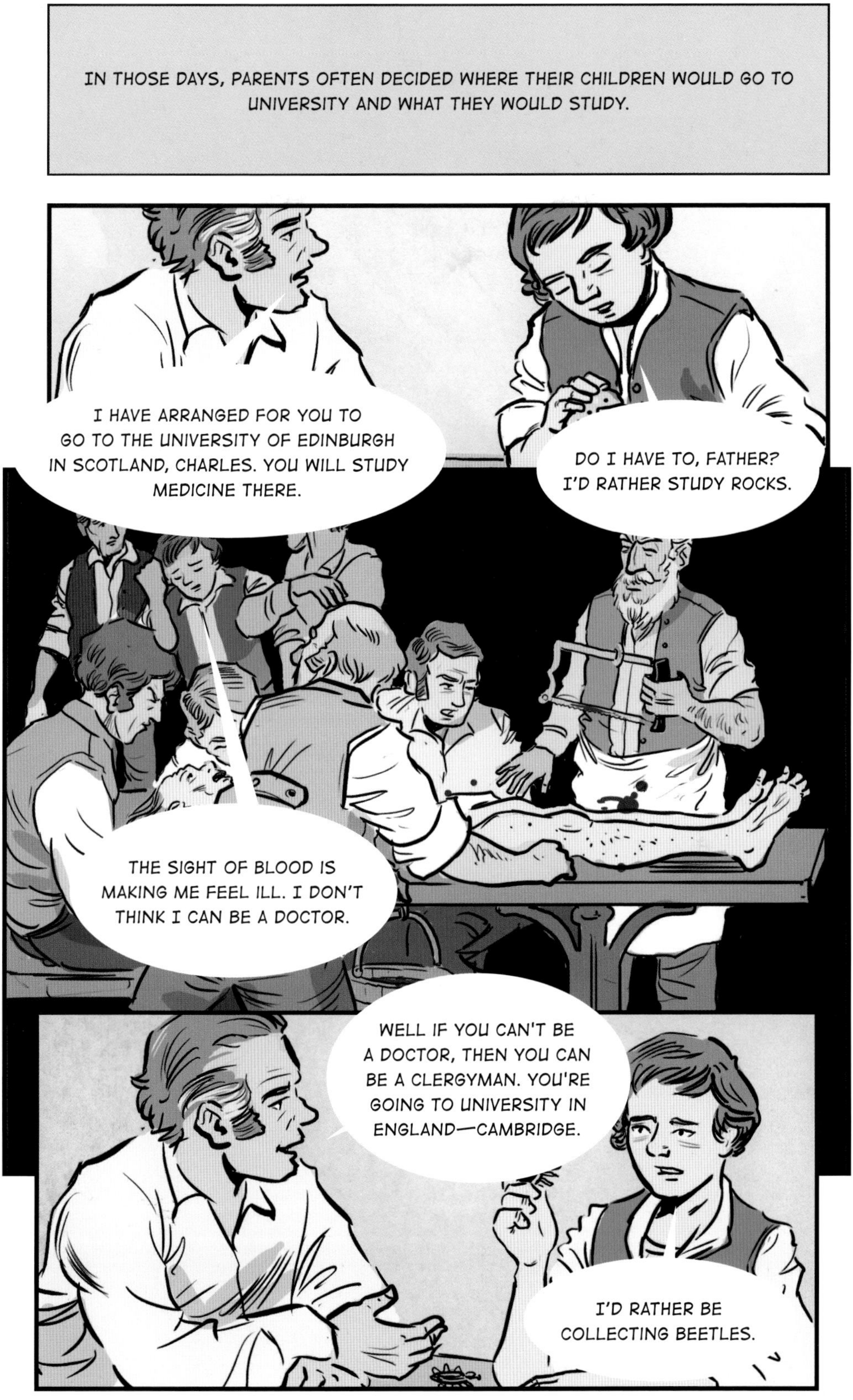
IN THOSE DAYS, PARENTS OFTEN DECIDED WHERE THEIR CHILDREN WOULD GO TO UNIVERSITY AND WHAT THEY WOULD STUDY.
I HAVE ARRANGED FOR YOU TO GO TO THE UNIVERSITY OF EDINBURGH IN SCOTLAND, CHARLES. YOU WILL STUDY MEDICINE THERE.
DO I HAVE TO, FATHER? I'D RATHER STUDY ROCKS.
THE SIGHT OF BLOOD IS MAKING ME FEEL ILL. I DON'T THINK I CAN BE A DOCTOR.
WELL IF YOU CAN'T BE A DOCTOR, THEN YOU CAN BE A CLERGYMAN. YOU'RE GOING TO UNIVERSITY IN ENGLAND—CAMBRIDGE.
I'D RATHER BE COLLECTING BEETLES.

CHARLES GRADUATED FROM THE UNIVERSITY OF CAMBRIDGE IN 1831. HIS KNOWLEDGE OF NATURE HAD GREATLY IMPRESSED HIS PROFESSOR, JOHN HENSLOW.

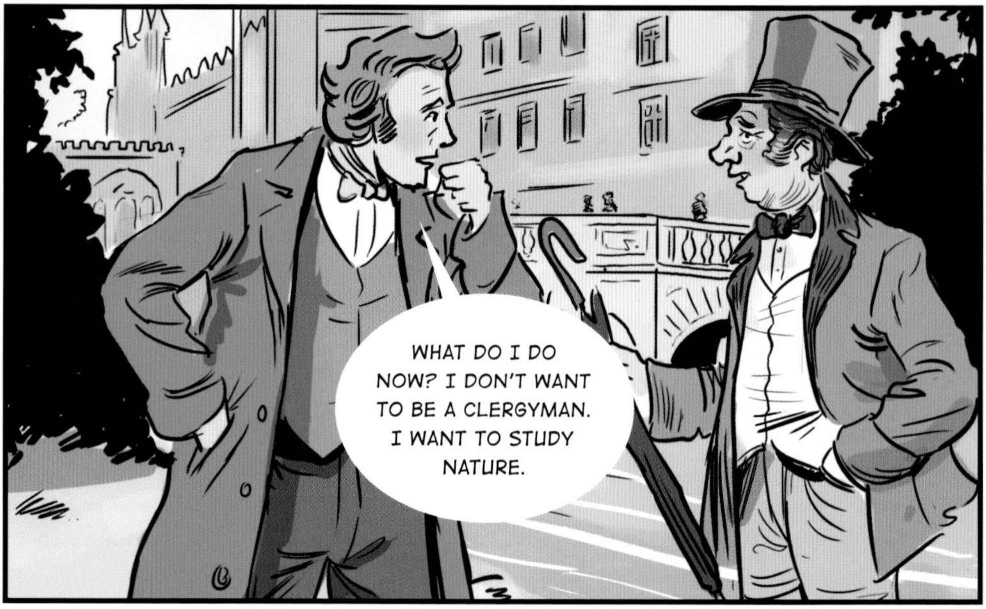
WHAT DO I DO NOW? I DON'T WANT TO BE A CLERGYMAN. I WANT TO STUDY NATURE.

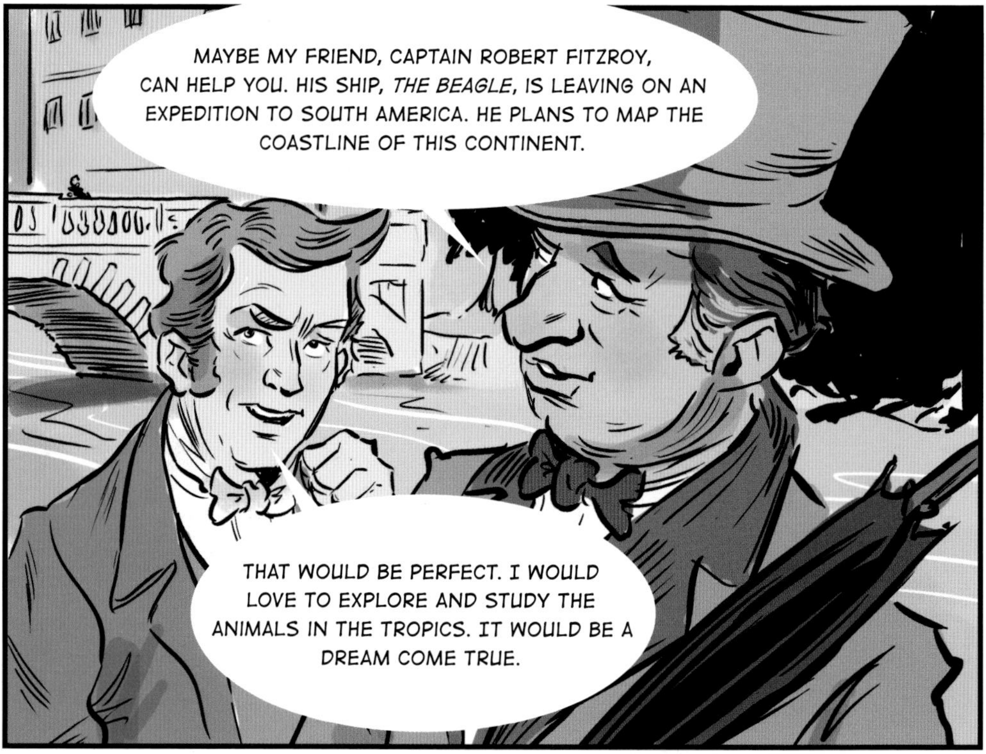
MAYBE MY FRIEND, CAPTAIN ROBERT FITZROY, CAN HELP YOU. HIS SHIP, *THE BEAGLE*, IS LEAVING ON AN EXPEDITION TO SOUTH AMERICA. HE PLANS TO MAP THE COASTLINE OF THIS CONTINENT.
THAT WOULD BE PERFECT. I WOULD LOVE TO EXPLORE AND STUDY THE ANIMALS IN THE TROPICS. IT WOULD BE A DREAM COME TRUE.

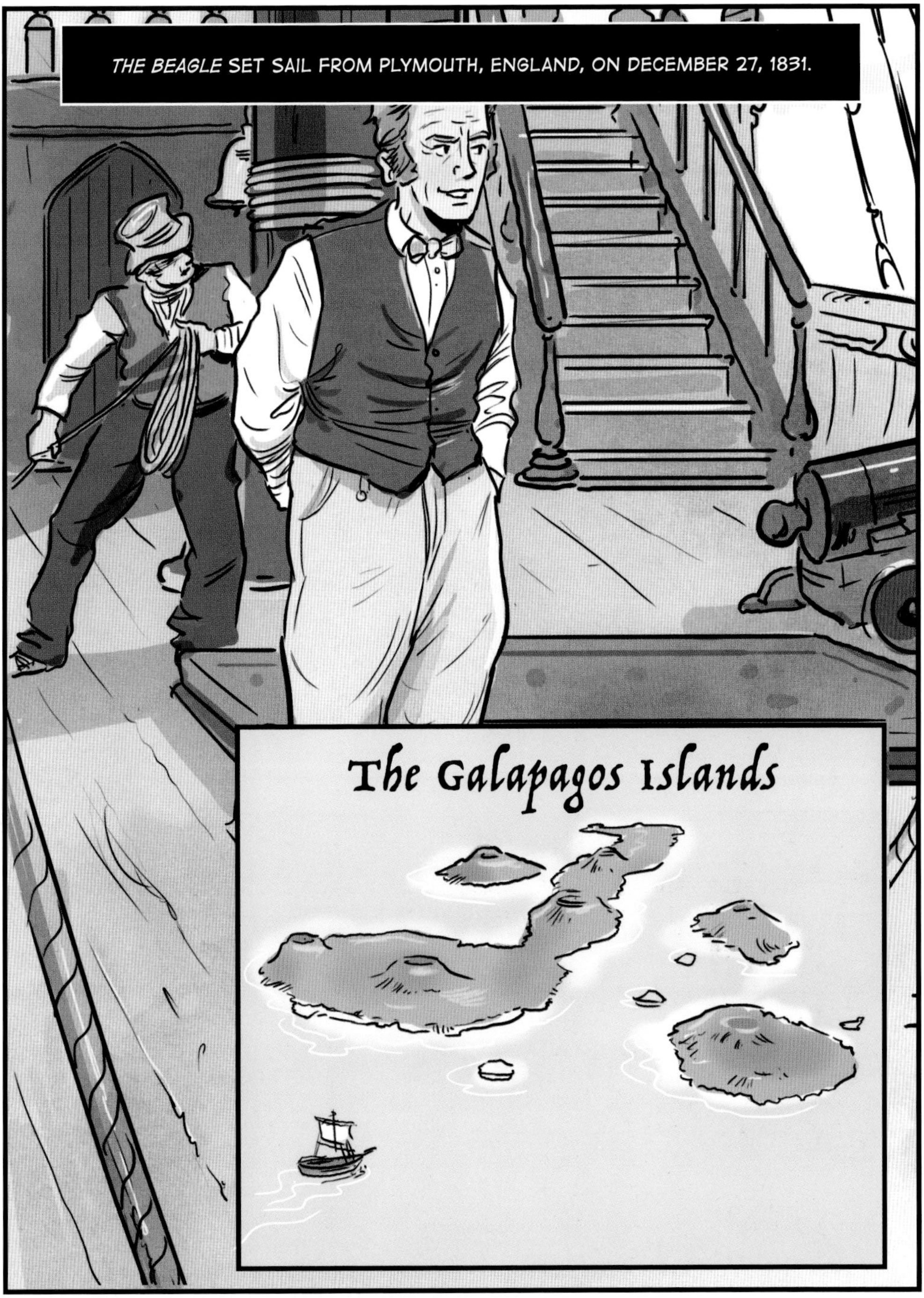
THE BEAGLE SET SAIL FROM PLYMOUTH, ENGLAND, ON DECEMBER 27, 1831.
The Galapagos Islands

DURING THE FIVE-YEAR EXPEDITION, CHARLES SPENT FIVE WEEKS IN THE GALAPAGOS ISLANDS NEAR ECUADOR, SOUTH AMERICA. HE WAS FASCINATED BY THE WILDLIFE THERE.

THE CABINBOY, SYMS COVINGTON, HELPED CHARLES COLLECT SPECIMENS AND CLASSIFY THE DIFFERENT SPECIES THEY DISCOVERED.

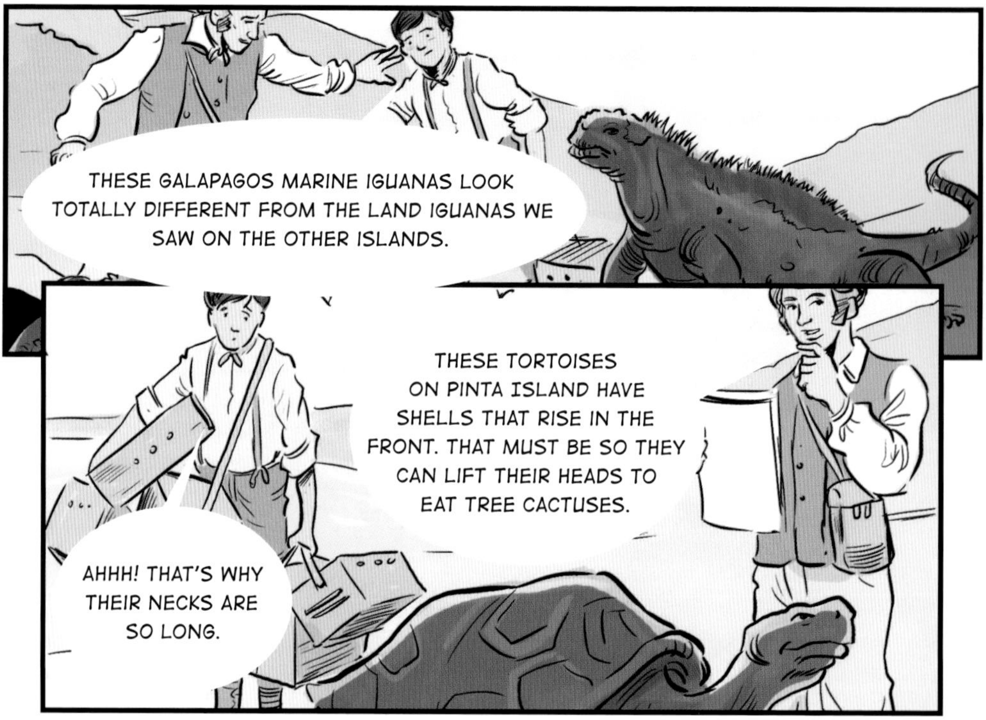
THESE GALAPAGOS MARINE IGUANAS LOOK TOTALLY DIFFERENT FROM THE LAND IGUANAS WE SAW ON THE OTHER ISLANDS.
THESE TORTOISES ON PINTA ISLAND HAVE SHELLS THAT RISE IN THE FRONT. THAT MUST BE SO THEY CAN LIFT THEIR HEADS TO EAT TREE CACTUSES.
AHHH! THAT'S WHY THEIR NECKS ARE SO LONG.

DURING HIS TIME IN THE GALAPAGOS, HE NOTICED DIFFERENCES AMONG THE TORTOISES FROM ISLAND TO ISLAND.

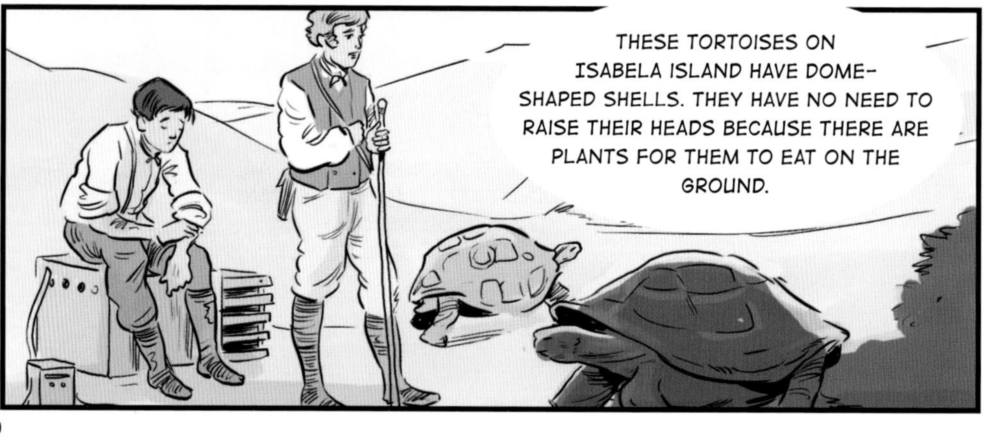
THESE TORTOISES ON ISABELA ISLAND HAVE DOME-SHAPED SHELLS. THEY HAVE NO NEED TO RAISE THEIR HEADS BECAUSE THERE ARE PLANTS FOR THEM TO EAT ON THE GROUND.

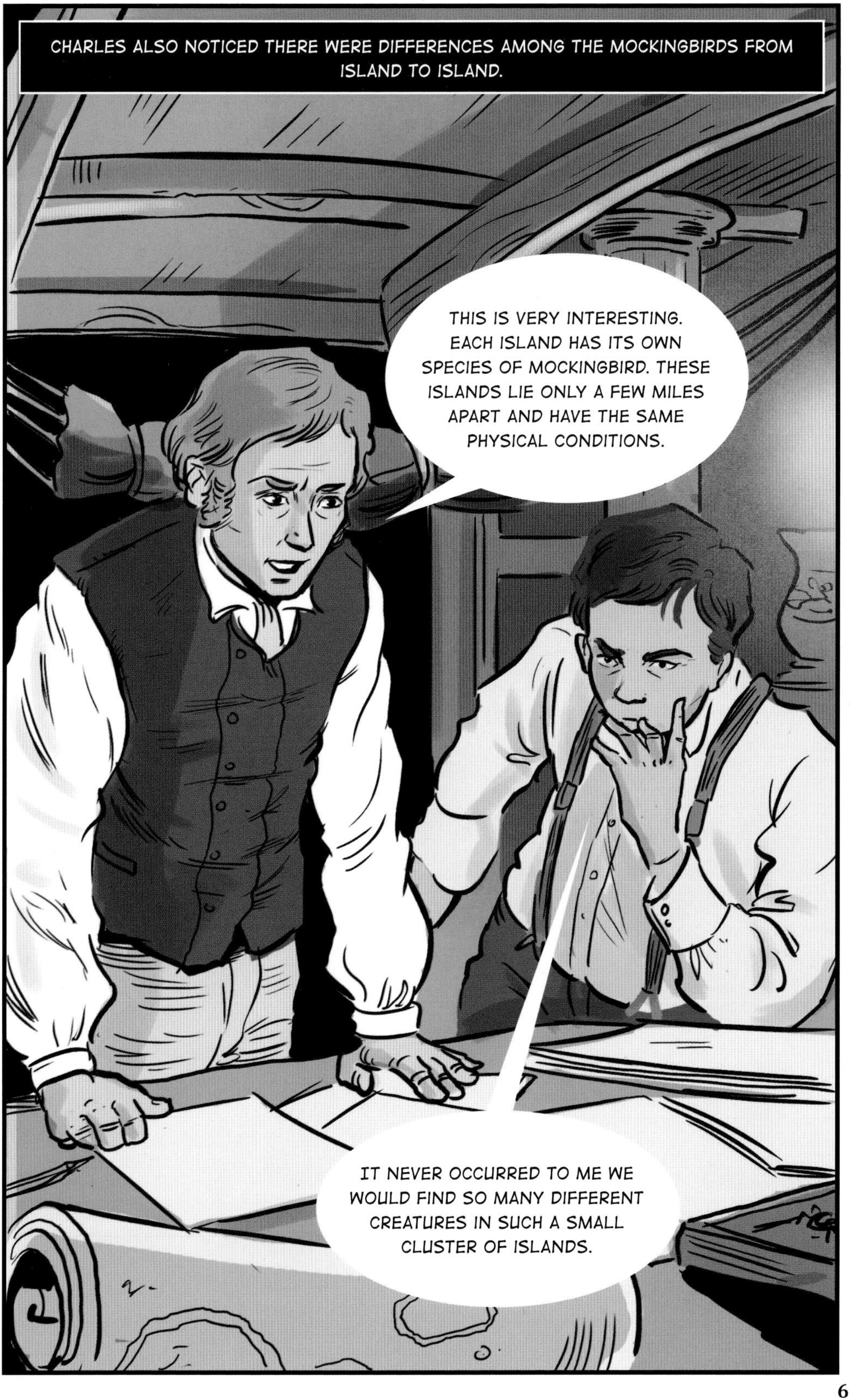
CHARLES ALSO NOTICED THERE WERE DIFFERENCES AMONG THE MOCKINGBIRDS FROM ISLAND TO ISLAND.
THIS IS VERY INTERESTING. EACH ISLAND HAS ITS OWN SPECIES OF MOCKINGBIRD. THESE ISLANDS LIE ONLY A FEW MILES APART AND HAVE THE SAME PHYSICAL CONDITIONS.
IT NEVER OCCURRED TO ME WE WOULD FIND SO MANY DIFFERENT CREATURES IN SUCH A SMALL CLUSTER OF ISLANDS.

WHEN CHARLES RETURNED HOME, HE EMPLOYED SYMS COVINGTON AS HIS ASSISTANT. THEY SPENT THREE YEARS TOGETHER, STUDYING AND LISTING ALL THE PLANTS AND CREATURES THEY HAD SEEN ON THE GALAPAGOS ISLANDS.

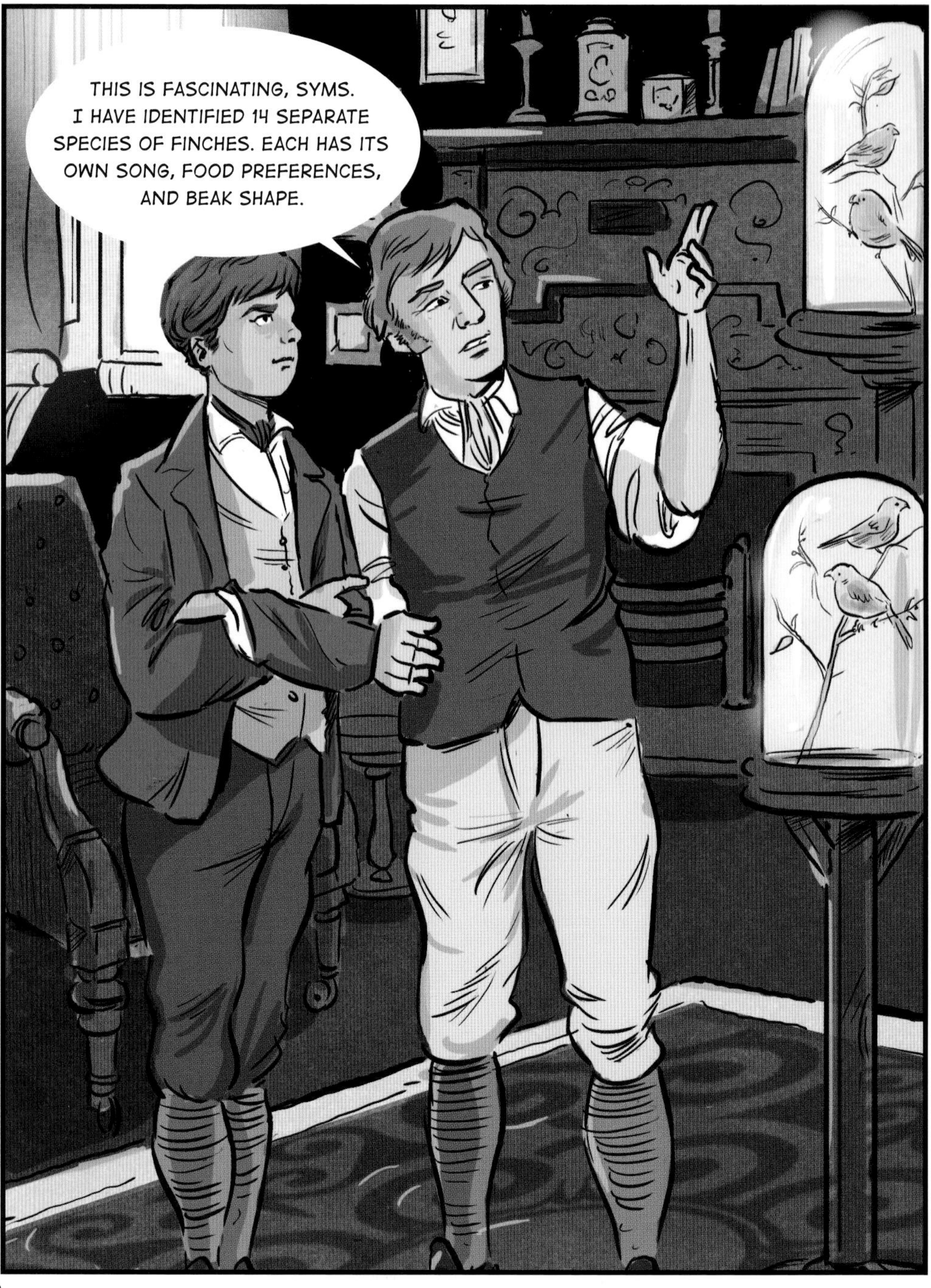
THIS IS FASCINATING, SYMS. I HAVE IDENTIFIED 14 SEPARATE SPECIES OF FINCHES. EACH HAS ITS OWN SONG, FOOD PREFERENCES, AND BEAK SHAPE.

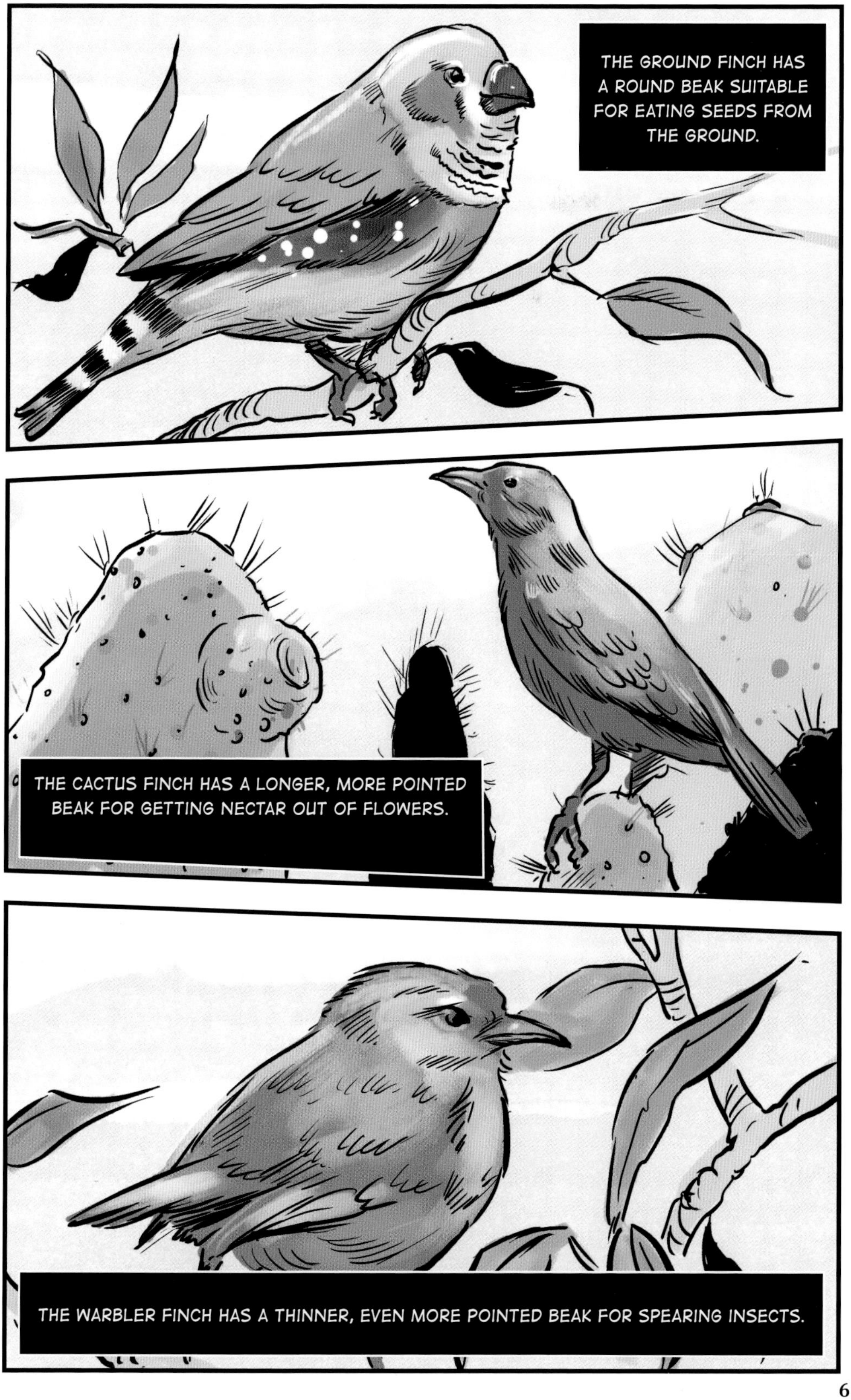
THE GROUND FINCH HAS A ROUND BEAK SUITABLE FOR EATING SEEDS FROM THE GROUND.
THE CACTUS FINCH HAS A LONGER, MORE POINTED BEAK FOR GETTING NECTAR OUT OF FLOWERS.
THE WARBLER FINCH HAS A THINNER, EVEN MORE POINTED BEAK FOR SPEARING INSECTS.

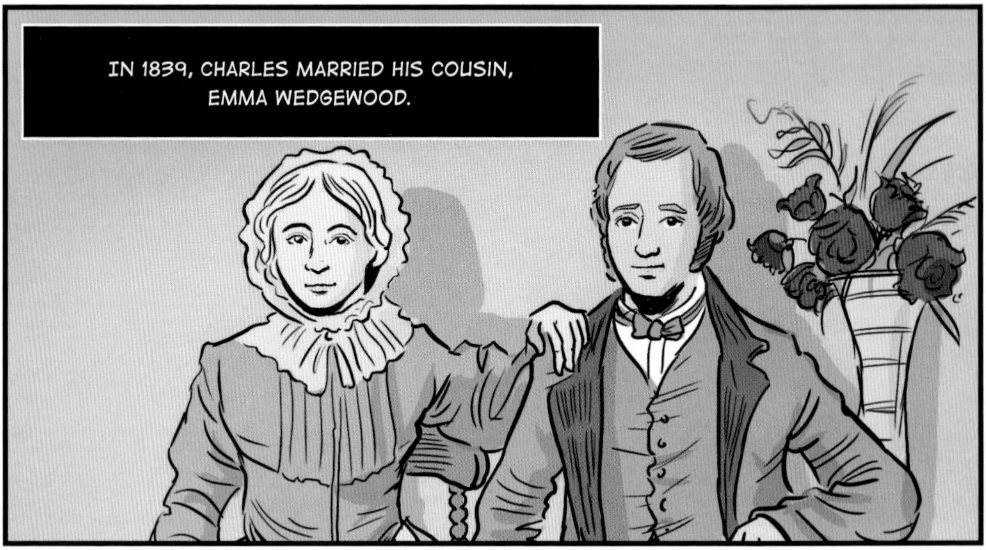
IN 1839, CHARLES MARRIED HIS COUSIN, EMMA WEDGEWOOD.

BY THE SUMMER OF 1858, CHARLES HAD FILLED HUNDREDS OF NOTEBOOKS WITH HIS THEORY OF NATURAL SELECTION, BUT HE HAD PUBLISHED NOTHING.

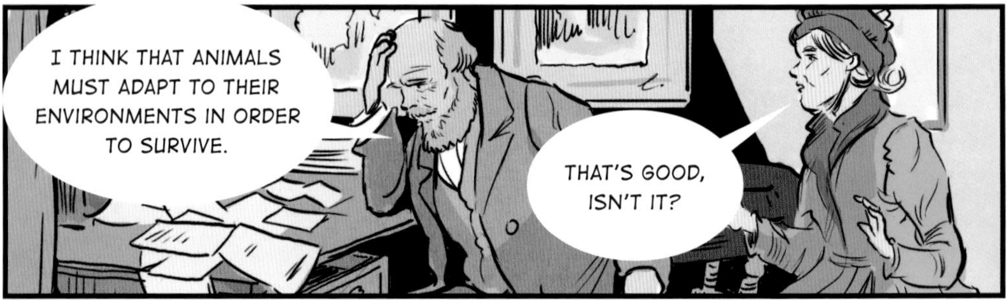
I THINK THAT ANIMALS MUST ADAPT TO THEIR ENVIRONMENTS IN ORDER TO SURVIVE.
THAT'S GOOD, ISN'T IT?

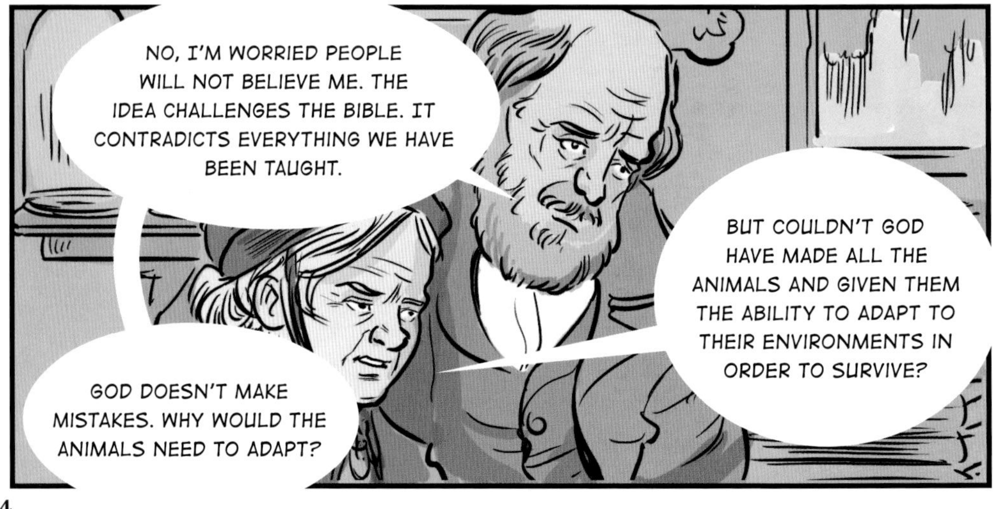
NO, I'M WORRIED PEOPLE WILL NOT BELIEVE ME. THE IDEA CHALLENGES THE BIBLE. IT CONTRADICTS EVERYTHING WE HAVE BEEN TAUGHT.
GOD DOESN'T MAKE MISTAKES. WHY WOULD THE ANIMALS NEED TO ADAPT?
BUT COULDN'T GOD HAVE MADE ALL THE ANIMALS AND GIVEN THEM THE ABILITY TO ADAPT TO THEIR ENVIRONMENTS IN ORDER TO SURVIVE?

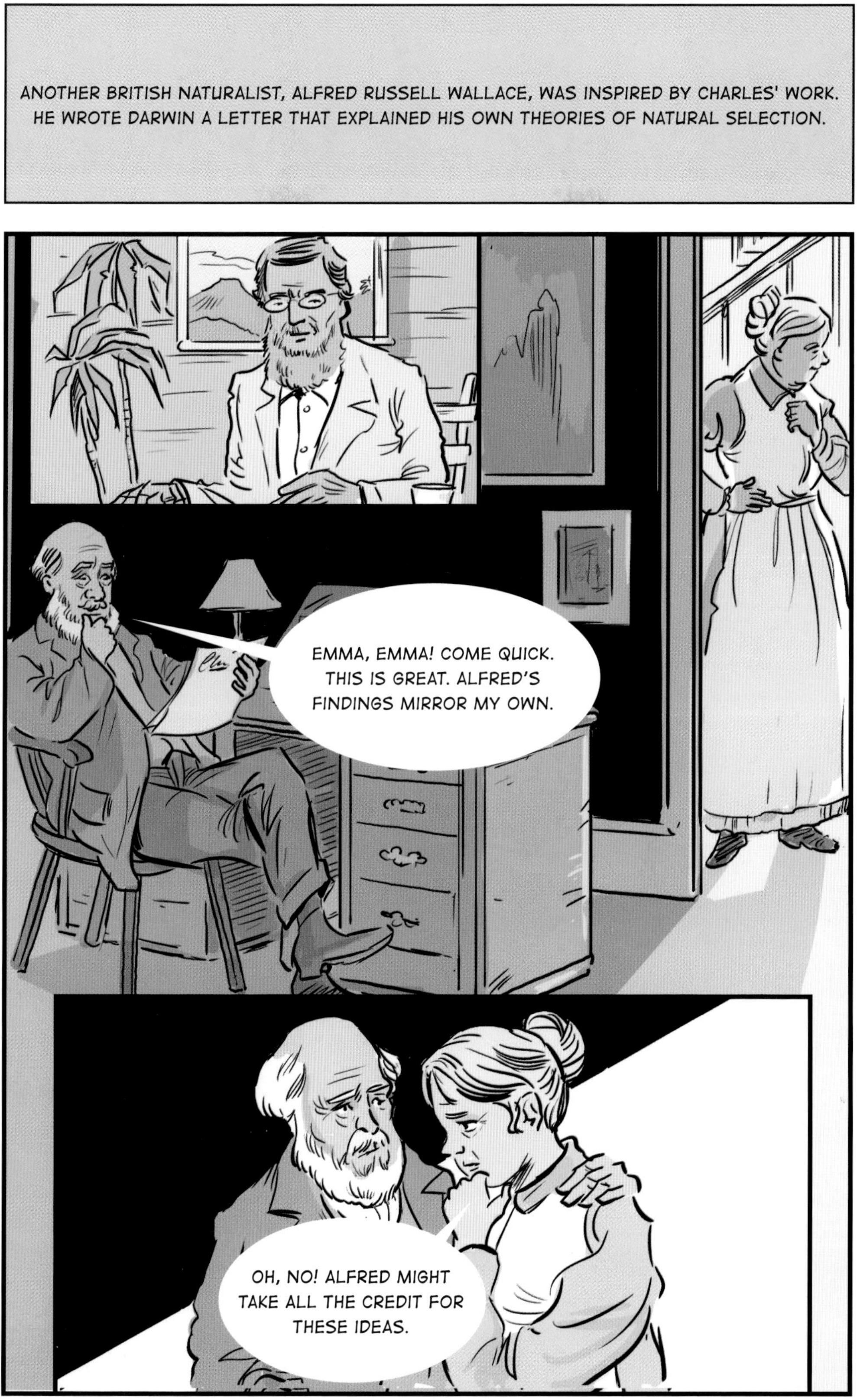
ANOTHER BRITISH NATURALIST, ALFRED RUSSELL WALLACE, WAS INSPIRED BY CHARLES' WORK. HE WROTE DARWIN A LETTER THAT EXPLAINED HIS OWN THEORIES OF NATURAL SELECTION.
EMMA, EMMA! COME QUICK. THIS IS GREAT. ALFRED'S FINDINGS MIRROR MY OWN.
OH, NO! ALFRED MIGHT TAKE ALL THE CREDIT FOR THESE IDEAS.

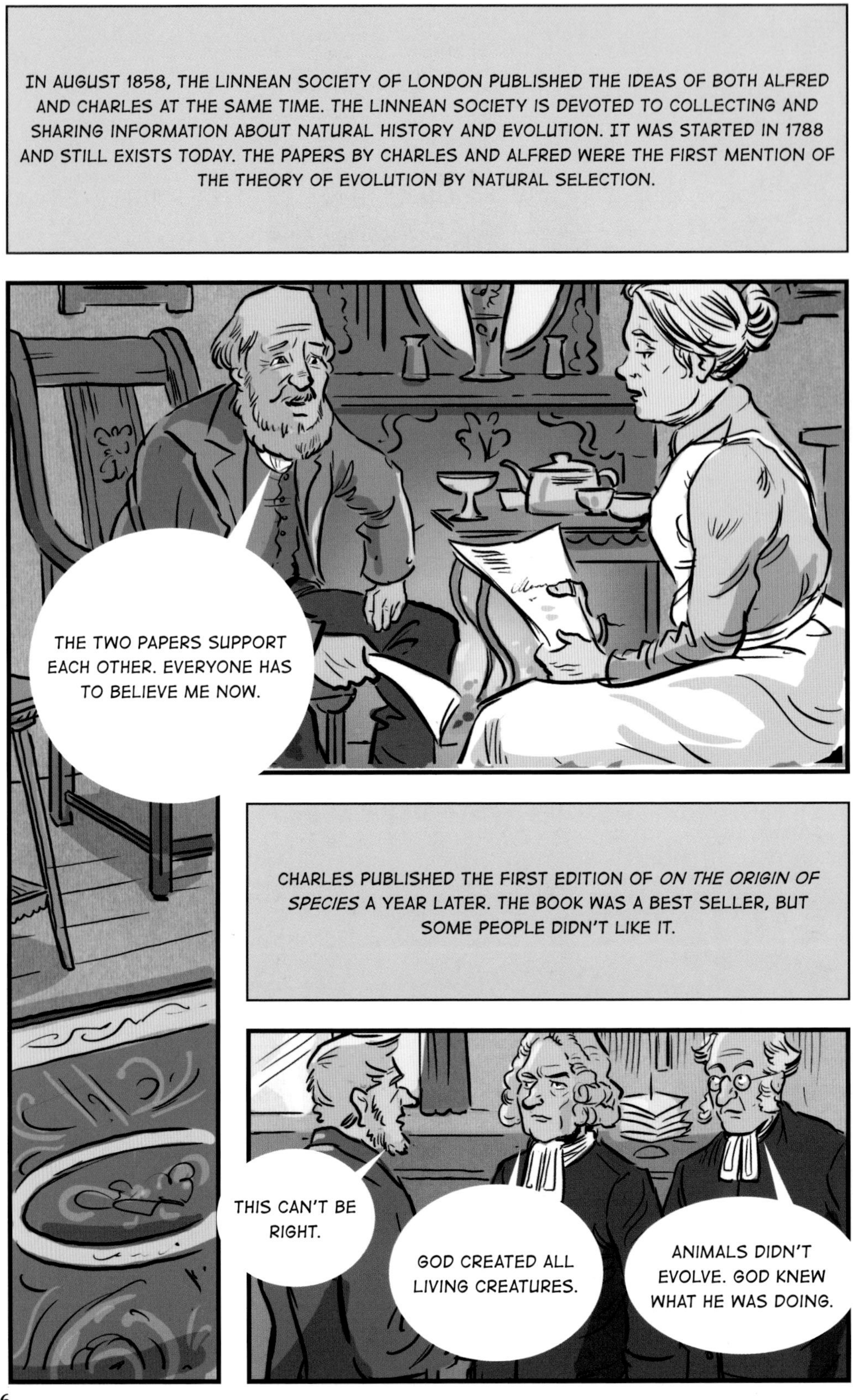
IN AUGUST 1858, THE LINNEAN SOCIETY OF LONDON PUBLISHED THE IDEAS OF BOTH ALFRED AND CHARLES AT THE SAME TIME. THE LINNEAN SOCIETY IS DEVOTED TO COLLECTING AND SHARING INFORMATION ABOUT NATURAL HISTORY AND EVOLUTION. IT WAS STARTED IN 1788 AND STILL EXISTS TODAY. THE PAPERS BY CHARLES AND ALFRED WERE THE FIRST MENTION OF THE THEORY OF EVOLUTION BY NATURAL SELECTION.
THE TWO PAPERS SUPPORT EACH OTHER. EVERYONE HAS TO BELIEVE ME NOW.
CHARLES PUBLISHED THE FIRST EDITION OF *ON THE ORIGIN OF SPECIES* A YEAR LATER. THE BOOK WAS A BEST SELLER, BUT SOME PEOPLE DIDN'T LIKE IT.
THIS CAN'T BE RIGHT.
GOD CREATED ALL LIVING CREATURES.
ANIMALS DIDN'T EVOLVE. GOD KNEW WHAT HE WAS DOING.

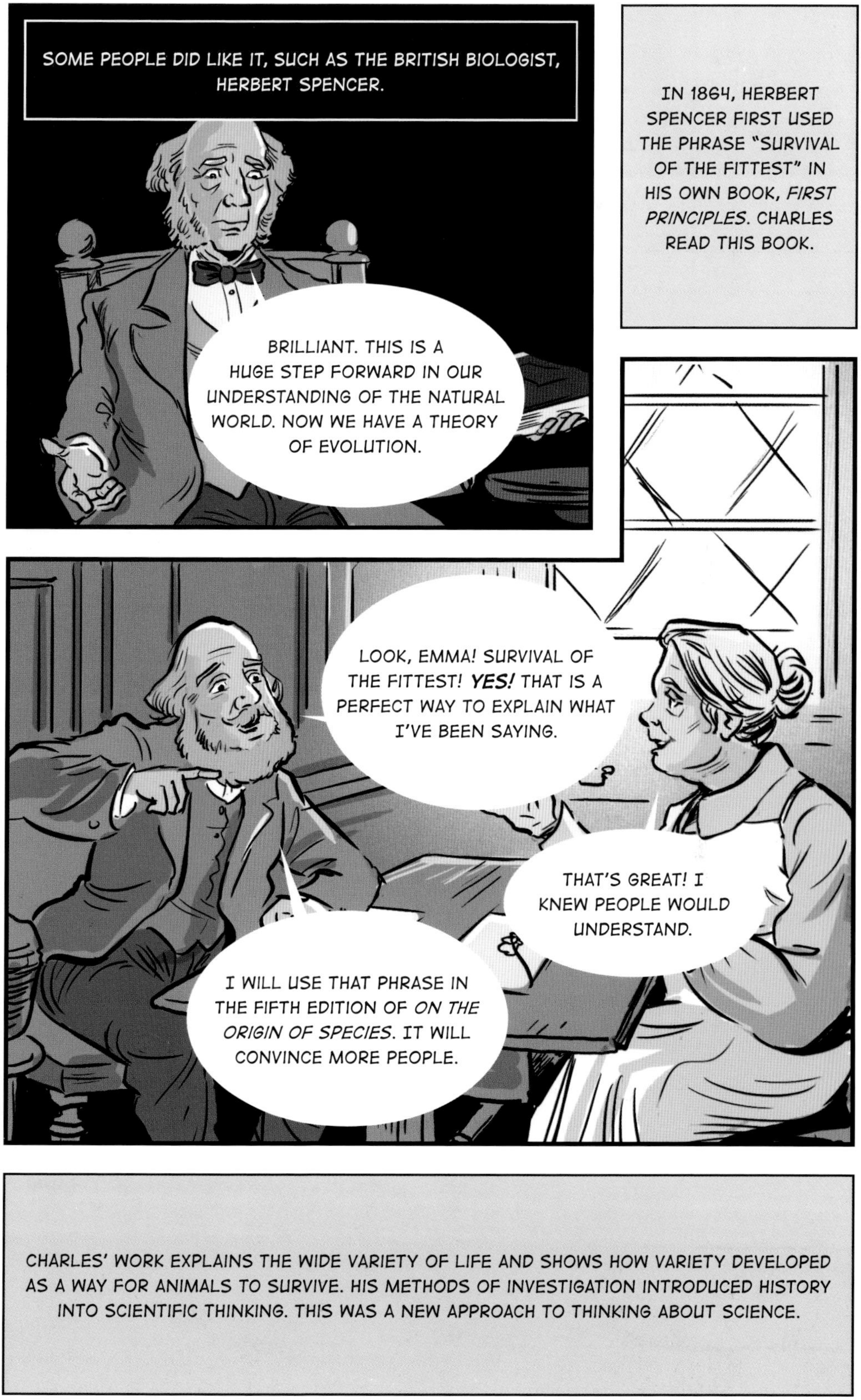
SOME PEOPLE DID LIKE IT, SUCH AS THE BRITISH BIOLOGIST, HERBERT SPENCER.
BRILLIANT. THIS IS A HUGE STEP FORWARD IN OUR UNDERSTANDING OF THE NATURAL WORLD. NOW WE HAVE A THEORY OF EVOLUTION.
IN 1864, HERBERT SPENCER FIRST USED THE PHRASE "SURVIVAL OF THE FITTEST" IN HIS OWN BOOK, *FIRST PRINCIPLES*. CHARLES READ THIS BOOK.
LOOK, EMMA! SURVIVAL OF THE FITTEST! ***YES!*** THAT IS A PERFECT WAY TO EXPLAIN WHAT I'VE BEEN SAYING.
THAT'S GREAT! I KNEW PEOPLE WOULD UNDERSTAND.
I WILL USE THAT PHRASE IN THE FIFTH EDITION OF *ON THE ORIGIN OF SPECIES*. IT WILL CONVINCE MORE PEOPLE.
CHARLES' WORK EXPLAINS THE WIDE VARIETY OF LIFE AND SHOWS HOW VARIETY DEVELOPED AS A WAY FOR ANIMALS TO SURVIVE. HIS METHODS OF INVESTIGATION INTRODUCED HISTORY INTO SCIENTIFIC THINKING. THIS WAS A NEW APPROACH TO THINKING ABOUT SCIENCE.

LOUIS PASTEUR
(1822–1895)
THE GERM DETECTIVE

LOUIS PASTEUR CAME FROM A POOR FAMILY IN FRANCE AND WAS AN AVERAGE STUDENT. HIS MAIN INTERESTS AS A CHILD WERE DRAWING AND PAINTING.

STAY STILL, FATHER.

THROUGH HARD WORK AND DETERMINATION, LOUIS BECAME HEAD OF THE FACULTY OF SCIENCE AT THE UNIVERSITY OF LILLE, FRANCE. IN 1856, DISTILLER M. BIGO, THE FATHER OF ONE OF HIS STUDENTS, WAS HAVING TROUBLE MAKING ALCOHOL FOR HIS BUSINESS. IT SEEMED LIKE A SCIENCE PROBLEM, SO HE ASKED LOUIS FOR HELP.

SOME OF THE SUGAR BEET ALCOHOL I AM TRYING TO PRODUCE IS TOO SOUR TO DRINK. NOBODY WANTS TO BUY ANY. IT IS COSTING ME THOUSANDS OF FRANCS A DAY.

I WONDER WHY YOUR FERMENTATION PROCESS IS FAILING?

THE PROCESS OF TURNING SUGARS IN VEGETABLES, FRUIT OR GRAINS INTO ALCOHOL IS CALLED FERMENTATION.

LOUIS SET UP A LABORATORY IN THE CELLAR OF AN OLD SUGAR FACTORY. HE BORROWED A MICROSCOPE FROM THE UNIVERSITY. HE WANTED TO SEE IN CLOSE DETAIL WHAT ACTUALLY HAPPENED DURING FERMENTATION. HIS WIFE, MARIE, WAS HIS SCIENTIFIC RESEARCH ASSISTANT.

THIS IS A SAMPLE OF ALCOHOL THAT CAME OUT WELL. I AM GOING TO LOOK AT THIS FIRST.

I PUT A SAMPLE OF THE GOOD ALCOHOL ONTO A SLIDE FOR YOU, SO YOU CAN TAKE A CLOSER LOOK AT IT THROUGH THE MICROSCOPE.

THIS IS A SURPRISE! THERE IS A LARGE NUMBER OF YEAST CELLS IN THE GOOD ALCOHOL. THESE YEAST CELLS ARE CHANGING SHAPE. A NEW CELL BUDS AND THEN BREAKS AWAY FROM THE ORIGINAL CELL. THEY ARE REPRODUCING. THIS MUST MEAN THEY ARE LIVING ORGANISMS.

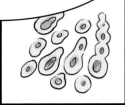

YEAST AND BACTERIA ARE BOTH SINGLE-CELLED LIVING MICROORGANISMS, OFTEN KNOWN AS MICROBES.

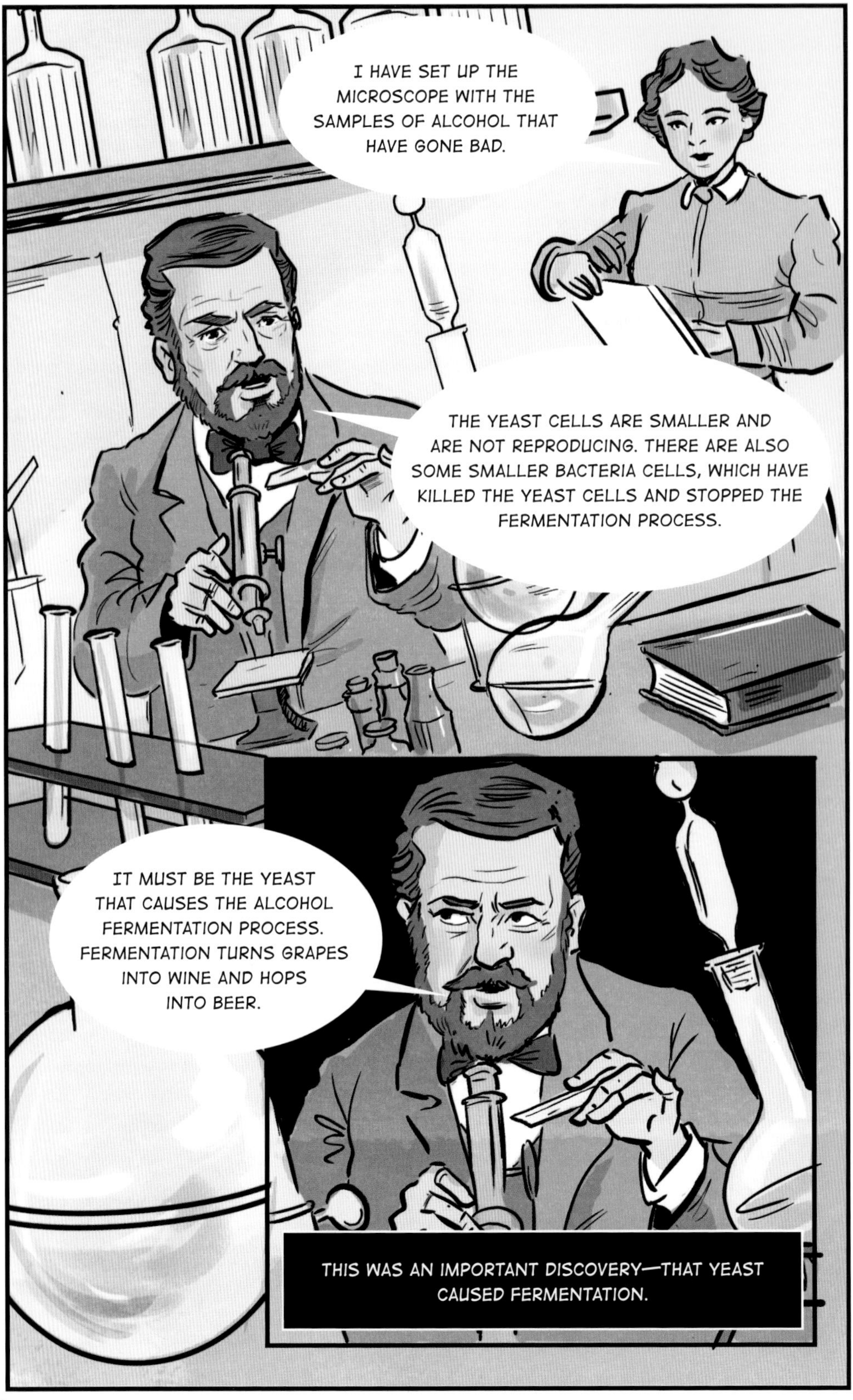
I HAVE SET UP THE MICROSCOPE WITH THE SAMPLES OF ALCOHOL THAT HAVE GONE BAD.
THE YEAST CELLS ARE SMALLER AND ARE NOT REPRODUCING. THERE ARE ALSO SOME SMALLER BACTERIA CELLS, WHICH HAVE KILLED THE YEAST CELLS AND STOPPED THE FERMENTATION PROCESS.
IT MUST BE THE YEAST THAT CAUSES THE ALCOHOL FERMENTATION PROCESS. FERMENTATION TURNS GRAPES INTO WINE AND HOPS INTO BEER.
THIS WAS AN IMPORTANT DISCOVERY—THAT YEAST CAUSED FERMENTATION.

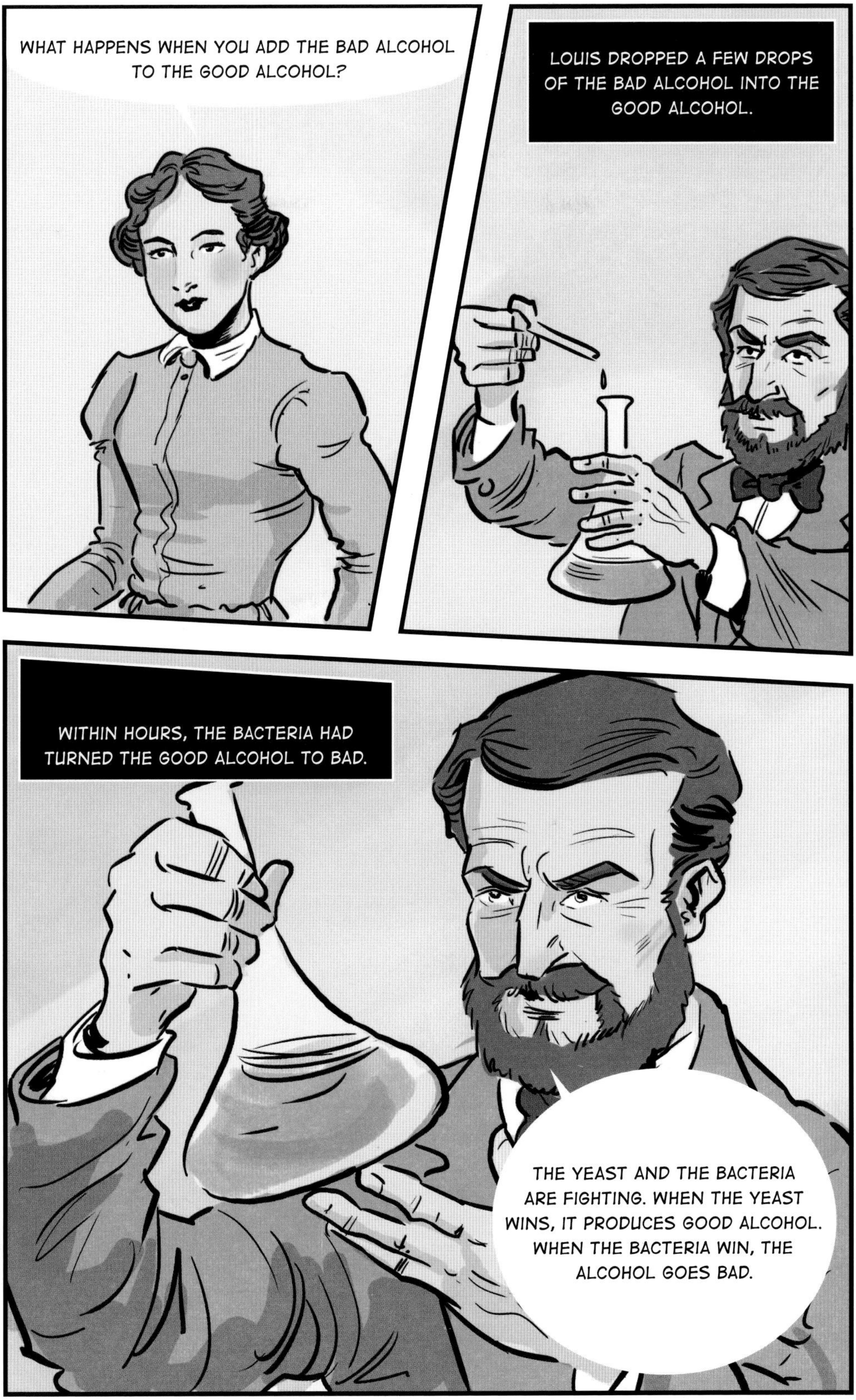
WHAT HAPPENS WHEN YOU ADD THE BAD ALCOHOL TO THE GOOD ALCOHOL?
LOUIS DROPPED A FEW DROPS OF THE BAD ALCOHOL INTO THE GOOD ALCOHOL.
WITHIN HOURS, THE BACTERIA HAD TURNED THE GOOD ALCOHOL TO BAD.
THE YEAST AND THE BACTERIA ARE FIGHTING. WHEN THE YEAST WINS, IT PRODUCES GOOD ALCOHOL. WHEN THE BACTERIA WIN, THE ALCOHOL GOES BAD.

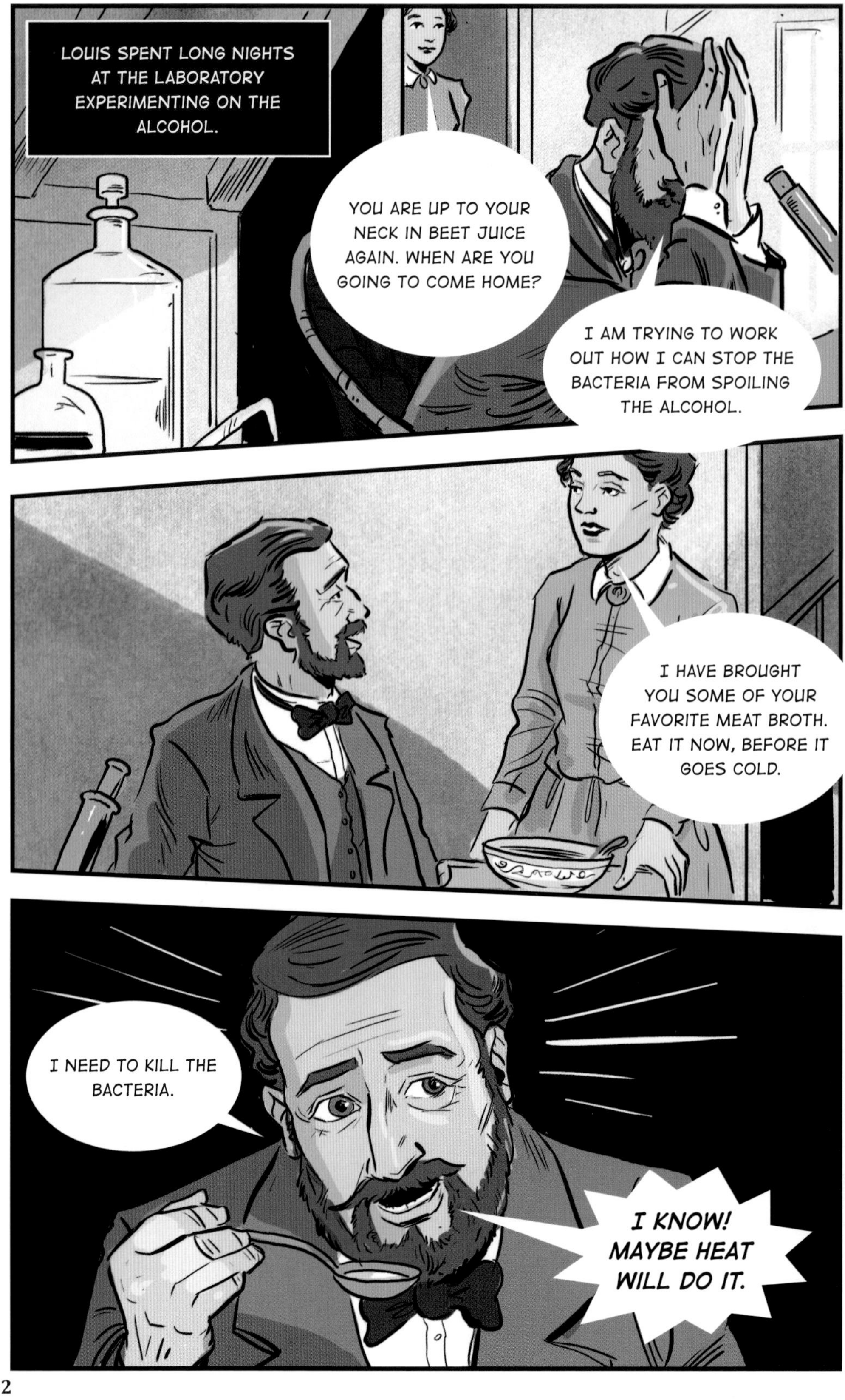
LOUIS SPENT LONG NIGHTS AT THE LABORATORY EXPERIMENTING ON THE ALCOHOL.
YOU ARE UP TO YOUR NECK IN BEET JUICE AGAIN. WHEN ARE YOU GOING TO COME HOME?
I AM TRYING TO WORK OUT HOW I CAN STOP THE BACTERIA FROM SPOILING THE ALCOHOL.
I HAVE BROUGHT YOU SOME OF YOUR FAVORITE MEAT BROTH. EAT IT NOW, BEFORE IT GOES COLD.
I NEED TO KILL THE BACTERIA.
I KNOW! MAYBE HEAT WILL DO IT.

IN 1857, LOUIS GOT A NEW JOB AS ADMINISTRATOR AND DIRECTOR OF SCIENTIFIC STUDIES AT A TOP UNIVERSITY IN PARIS, FRANCE. HE SET UP A LABORATORY IN THE ATTIC OF THE UNIVERSITY TO CONTINUE HIS RESEARCH. MARIE WAS PREGNANT WITH THEIR FOURTH CHILD, SO LOUIS HIRED A RESEARCH ASSISTANT. HE PARTIALLY FILLED SOME BOTTLES WITH MILK, THEN SEALED AND STERILIZED THEM IN BOILING WATER. BACTERIA SUCH AS TUBERCULOSIS, SALMONELLA, TYPHOID, AND DIPHTHERIA THRIVE IN MILK.

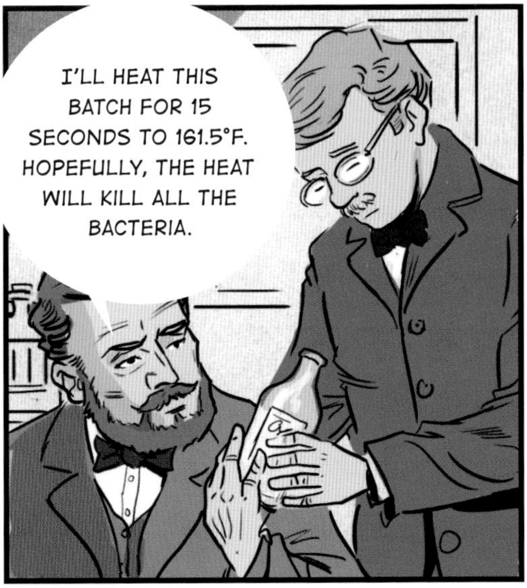
I'LL HEAT THIS BATCH FOR 15 SECONDS TO 161.5°F. HOPEFULLY, THE HEAT WILL KILL ALL THE BACTERIA.

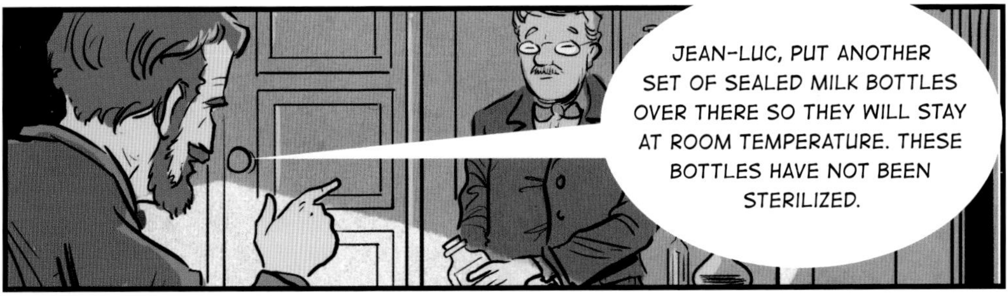
JEAN-LUC, PUT ANOTHER SET OF SEALED MILK BOTTLES OVER THERE SO THEY WILL STAY AT ROOM TEMPERATURE. THESE BOTTLES HAVE NOT BEEN STERILIZED.

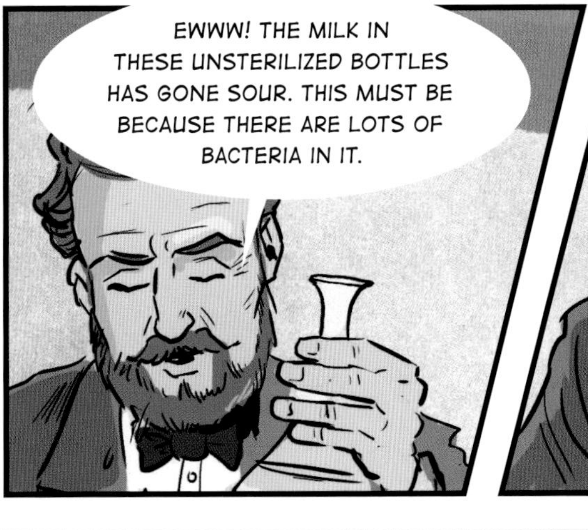
EWWW! THE MILK IN THESE UNSTERILIZED BOTTLES HAS GONE SOUR. THIS MUST BE BECAUSE THERE ARE LOTS OF BACTERIA IN IT.

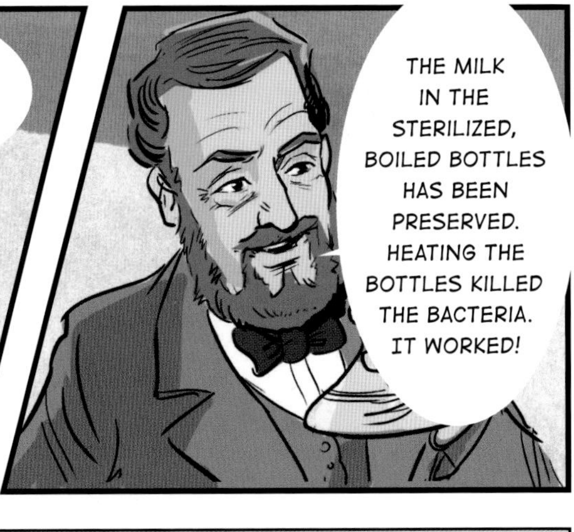
THE MILK IN THE STERILIZED, BOILED BOTTLES HAS BEEN PRESERVED. HEATING THE BOTTLES KILLED THE BACTERIA. IT WORKED!

THIS METHOD OF HEATING FOOD IS CALLED PASTEURIZATION. IT HAS SAVED MILLIONS OF LIVES BY KILLING BACTERIA THAT CAN MAKE PEOPLE SICK. BEFORE LOUIS' DISCOVERY, PEOPLE DID NOT KNOW GERMS MADE PEOPLE SICK.

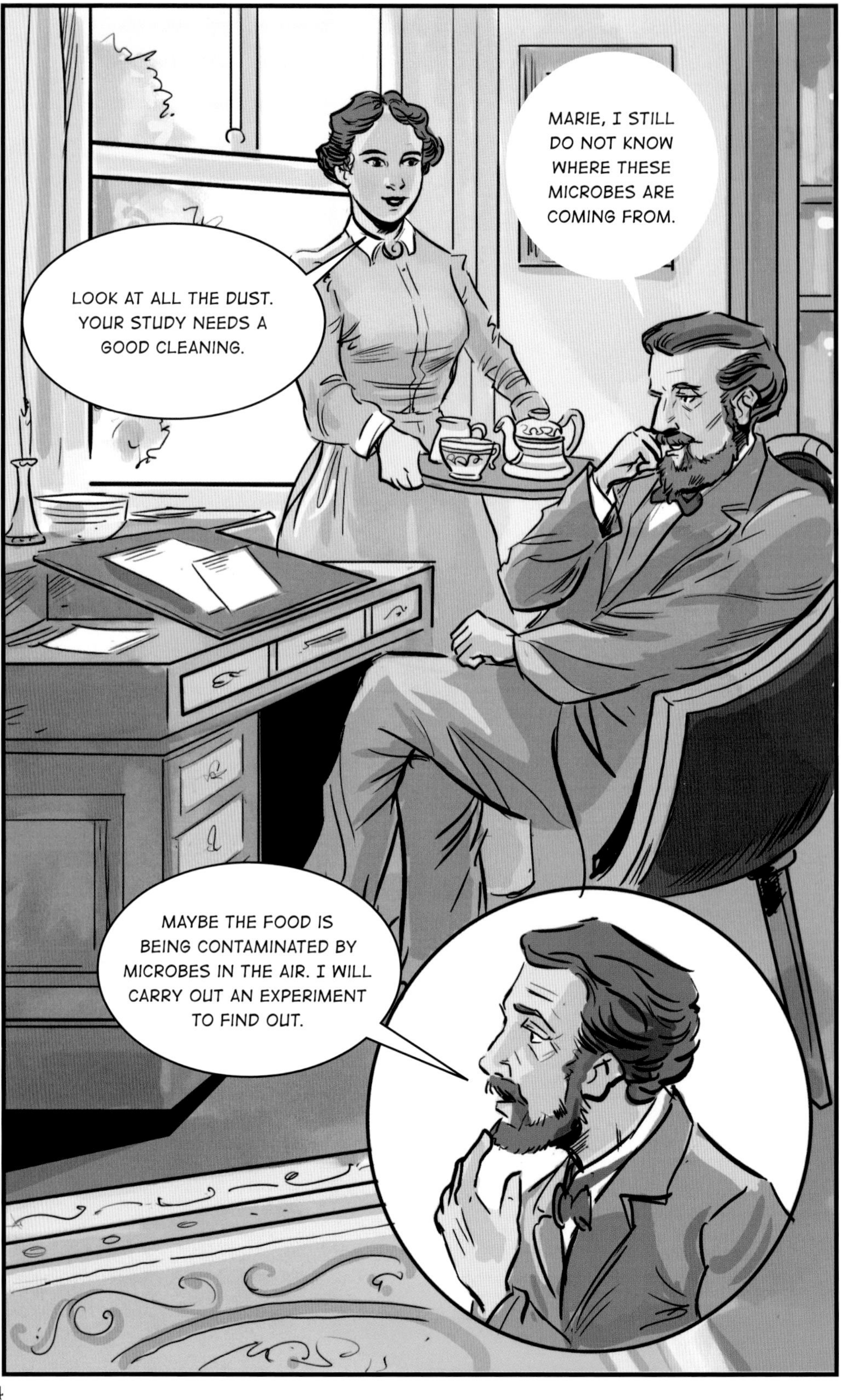
MARIE, I STILL DO NOT KNOW WHERE THESE MICROBES ARE COMING FROM.
LOOK AT ALL THE DUST. YOUR STUDY NEEDS A GOOD CLEANING.
MAYBE THE FOOD IS BEING CONTAMINATED BY MICROBES IN THE AIR. I WILL CARRY OUT AN EXPERIMENT TO FIND OUT.

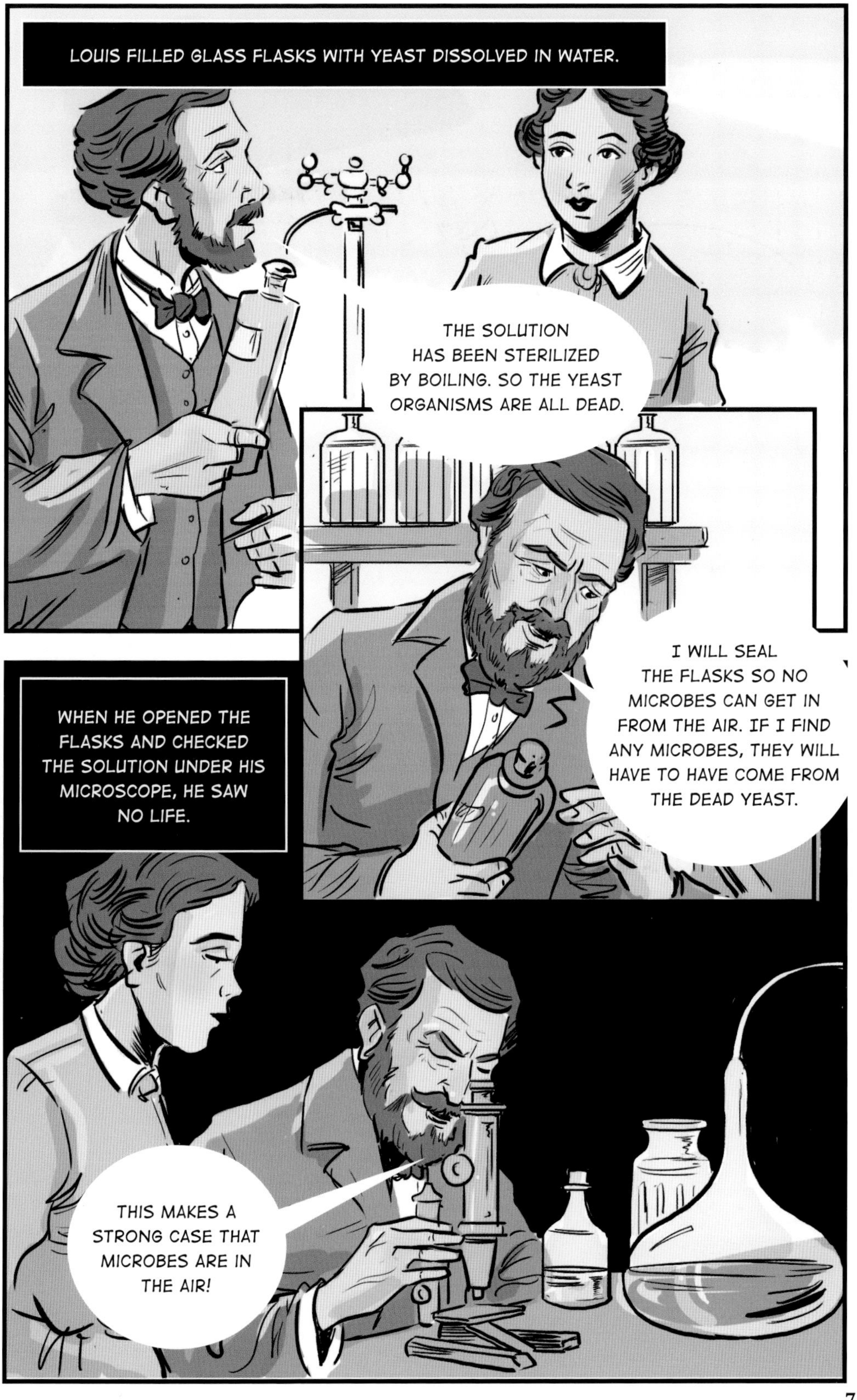
LOUIS FILLED GLASS FLASKS WITH YEAST DISSOLVED IN WATER.
THE SOLUTION HAS BEEN STERILIZED BY BOILING. SO THE YEAST ORGANISMS ARE ALL DEAD.
I WILL SEAL THE FLASKS SO NO MICROBES CAN GET IN FROM THE AIR. IF I FIND ANY MICROBES, THEY WILL HAVE TO HAVE COME FROM THE DEAD YEAST.
WHEN HE OPENED THE FLASKS AND CHECKED THE SOLUTION UNDER HIS MICROSCOPE, HE SAW NO LIFE.
THIS MAKES A STRONG CASE THAT MICROBES ARE IN THE AIR!

OTHER SCIENTISTS DID NOT AGREE WITH HIS THEORY. FELIX POUCHET BELIEVED IN SPONTANEOUS GENERATION. HE WAS AN OLDER AND INFLUENTIAL FRENCH SCIENTIST WITH MANY FOLLOWERS. ACCORDING TO HIS THEORY, ORGANISMS COULD APPEAR OUT OF DEAD MATTER.

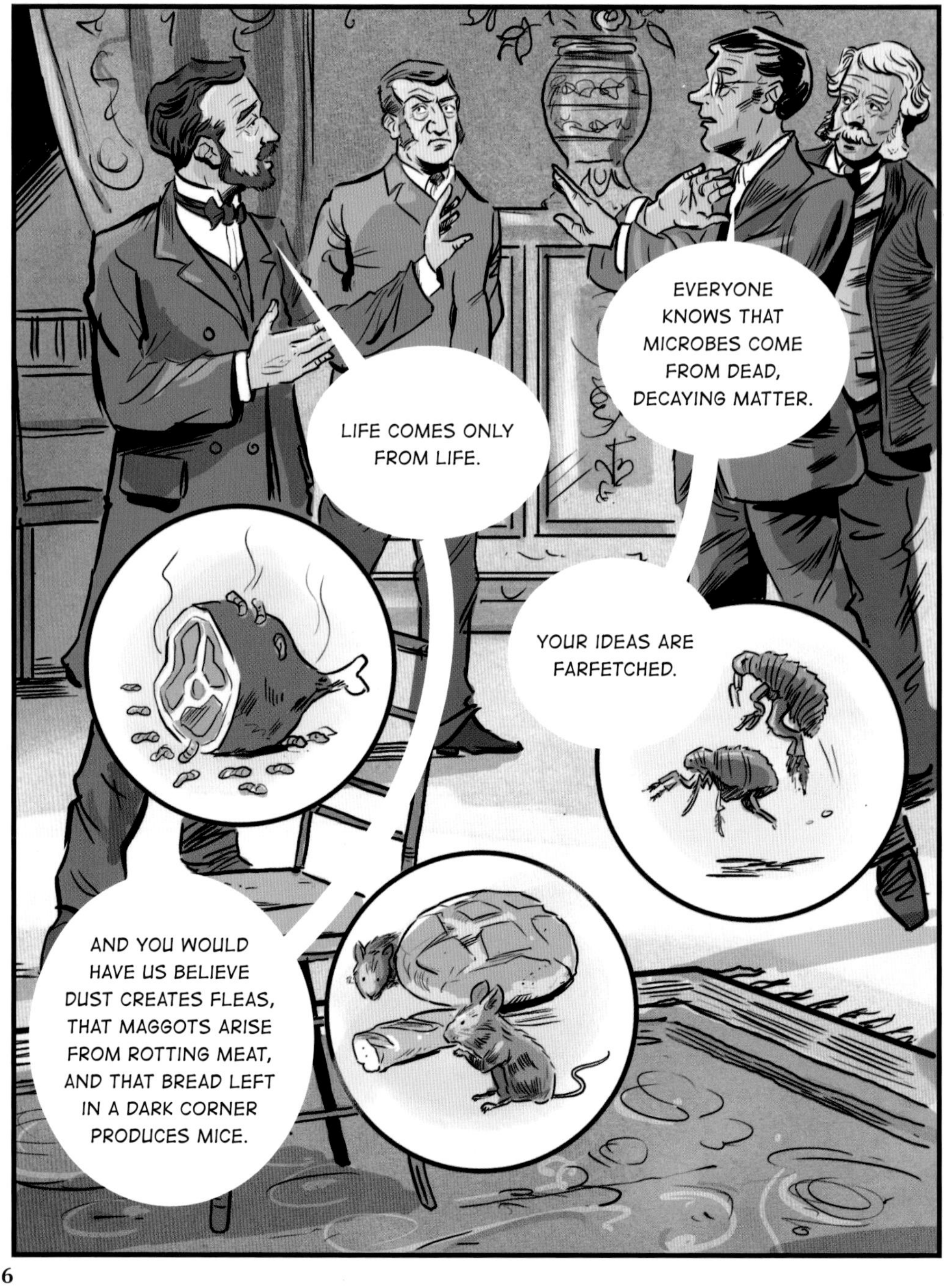

LIFE COMES ONLY FROM LIFE.
EVERYONE KNOWS THAT MICROBES COME FROM DEAD, DECAYING MATTER.
YOUR IDEAS ARE FARFETCHED.
AND YOU WOULD HAVE US BELIEVE DUST CREATES FLEAS, THAT MAGGOTS ARISE FROM ROTTING MEAT, AND THAT BREAD LEFT IN A DARK CORNER PRODUCES MICE.

LOUIS REFUSED TO GIVE UP. IN THE EARLY 1860s, HE DEVISED ANOTHER TEST TO PROVE HIS THEORIES. HE USED FLASKS WITH LONG BENDING GLASS NECKS THAT LOOKED LIKE SWANS. DUST AND MICROBES WOULD GET TRAPPED IN THE BEND OF THE NECK. HE PUT SOME OF HIS WIFE'S DELICIOUS BOILED MEAT BROTH IN THE FLASK. WHEN THE BROTH WAS KEPT AWAY FROM DUST IN THE AIR, IT STAYED STERILE. THERE WERE NO BACTERIA PRESENT.

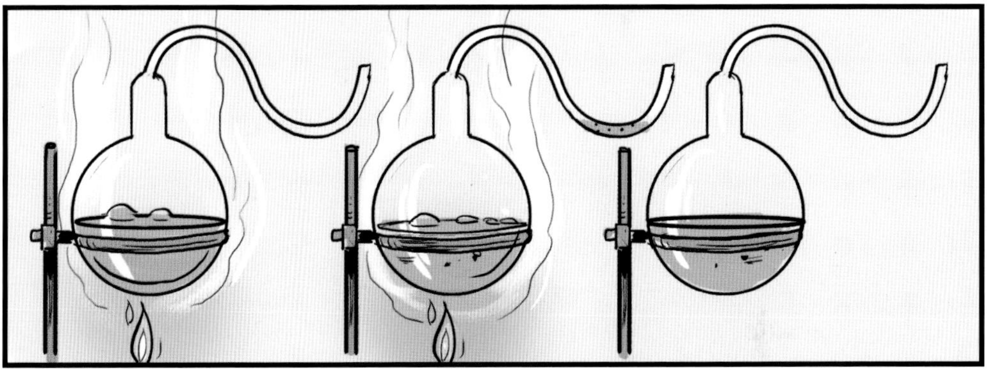

WHEN LOUIS HEATED THE BROTH AND THEN SNAPPED OFF THE NECKS OF THE FLASKS, THE BROTH BECAME CLOUDY AFTER A FEW HOURS. THERE WERE BACTERIA PRESENT. WHEN LOUIS TILTED THE FLASK SO THE BROTH CAME INTO CONTACT WITH THE DUST AND MICROBES, THE BROTH ALSO BECAME CLOUDY AFTER A FEW HOURS. AGAIN, THERE WERE BACTERIA PRESENT. THESE EXPERIMENTS PROVED THAT THE MEAT BROTH HAD BEEN CONTAMINATED WITH MICROBES FROM THE AIR.

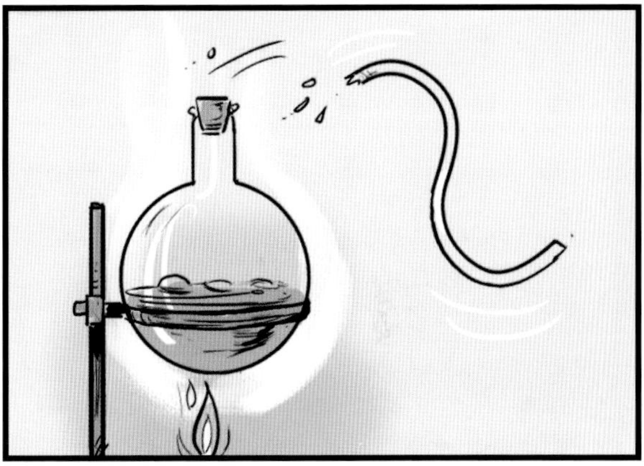

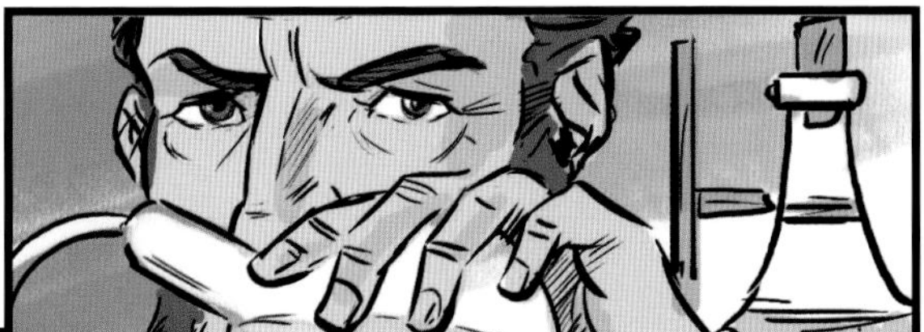

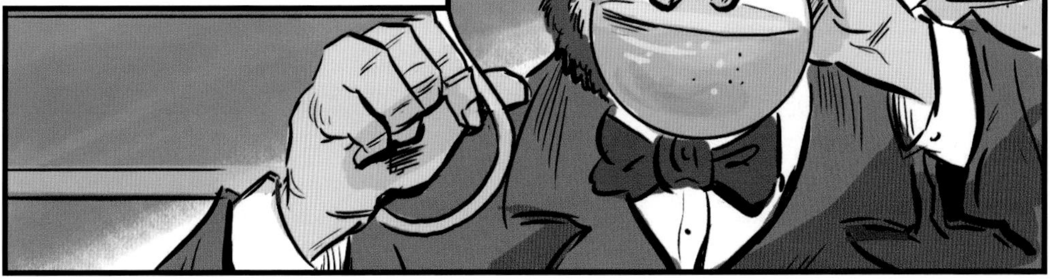

IN 1863, THE EMPEROR OF FRANCE, NAPOLEON III, WAS WORRIED BECAUSE LARGE QUANTITIES OF WINE WERE GOING BAD ALL OVER FRANCE. HE BELIEVED WINE WAS IMPORTANT TO THE MORALE OF HIS SOLDIERS. WHEN HE HEARD ABOUT LOUIS PASTEUR'S WORK, HE REQUESTED A MEETING WITH HIM.

YOU NEED TO FIND A WAY TO STOP THE WINE FROM GOING BAD.

I HAVE HAD SUCCESS WITH HEATING MILK TO KILL BACTERIA. MAYBE I COULD TRY HEATING THE WINE.

BUT WHAT TEMPERATURE WOULD DO THE JOB WITHOUT SPOILING THE TASTE OF THE WINE?

I'VE DONE HUNDREDS OF EXPERIMENTS AND I'VE DISCOVERED THAT IF WINE IS HEATED TO BETWEEN 122°F AND 140°F, IT DOES NOT GO BAD.

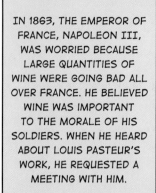

LOUIS ALSO DEVELOPED A WAY OF MAKING BEER BY PREVENTING AIR FROM GETTING INTO THE BARRELS. THIS ALLOWED THE BEVERAGE TO BE TRANSPORTED OVERSEAS FOR THE FIRST TIME. THE PASTEURIZATION PROCESS HE DEVELOPED IS STILL USED ALL OVER THE WORLD. THIS DISCOVERY HAS SAVED MILLIONS OF LIVES BY PREVENTING BACTERIA BEING SPREAD IN OUR FOOD. UNDERSTANDING MICROBES HAS LED TO MAJOR ADVANCES IN HUMAN HEALTH.

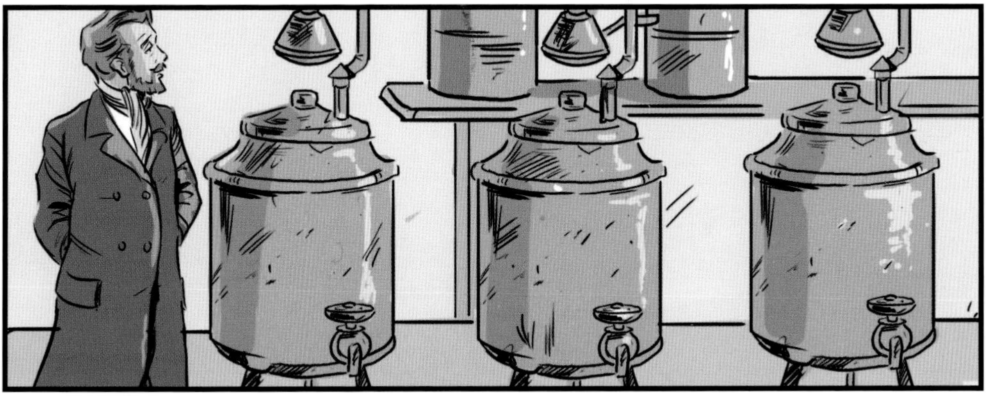

LOUIS PASTEUR'S FASCINATION WITH GERMS, AS WELL AS THE DEATH OF THREE OF HIS CHILDREN TO TUBERCULOSIS, LED HIM TO CONTINUE THE WORK OF THE BRITISH DOCTOR, EDWARD JENNER. ON JULY 6, 1885, LOUIS SUPERVISED THE VACCINATION OF JOSEPH MEISTER, A NINE-YEAR-OLD BOY WHO HAD BEEN BITTEN BY A RABID DOG. THIS SAVED THE BOY'S LIFE. LOUIS ALSO DEVELOPED VACCINES FOR OTHER GLOBAL DISEASES, SUCH AS TUBERCULOSIS AND CHOLERA.

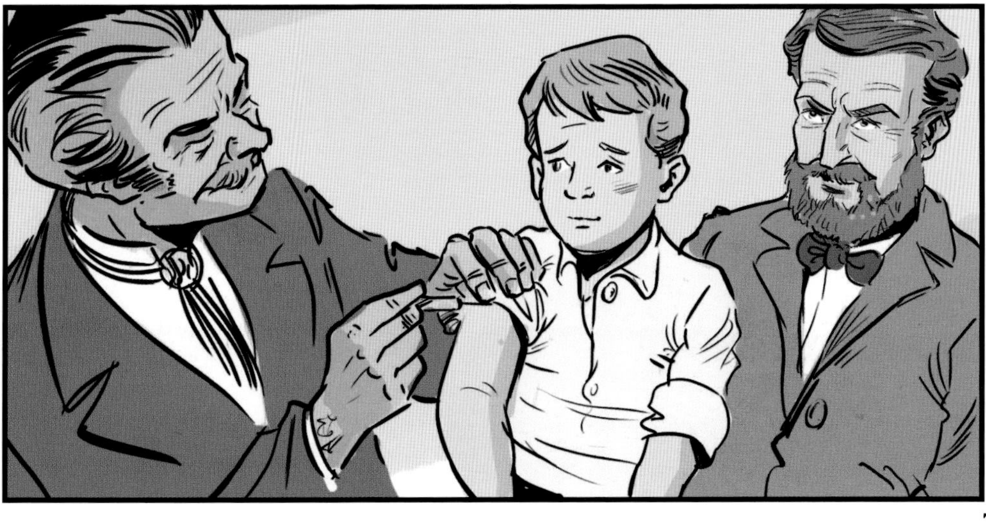

ALBERT EINSTEIN
(1879–1955)
EVERYTHING IS RELATIVE

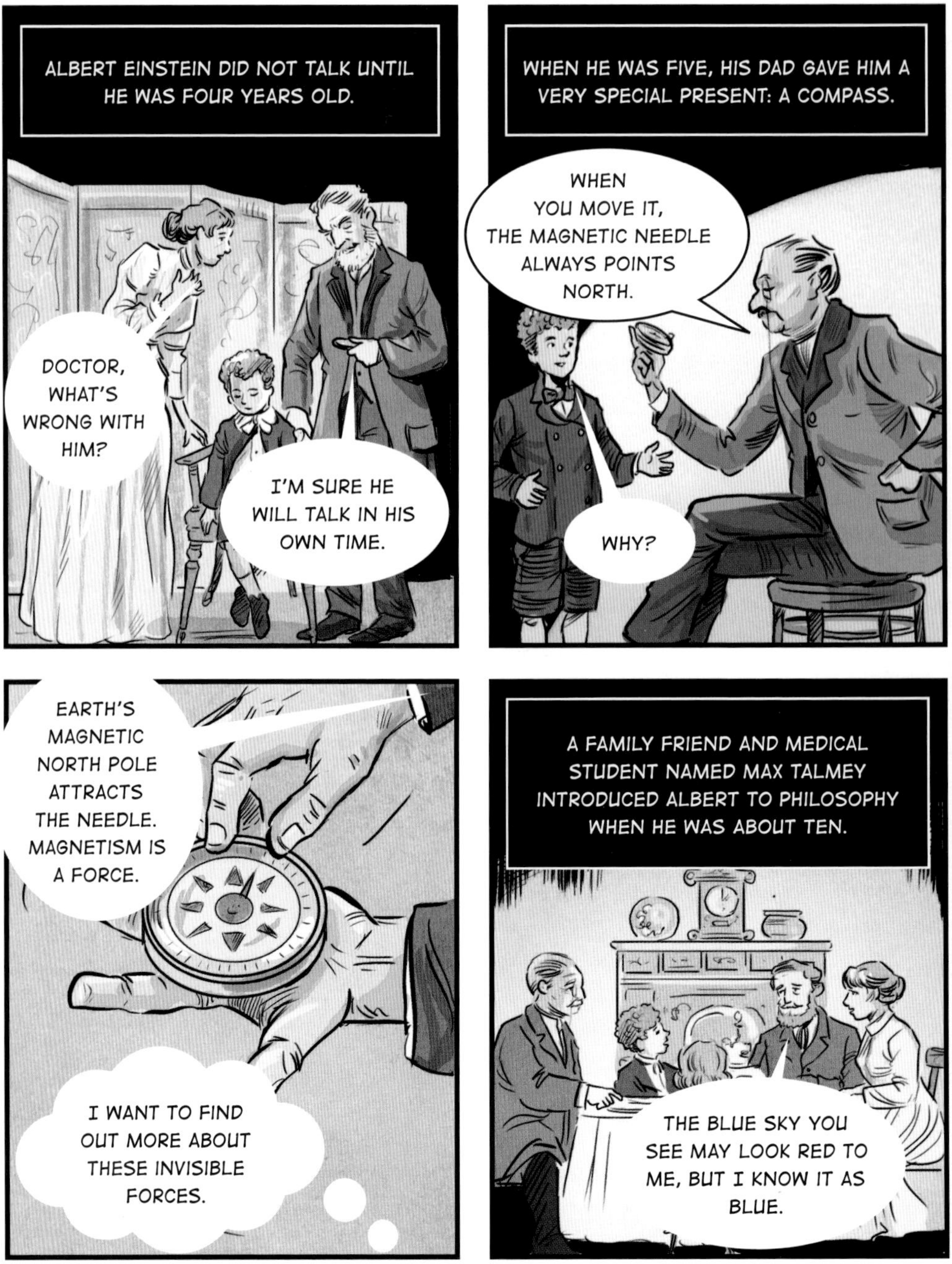
ALBERT EINSTEIN DID NOT TALK UNTIL HE WAS FOUR YEARS OLD.
DOCTOR, WHAT'S WRONG WITH HIM?
I'M SURE HE WILL TALK IN HIS OWN TIME.
WHEN HE WAS FIVE, HIS DAD GAVE HIM A VERY SPECIAL PRESENT: A COMPASS.
WHEN YOU MOVE IT, THE MAGNETIC NEEDLE ALWAYS POINTS NORTH.
WHY?
EARTH'S MAGNETIC NORTH POLE ATTRACTS THE NEEDLE. MAGNETISM IS A FORCE.
I WANT TO FIND OUT MORE ABOUT THESE INVISIBLE FORCES.
A FAMILY FRIEND AND MEDICAL STUDENT NAMED MAX TALMEY INTRODUCED ALBERT TO PHILOSOPHY WHEN HE WAS ABOUT TEN.
THE BLUE SKY YOU SEE MAY LOOK RED TO ME, BUT I KNOW IT AS BLUE.

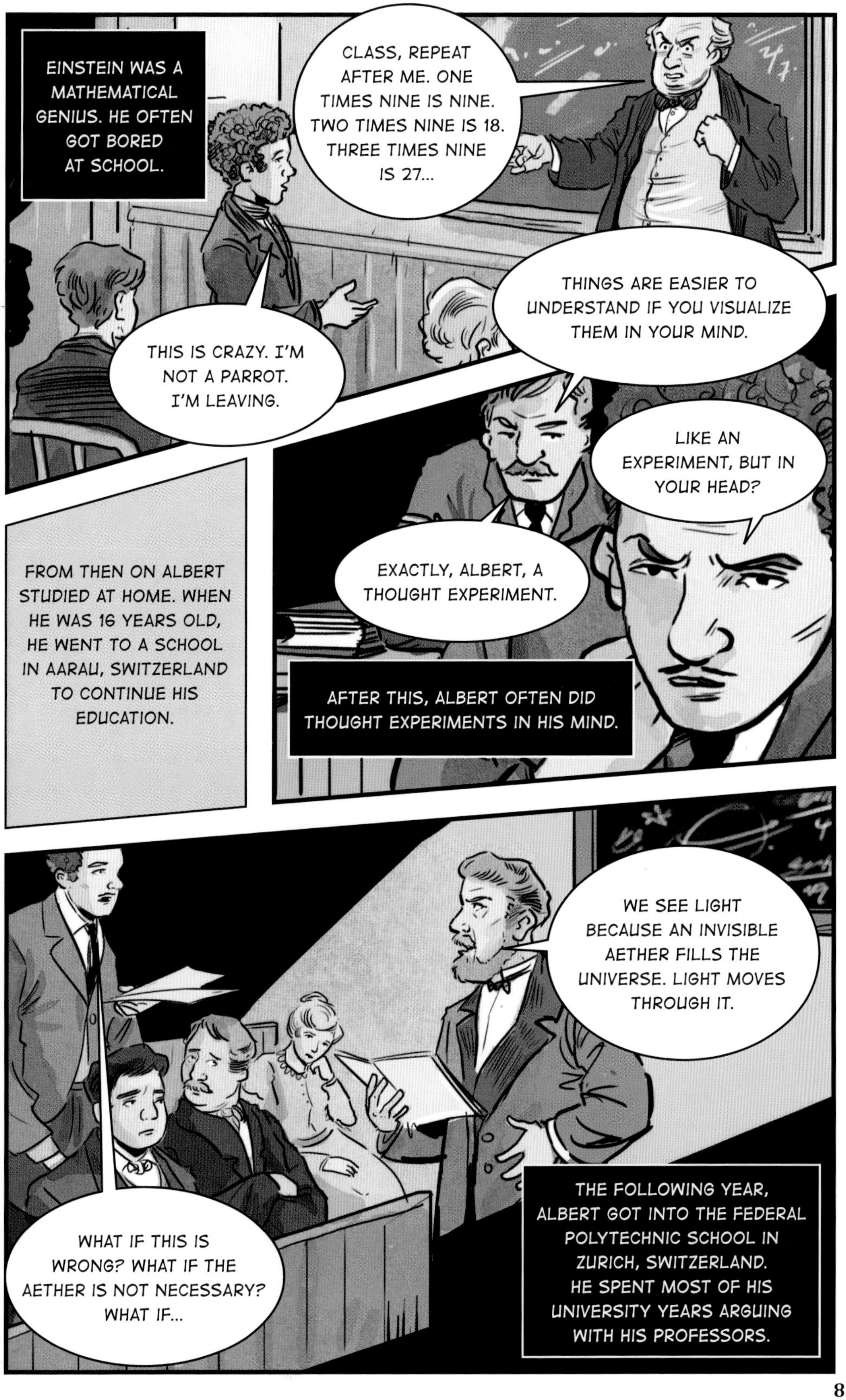
EINSTEIN WAS A MATHEMATICAL GENIUS. HE OFTEN GOT BORED AT SCHOOL.
CLASS, REPEAT AFTER ME. ONE TIMES NINE IS NINE. TWO TIMES NINE IS 18. THREE TIMES NINE IS 27...
THIS IS CRAZY. I'M NOT A PARROT. I'M LEAVING.
FROM THEN ON ALBERT STUDIED AT HOME. WHEN HE WAS 16 YEARS OLD, HE WENT TO A SCHOOL IN AARAU, SWITZERLAND TO CONTINUE HIS EDUCATION.
THINGS ARE EASIER TO UNDERSTAND IF YOU VISUALIZE THEM IN YOUR MIND.
LIKE AN EXPERIMENT, BUT IN YOUR HEAD?
EXACTLY, ALBERT, A THOUGHT EXPERIMENT.
AFTER THIS, ALBERT OFTEN DID THOUGHT EXPERIMENTS IN HIS MIND.
WE SEE LIGHT BECAUSE AN INVISIBLE AETHER FILLS THE UNIVERSE. LIGHT MOVES THROUGH IT.
WHAT IF THIS IS WRONG? WHAT IF THE AETHER IS NOT NECESSARY? WHAT IF...
THE FOLLOWING YEAR, ALBERT GOT INTO THE FEDERAL POLYTECHNIC SCHOOL IN ZURICH, SWITZERLAND. HE SPENT MOST OF HIS UNIVERSITY YEARS ARGUING WITH HIS PROFESSORS.

AFTER UNIVERSITY, ALBERT WORKED AT THE PATENT OFFICE IN BERN, SWITZERLAND. HE FOUND THE WORK EASY, WHICH GAVE HIM A LOT OF FREE TIME TO CONCENTRATE ON PHYSICS AND HIS THOUGHT EXPERIMENTS. IN 1905, HE HAD A "MIRACLE YEAR." HE PUBLISHED FOUR IMPORTANT PAPERS. HIS FIRST PAPER OUTLINED A PHOTOELECTRIC EFFECT.

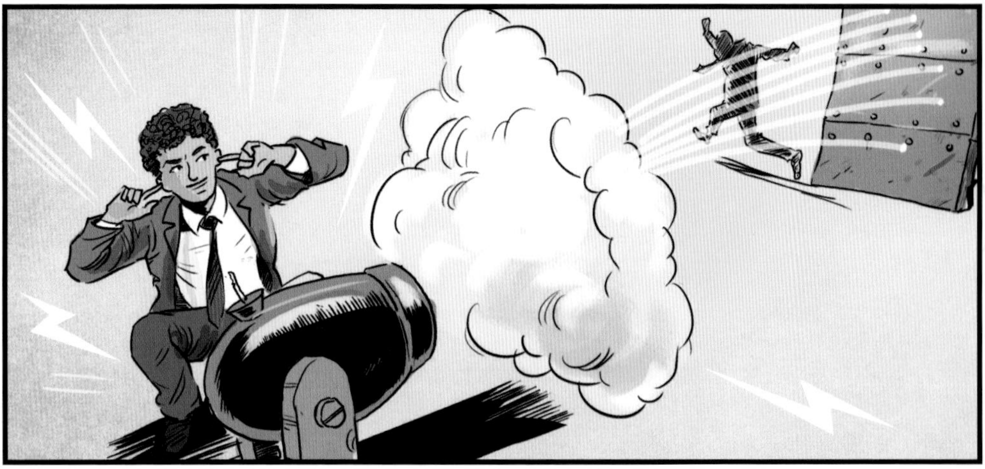

THE SECOND PAPER PROVED THE EXISTENCE OF ATOMS USING OBSERVATIONS BY THE SCIENTIST ROBERT BROWN, WHO NOTICED THAT POLLEN GRAINS ZIGZAG IN WATER. THIS IS KNOWN AS BROWNIAN MOTION.

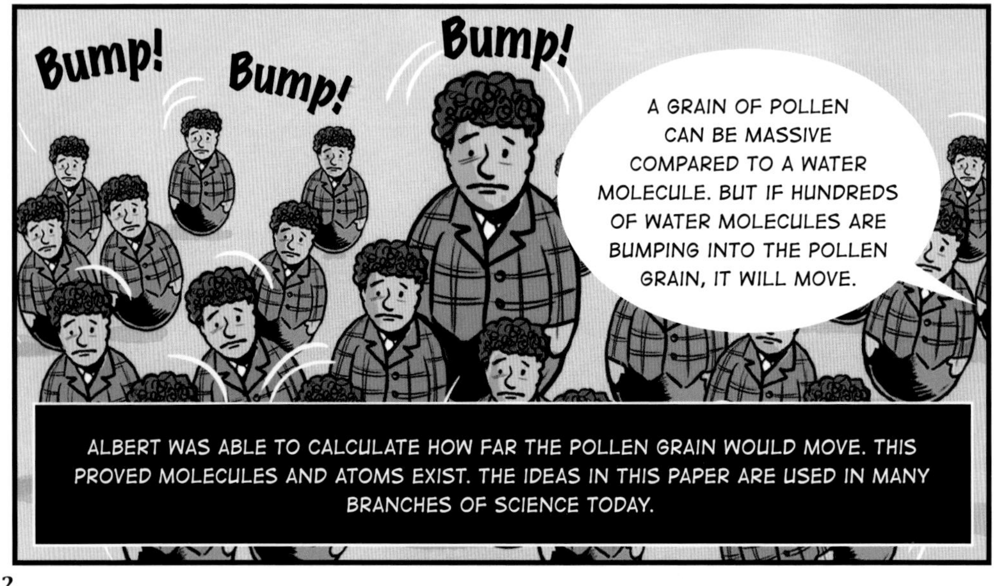
Bump!
Bump!
Bump!
A GRAIN OF POLLEN CAN BE MASSIVE COMPARED TO A WATER MOLECULE. BUT IF HUNDREDS OF WATER MOLECULES ARE BUMPING INTO THE POLLEN GRAIN, IT WILL MOVE.
ALBERT WAS ABLE TO CALCULATE HOW FAR THE POLLEN GRAIN WOULD MOVE. THIS PROVED MOLECULES AND ATOMS EXIST. THE IDEAS IN THIS PAPER ARE USED IN MANY BRANCHES OF SCIENCE TODAY.

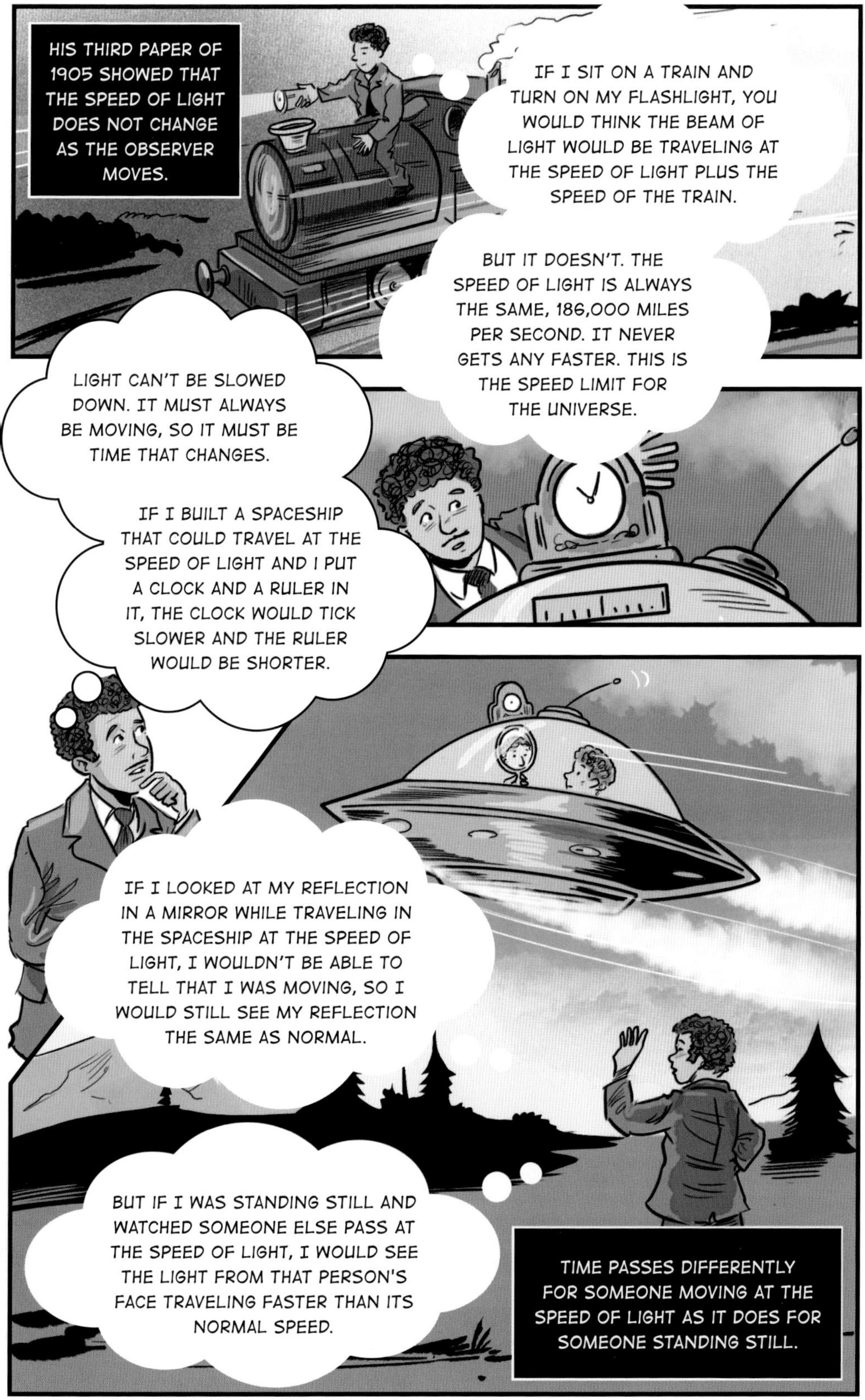
HIS THIRD PAPER OF 1905 SHOWED THAT THE SPEED OF LIGHT DOES NOT CHANGE AS THE OBSERVER MOVES.
IF I SIT ON A TRAIN AND TURN ON MY FLASHLIGHT, YOU WOULD THINK THE BEAM OF LIGHT WOULD BE TRAVELING AT THE SPEED OF LIGHT PLUS THE SPEED OF THE TRAIN.
BUT IT DOESN'T. THE SPEED OF LIGHT IS ALWAYS THE SAME, 186,000 MILES PER SECOND. IT NEVER GETS ANY FASTER. THIS IS THE SPEED LIMIT FOR THE UNIVERSE.
LIGHT CAN'T BE SLOWED DOWN. IT MUST ALWAYS BE MOVING, SO IT MUST BE TIME THAT CHANGES.
IF I BUILT A SPACESHIP THAT COULD TRAVEL AT THE SPEED OF LIGHT AND I PUT A CLOCK AND A RULER IN IT, THE CLOCK WOULD TICK SLOWER AND THE RULER WOULD BE SHORTER.
IF I LOOKED AT MY REFLECTION IN A MIRROR WHILE TRAVELING IN THE SPACESHIP AT THE SPEED OF LIGHT, I WOULDN'T BE ABLE TO TELL THAT I WAS MOVING, SO I WOULD STILL SEE MY REFLECTION THE SAME AS NORMAL.
BUT IF I WAS STANDING STILL AND WATCHED SOMEONE ELSE PASS AT THE SPEED OF LIGHT, I WOULD SEE THE LIGHT FROM THAT PERSON'S FACE TRAVELING FASTER THAN ITS NORMAL SPEED.
TIME PASSES DIFFERENTLY FOR SOMEONE MOVING AT THE SPEED OF LIGHT AS IT DOES FOR SOMEONE STANDING STILL.

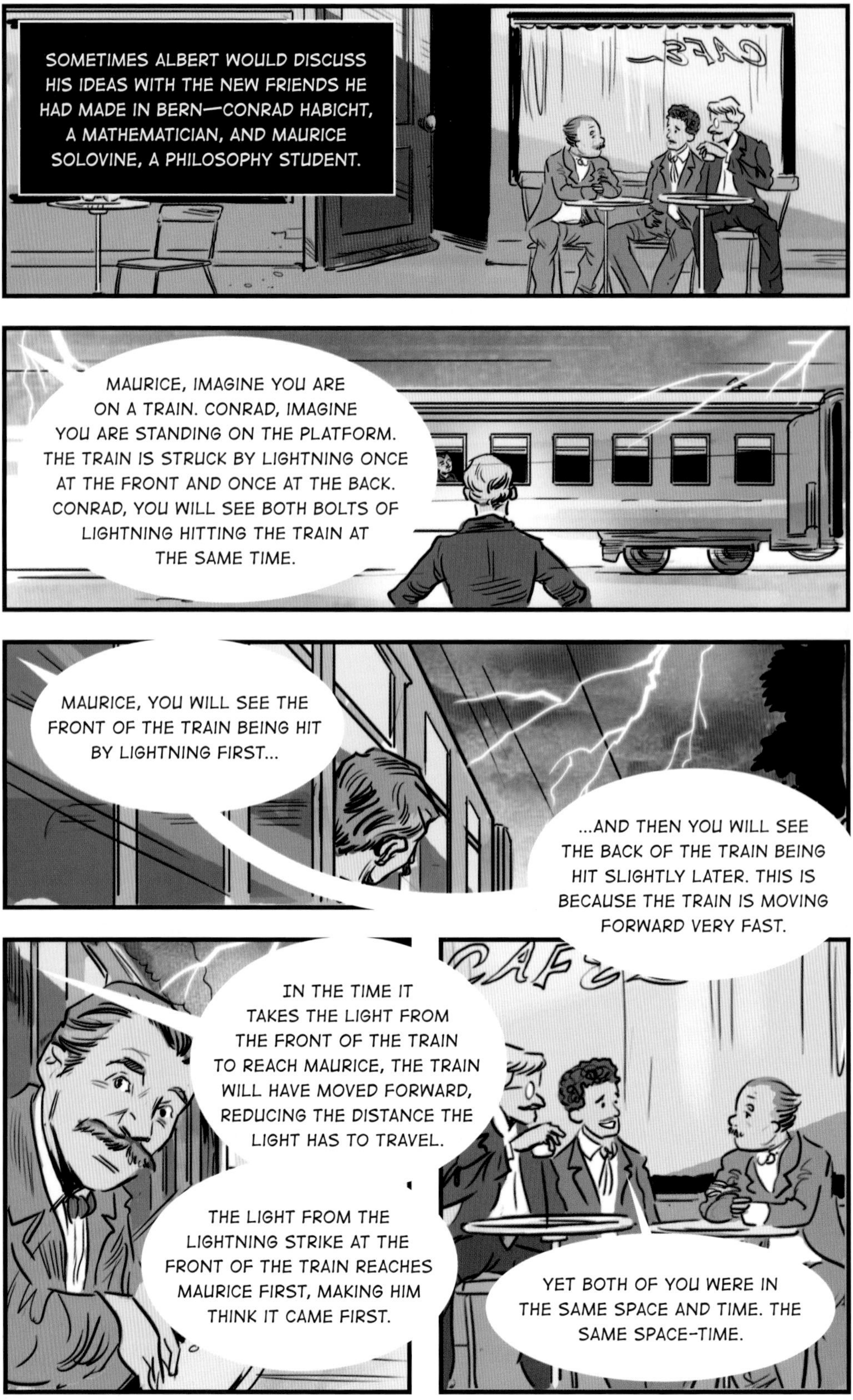
SOMETIMES ALBERT WOULD DISCUSS HIS IDEAS WITH THE NEW FRIENDS HE HAD MADE IN BERN—CONRAD HABICHT, A MATHEMATICIAN, AND MAURICE SOLOVINE, A PHILOSOPHY STUDENT.
CAFE
MAURICE, IMAGINE YOU ARE ON A TRAIN. CONRAD, IMAGINE YOU ARE STANDING ON THE PLATFORM. THE TRAIN IS STRUCK BY LIGHTNING ONCE AT THE FRONT AND ONCE AT THE BACK. CONRAD, YOU WILL SEE BOTH BOLTS OF LIGHTNING HITTING THE TRAIN AT THE SAME TIME.
MAURICE, YOU WILL SEE THE FRONT OF THE TRAIN BEING HIT BY LIGHTNING FIRST...
...AND THEN YOU WILL SEE THE BACK OF THE TRAIN BEING HIT SLIGHTLY LATER. THIS IS BECAUSE THE TRAIN IS MOVING FORWARD VERY FAST.
IN THE TIME IT TAKES THE LIGHT FROM THE FRONT OF THE TRAIN TO REACH MAURICE, THE TRAIN WILL HAVE MOVED FORWARD, REDUCING THE DISTANCE THE LIGHT HAS TO TRAVEL.
THE LIGHT FROM THE LIGHTNING STRIKE AT THE FRONT OF THE TRAIN REACHES MAURICE FIRST, MAKING HIM THINK IT CAME FIRST.
YET BOTH OF YOU WERE IN THE SAME SPACE AND TIME. THE SAME SPACE-TIME.

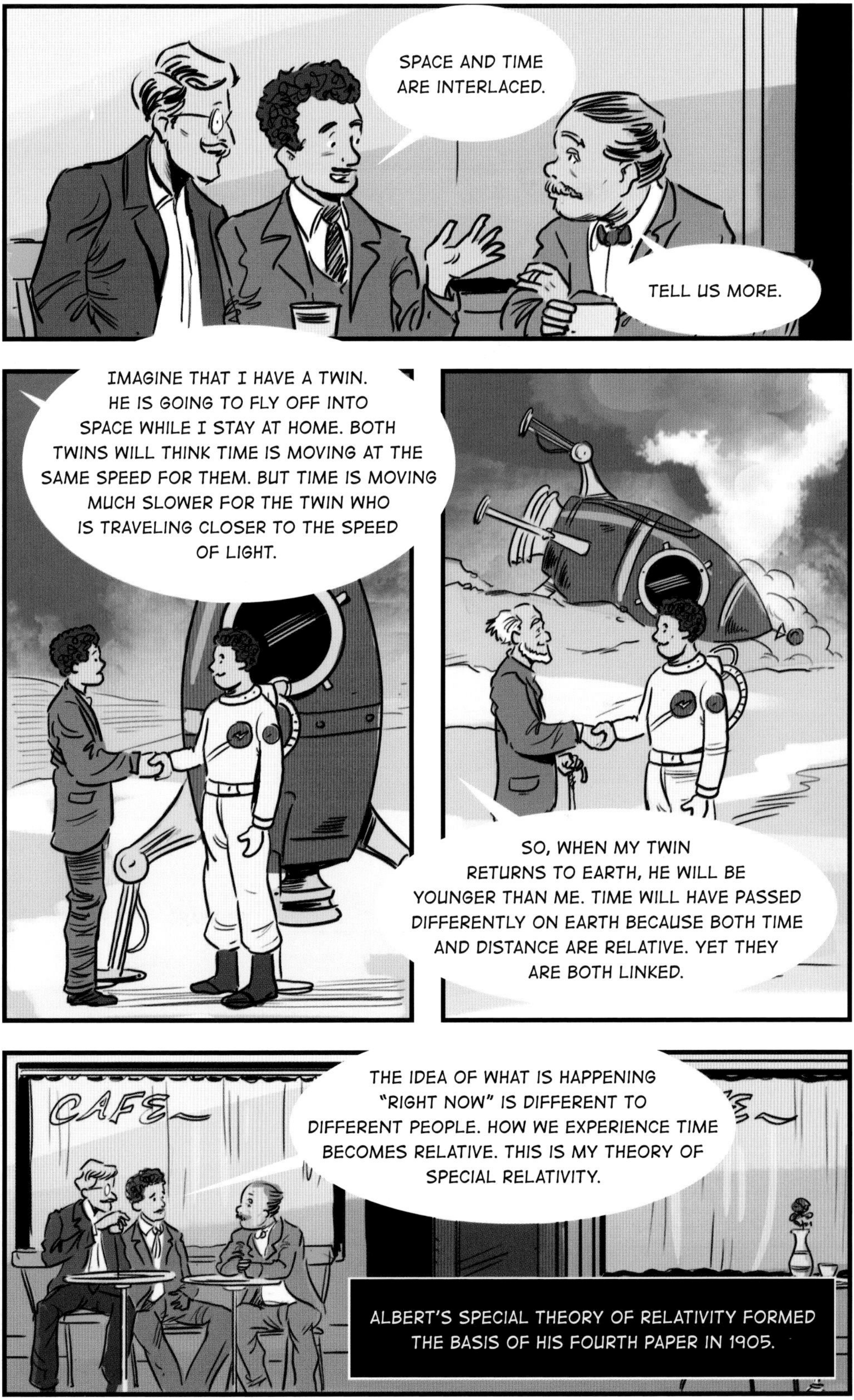
SPACE AND TIME ARE INTERLACED.
TELL US MORE.
IMAGINE THAT I HAVE A TWIN. HE IS GOING TO FLY OFF INTO SPACE WHILE I STAY AT HOME. BOTH TWINS WILL THINK TIME IS MOVING AT THE SAME SPEED FOR THEM. BUT TIME IS MOVING MUCH SLOWER FOR THE TWIN WHO IS TRAVELING CLOSER TO THE SPEED OF LIGHT.
SO, WHEN MY TWIN RETURNS TO EARTH, HE WILL BE YOUNGER THAN ME. TIME WILL HAVE PASSED DIFFERENTLY ON EARTH BECAUSE BOTH TIME AND DISTANCE ARE RELATIVE. YET THEY ARE BOTH LINKED.
CAFE
THE IDEA OF WHAT IS HAPPENING "RIGHT NOW" IS DIFFERENT TO DIFFERENT PEOPLE. HOW WE EXPERIENCE TIME BECOMES RELATIVE. THIS IS MY THEORY OF SPECIAL RELATIVITY.
ALBERT'S SPECIAL THEORY OF RELATIVITY FORMED THE BASIS OF HIS FOURTH PAPER IN 1905.

ALBERT'S FOURTH PAPER SHOWED THAT ENERGY AND MASS ARE CONNECTED. EVEN WHEN SOMETHING IS NOT MOVING, ITS ENERGY AND ITS MASS ARE RELATED.

$$E=MC^2$$

THE EQUATION ALBERT DISCOVERED HELPED SCIENTISTS UNDERSTAND NUCLEAR ENERGY TO CREATE ELECTRICITY.

HIS MASS-ENERGY EQUIVALENCE THEORY WAS ALSO USED TO MAKE ATOMIC BOMBS.

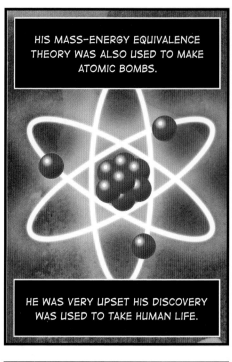

HE WAS VERY UPSET HIS DISCOVERY WAS USED TO TAKE HUMAN LIFE.

ALBERT LOVED TO PLAY CHESS. HE OFTEN PLAYED WITH HIS FRIEND MARCEL GROSSMAN. ONE DAY, HE WAS CYCLING THROUGH THE PARK TO MEET HIS FRIEND.

MY THEORY IS ONLY TRUE WHEN OBJECTS ARE MOVING AT THE SAME SPEED.

AS HE RODE, HE TRIED TO RECONCILE HIS SPECIAL THEORY OF RELATIVITY WITH ISAAC NEWTON'S LAW OF GRAVITY.

ALBERT WAS NOT CONCENTRATING ON WHERE HE WAS GOING. HE HIT A CURB AND FLEW OVER THE HANDLEBARS.

THIS IS FANTASTIC. NOW I KNOW THE SECRET OF GRAVITY.

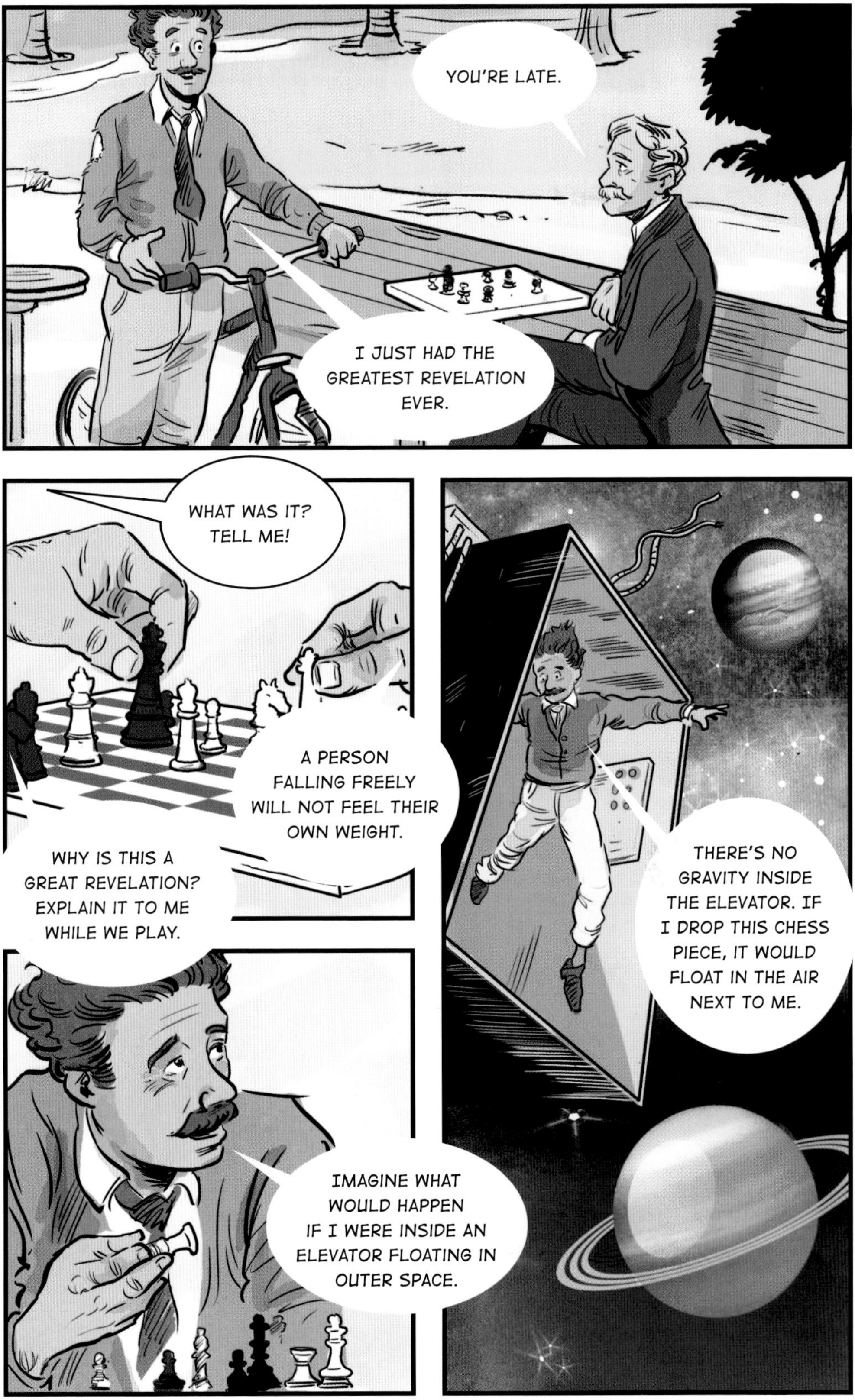

YOU'RE LATE.
I JUST HAD THE GREATEST REVELATION EVER.
WHAT WAS IT? TELL ME!
A PERSON FALLING FREELY WILL NOT FEEL THEIR OWN WEIGHT.
WHY IS THIS A GREAT REVELATION? EXPLAIN IT TO ME WHILE WE PLAY.
IMAGINE WHAT WOULD HAPPEN IF I WERE INSIDE AN ELEVATOR FLOATING IN OUTER SPACE.
THERE'S NO GRAVITY INSIDE THE ELEVATOR. IF I DROP THIS CHESS PIECE, IT WOULD FLOAT IN THE AIR NEXT TO ME.

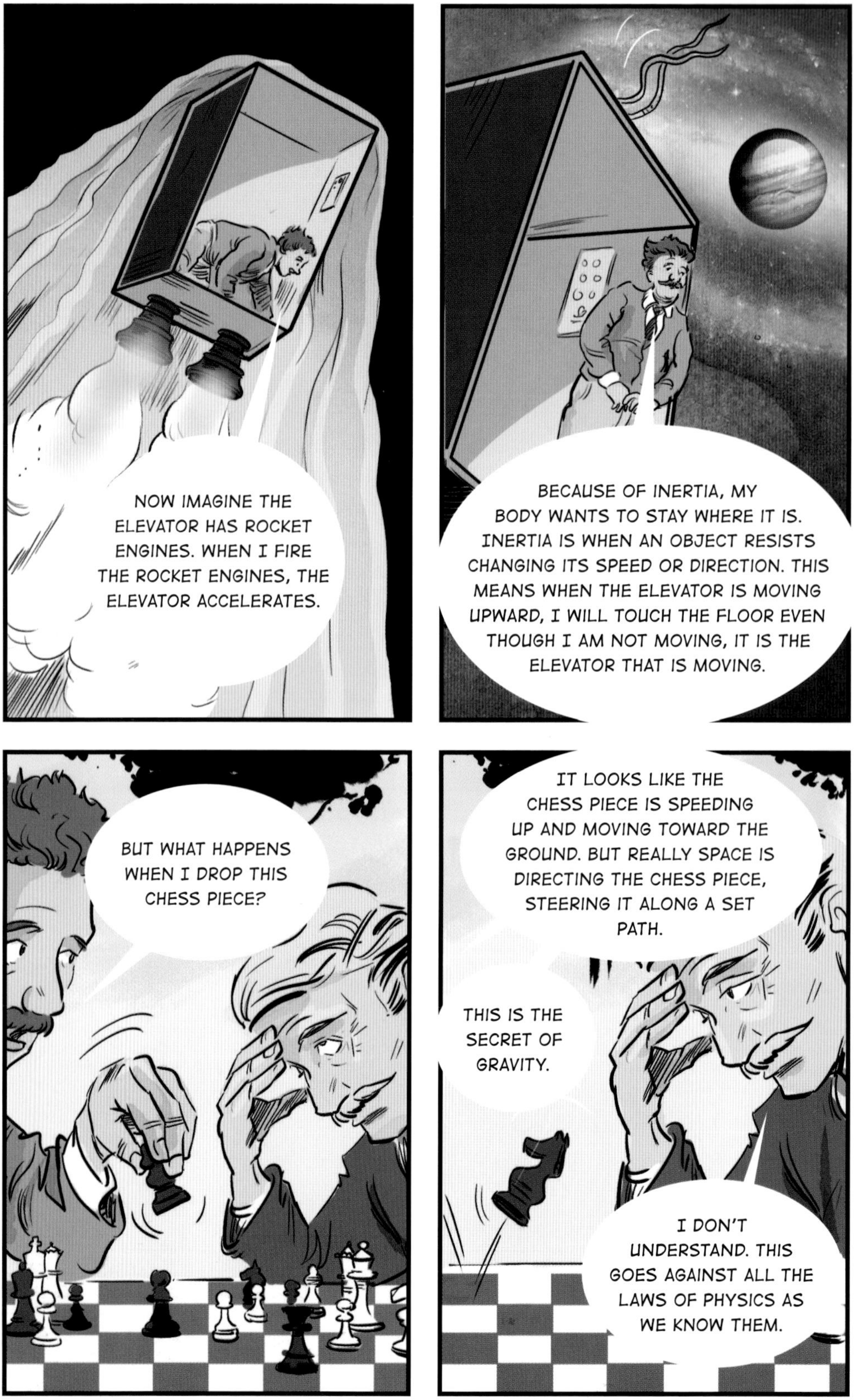
NOW IMAGINE THE ELEVATOR HAS ROCKET ENGINES. WHEN I FIRE THE ROCKET ENGINES, THE ELEVATOR ACCELERATES.
BECAUSE OF INERTIA, MY BODY WANTS TO STAY WHERE IT IS. INERTIA IS WHEN AN OBJECT RESISTS CHANGING ITS SPEED OR DIRECTION. THIS MEANS WHEN THE ELEVATOR IS MOVING UPWARD, I WILL TOUCH THE FLOOR EVEN THOUGH I AM NOT MOVING, IT IS THE ELEVATOR THAT IS MOVING.
BUT WHAT HAPPENS WHEN I DROP THIS CHESS PIECE?
IT LOOKS LIKE THE CHESS PIECE IS SPEEDING UP AND MOVING TOWARD THE GROUND. BUT REALLY SPACE IS DIRECTING THE CHESS PIECE, STEERING IT ALONG A SET PATH.
THIS IS THE SECRET OF GRAVITY.
I DON'T UNDERSTAND. THIS GOES AGAINST ALL THE LAWS OF PHYSICS AS WE KNOW THEM.

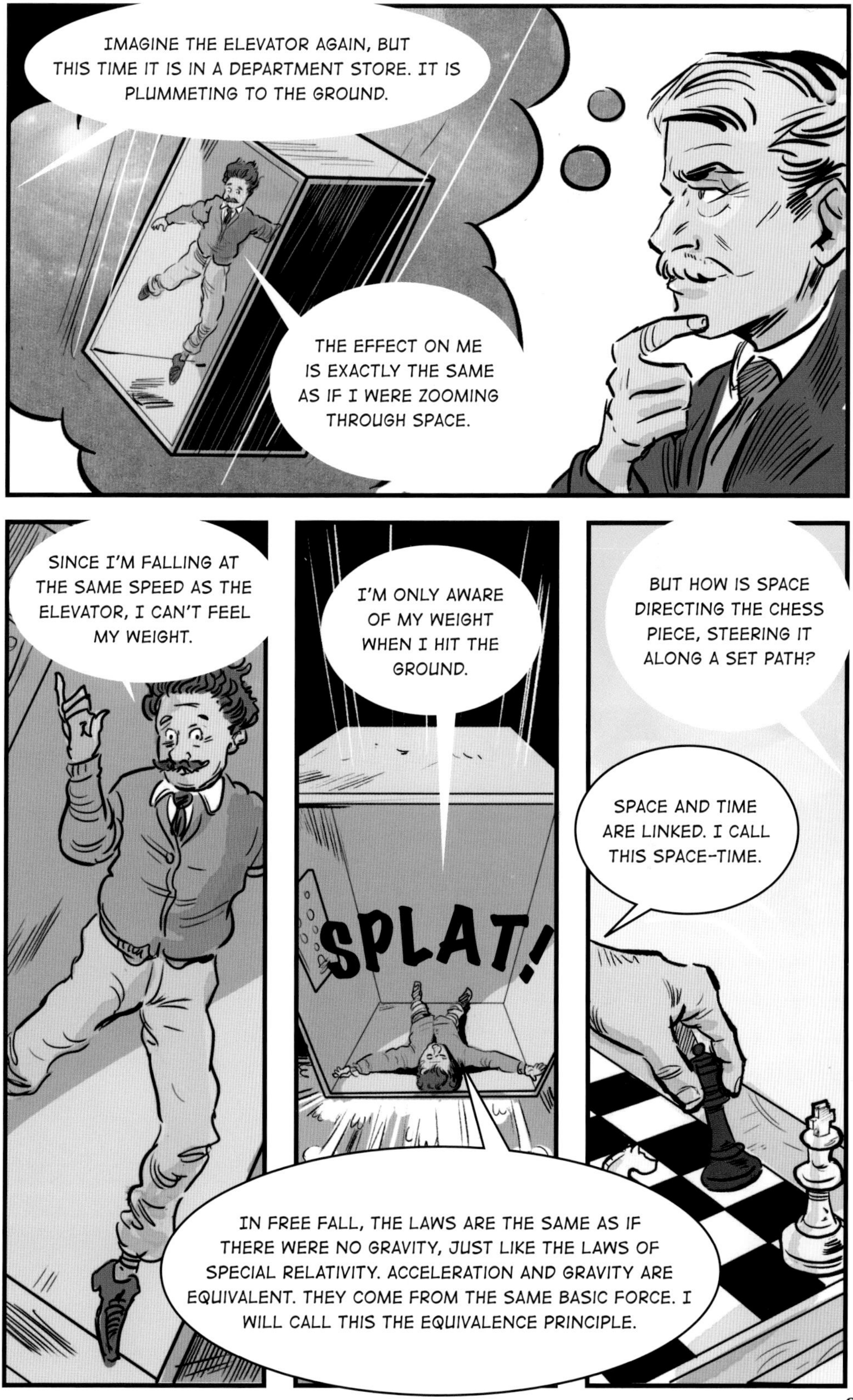
IMAGINE THE ELEVATOR AGAIN, BUT THIS TIME IT IS IN A DEPARTMENT STORE. IT IS PLUMMETING TO THE GROUND.
THE EFFECT ON ME IS EXACTLY THE SAME AS IF I WERE ZOOMING THROUGH SPACE.
SINCE I'M FALLING AT THE SAME SPEED AS THE ELEVATOR, I CAN'T FEEL MY WEIGHT.
I'M ONLY AWARE OF MY WEIGHT WHEN I HIT THE GROUND.
SPLAT!
BUT HOW IS SPACE DIRECTING THE CHESS PIECE, STEERING IT ALONG A SET PATH?
SPACE AND TIME ARE LINKED. I CALL THIS SPACE-TIME.
IN FREE FALL, THE LAWS ARE THE SAME AS IF THERE WERE NO GRAVITY, JUST LIKE THE LAWS OF SPECIAL RELATIVITY. ACCELERATION AND GRAVITY ARE EQUIVALENT. THEY COME FROM THE SAME BASIC FORCE. I WILL CALL THIS THE EQUIVALENCE PRINCIPLE.

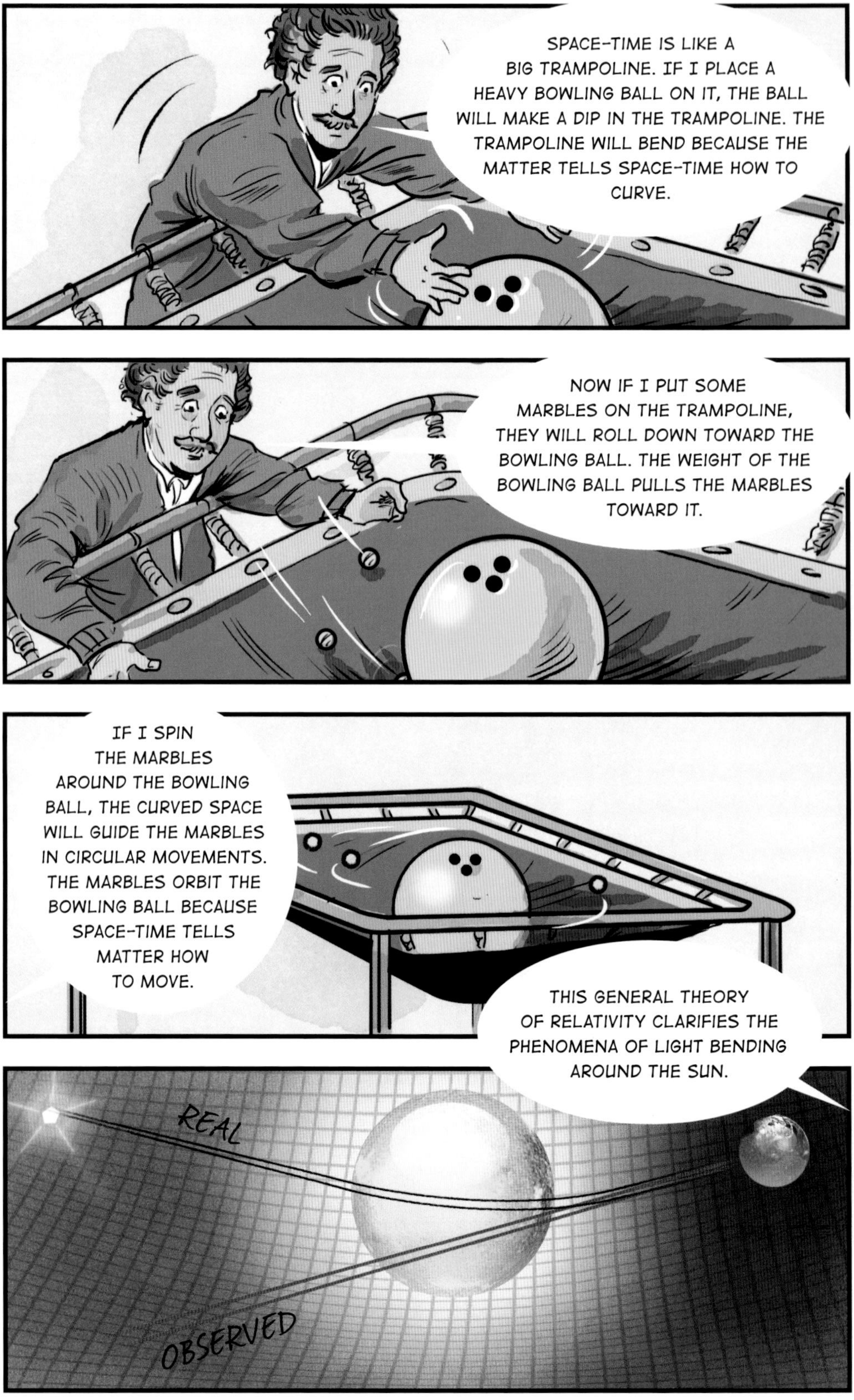
SPACE-TIME IS LIKE A BIG TRAMPOLINE. IF I PLACE A HEAVY BOWLING BALL ON IT, THE BALL WILL MAKE A DIP IN THE TRAMPOLINE. THE TRAMPOLINE WILL BEND BECAUSE THE MATTER TELLS SPACE-TIME HOW TO CURVE.
NOW IF I PUT SOME MARBLES ON THE TRAMPOLINE, THEY WILL ROLL DOWN TOWARD THE BOWLING BALL. THE WEIGHT OF THE BOWLING BALL PULLS THE MARBLES TOWARD IT.
IF I SPIN THE MARBLES AROUND THE BOWLING BALL, THE CURVED SPACE WILL GUIDE THE MARBLES IN CIRCULAR MOVEMENTS. THE MARBLES ORBIT THE BOWLING BALL BECAUSE SPACE-TIME TELLS MATTER HOW TO MOVE.
THIS GENERAL THEORY OF RELATIVITY CLARIFIES THE PHENOMENA OF LIGHT BENDING AROUND THE SUN.
REAL
OBSERVED

IT PREDICTS BLACK HOLES AND IT EXPLAINS THE COSMIC BACKGROUND RADIATION LEFT FROM THE BIG BANG.

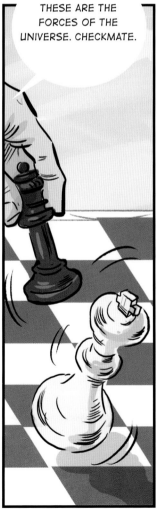

THESE ARE THE FORCES OF THE UNIVERSE. CHECKMATE.

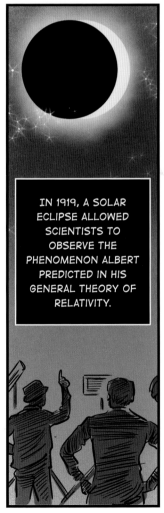

IN 1919, A SOLAR ECLIPSE ALLOWED SCIENTISTS TO OBSERVE THE PHENOMENON ALBERT PREDICTED IN HIS GENERAL THEORY OF RELATIVITY.

IN 1922, HE WON THE NOBEL PRIZE FOR HIS WORK ON QUANTUM THEORY.

THE THEORIES ALBERT EINSTEIN PUBLISHED IN HIS FOUR PAPERS ARE STILL USED BY SCIENTISTS TODAY.

MARIE CURIE
(1867–1934)
THE X-RAY HEROINE

MARIE AND HER SISTER HELENA WERE NOT ALLOWED TO ATTEND UNIVERSITIES IN THEIR HOME CITY OF WARSAW IN POLAND. THESE UNIVERSITIES WERE ONLY FOR MALES. INSTEAD, THE SISTERS WENT TO SECRET "FLYING UNIVERSITIES" THAT HELD CLASSES IN PRIVATE HOMES AROUND WARSAW.

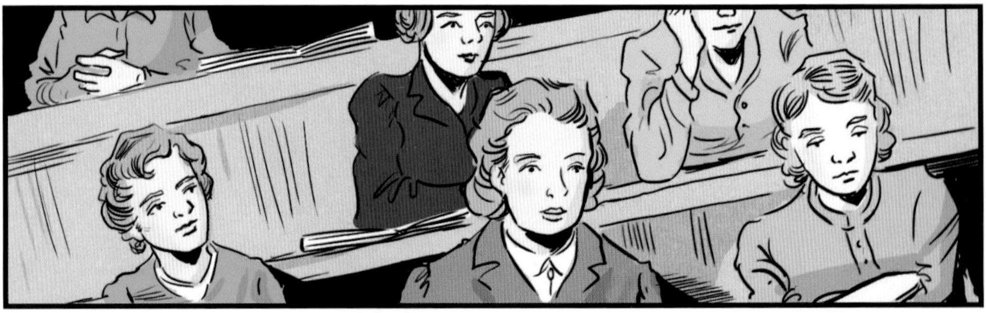

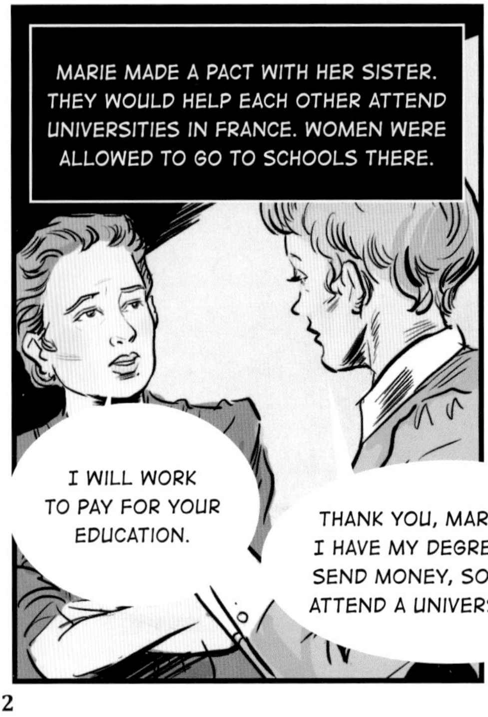
MARIE MADE A PACT WITH HER SISTER. THEY WOULD HELP EACH OTHER ATTEND UNIVERSITIES IN FRANCE. WOMEN WERE ALLOWED TO GO TO SCHOOLS THERE.
I WILL WORK TO PAY FOR YOUR EDUCATION.
THANK YOU, MARIE. WHEN I HAVE MY DEGREE, I WILL SEND MONEY, SO YOU CAN ATTEND A UNIVERSITY, TOO.

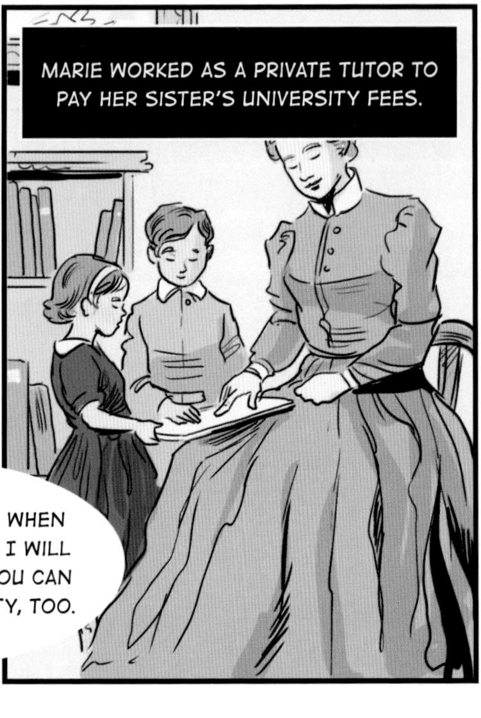
MARIE WORKED AS A PRIVATE TUTOR TO PAY HER SISTER'S UNIVERSITY FEES.

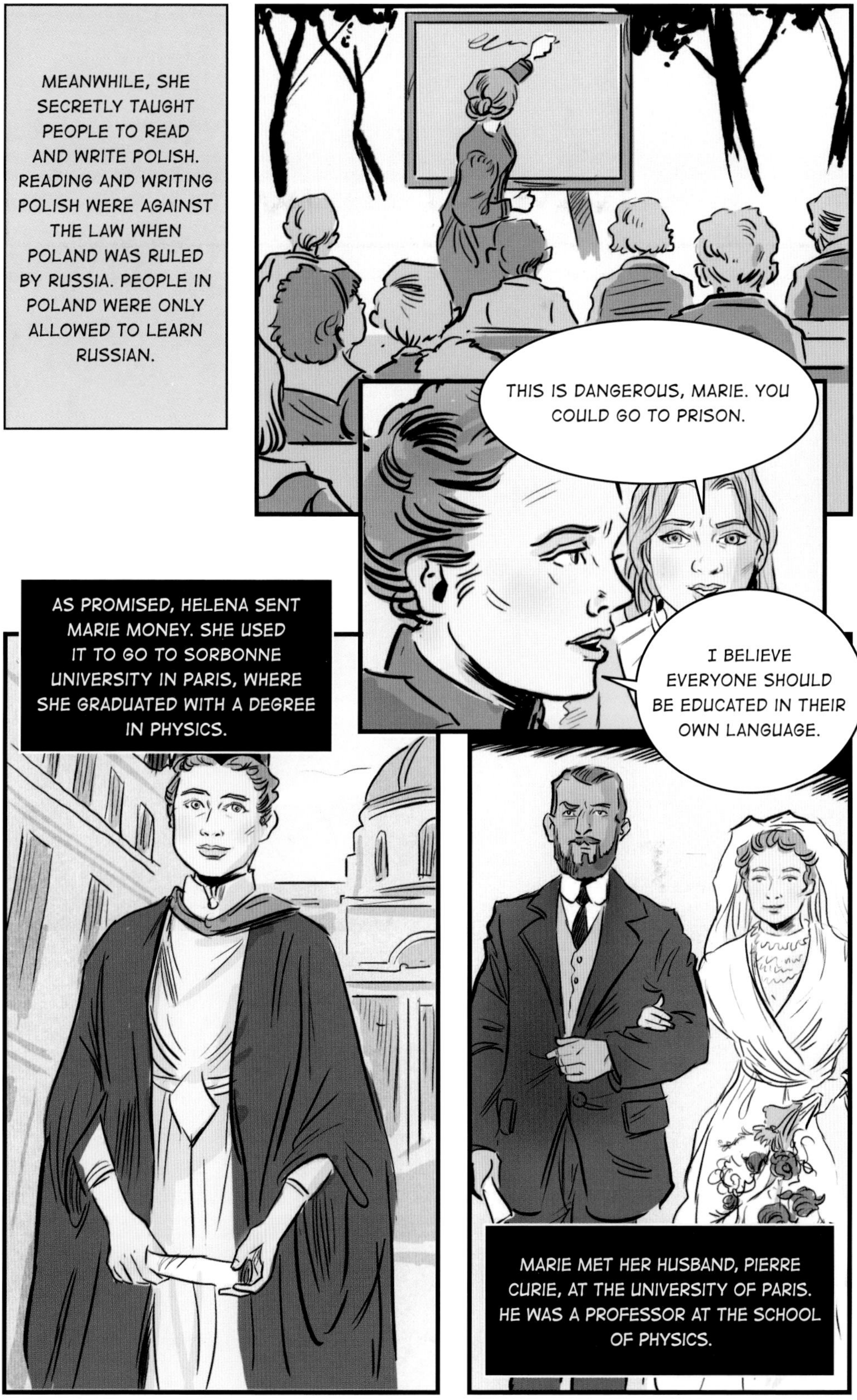
MEANWHILE, SHE SECRETLY TAUGHT PEOPLE TO READ AND WRITE POLISH. READING AND WRITING POLISH WERE AGAINST THE LAW WHEN POLAND WAS RULED BY RUSSIA. PEOPLE IN POLAND WERE ONLY ALLOWED TO LEARN RUSSIAN.
THIS IS DANGEROUS, MARIE. YOU COULD GO TO PRISON.
I BELIEVE EVERYONE SHOULD BE EDUCATED IN THEIR OWN LANGUAGE.
AS PROMISED, HELENA SENT MARIE MONEY. SHE USED IT TO GO TO SORBONNE UNIVERSITY IN PARIS, WHERE SHE GRADUATED WITH A DEGREE IN PHYSICS.
MARIE MET HER HUSBAND, PIERRE CURIE, AT THE UNIVERSITY OF PARIS. HE WAS A PROFESSOR AT THE SCHOOL OF PHYSICS.

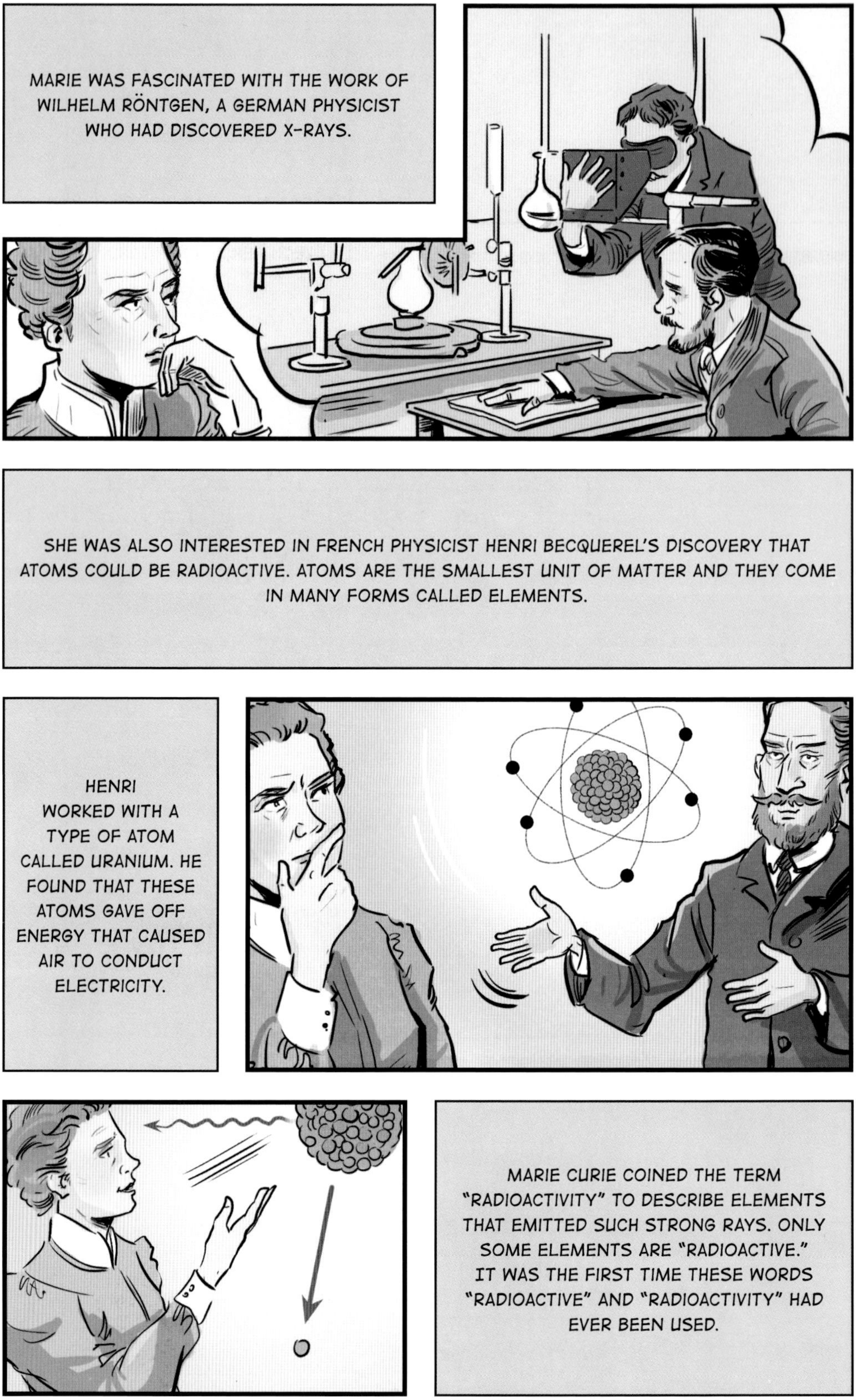
MARIE WAS FASCINATED WITH THE WORK OF WILHELM RÖNTGEN, A GERMAN PHYSICIST WHO HAD DISCOVERED X-RAYS.
SHE WAS ALSO INTERESTED IN FRENCH PHYSICIST HENRI BECQUEREL'S DISCOVERY THAT ATOMS COULD BE RADIOACTIVE. ATOMS ARE THE SMALLEST UNIT OF MATTER AND THEY COME IN MANY FORMS CALLED ELEMENTS.
HENRI WORKED WITH A TYPE OF ATOM CALLED URANIUM. HE FOUND THAT THESE ATOMS GAVE OFF ENERGY THAT CAUSED AIR TO CONDUCT ELECTRICITY.
MARIE CURIE COINED THE TERM "RADIOACTIVITY" TO DESCRIBE ELEMENTS THAT EMITTED SUCH STRONG RAYS. ONLY SOME ELEMENTS ARE "RADIOACTIVE." IT WAS THE FIRST TIME THESE WORDS "RADIOACTIVE" AND "RADIOACTIVITY" HAD EVER BEEN USED.

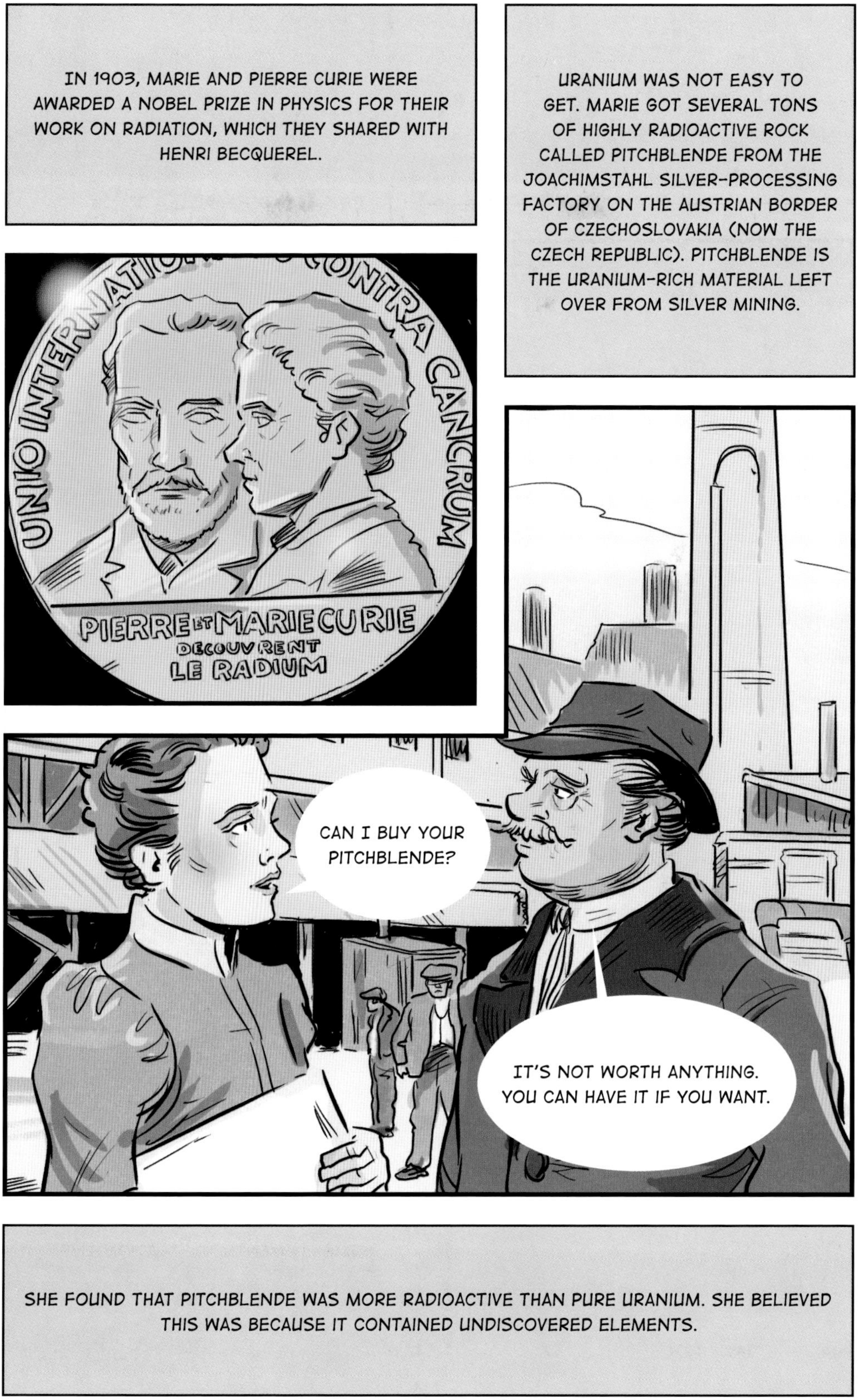
IN 1903, MARIE AND PIERRE CURIE WERE AWARDED A NOBEL PRIZE IN PHYSICS FOR THEIR WORK ON RADIATION, WHICH THEY SHARED WITH HENRI BECQUEREL.
URANIUM WAS NOT EASY TO GET. MARIE GOT SEVERAL TONS OF HIGHLY RADIOACTIVE ROCK CALLED PITCHBLENDE FROM THE JOACHIMSTAHL SILVER-PROCESSING FACTORY ON THE AUSTRIAN BORDER OF CZECHOSLOVAKIA (NOW THE CZECH REPUBLIC). PITCHBLENDE IS THE URANIUM-RICH MATERIAL LEFT OVER FROM SILVER MINING.
UNIO INTERNATIO... CONTRA CANCRUM
PIERRE ET MARIE CURIE
DECOUVRENT
LE RADIUM
CAN I BUY YOUR PITCHBLENDE?
IT'S NOT WORTH ANYTHING. YOU CAN HAVE IT IF YOU WANT.
SHE FOUND THAT PITCHBLENDE WAS MORE RADIOACTIVE THAN PURE URANIUM. SHE BELIEVED THIS WAS BECAUSE IT CONTAINED UNDISCOVERED ELEMENTS.

MARIE AND PIERRE BEGAN TO DO EXPERIMENTS WITH THE PITCHBLENDE—GRINDING, DISSOLVING, FILTERING, PRECIPITATING, AND CRYSTALLIZING.

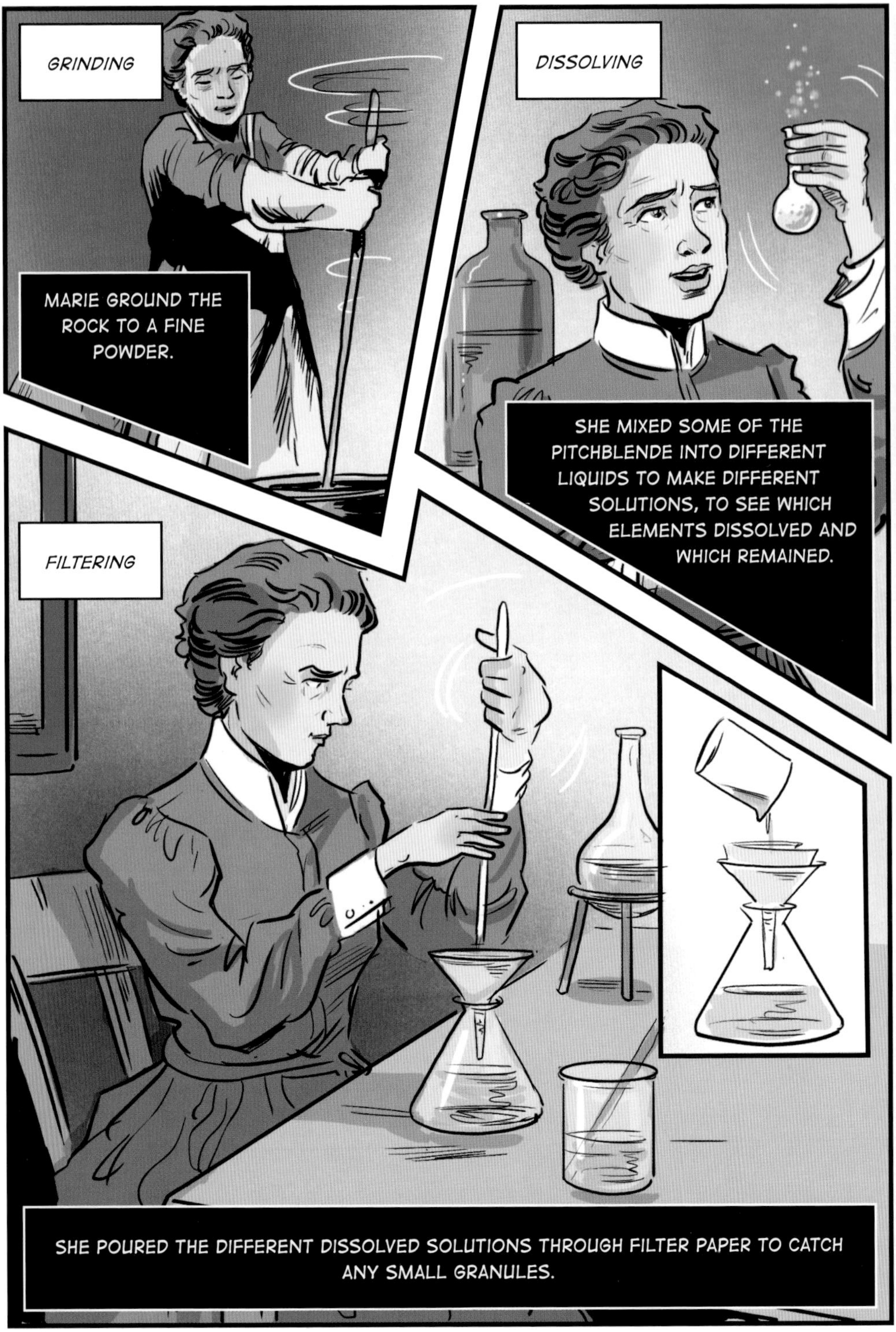
GRINDING
MARIE GROUND THE ROCK TO A FINE POWDER.
DISSOLVING
SHE MIXED SOME OF THE PITCHBLENDE INTO DIFFERENT LIQUIDS TO MAKE DIFFERENT SOLUTIONS, TO SEE WHICH ELEMENTS DISSOLVED AND WHICH REMAINED.
FILTERING
SHE POURED THE DIFFERENT DISSOLVED SOLUTIONS THROUGH FILTER PAPER TO CATCH ANY SMALL GRANULES.

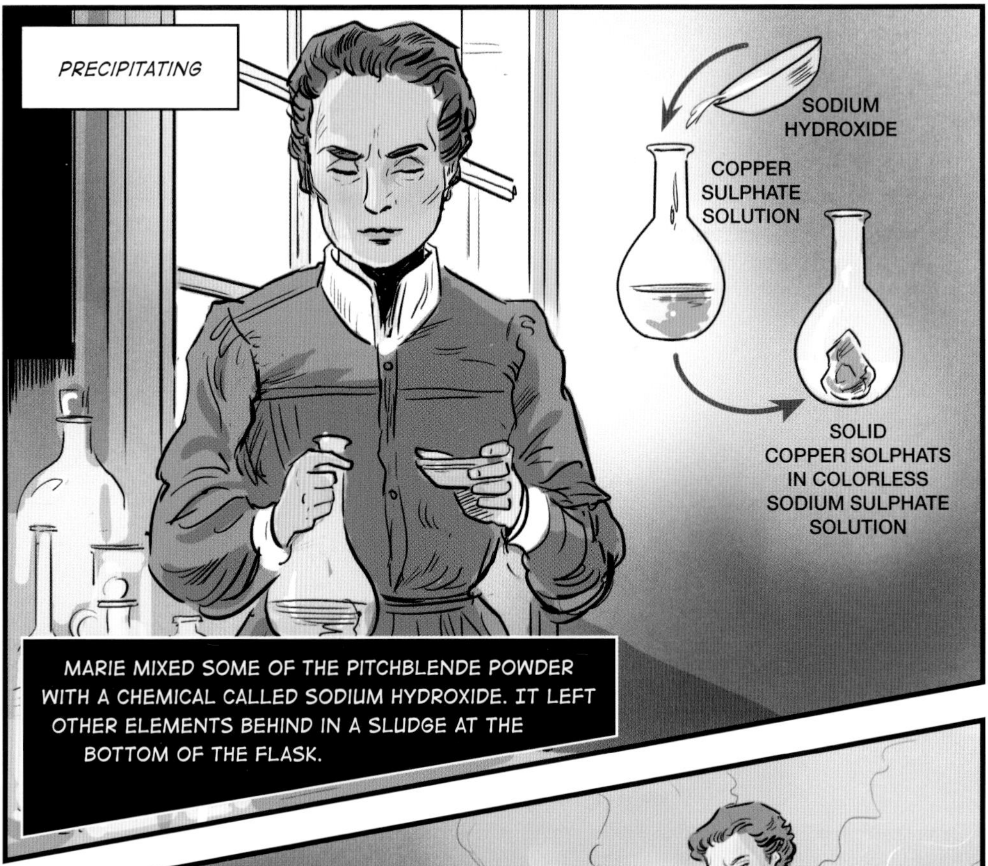
PRECIPITATING
SODIUM HYDROXIDE
COPPER SULPHATE SOLUTION
SOLID COPPER SOLPHATS IN COLORLESS SODIUM SULPHATE SOLUTION
MARIE MIXED SOME OF THE PITCHBLENDE POWDER WITH A CHEMICAL CALLED SODIUM HYDROXIDE. IT LEFT OTHER ELEMENTS BEHIND IN A SLUDGE AT THE BOTTOM OF THE FLASK.

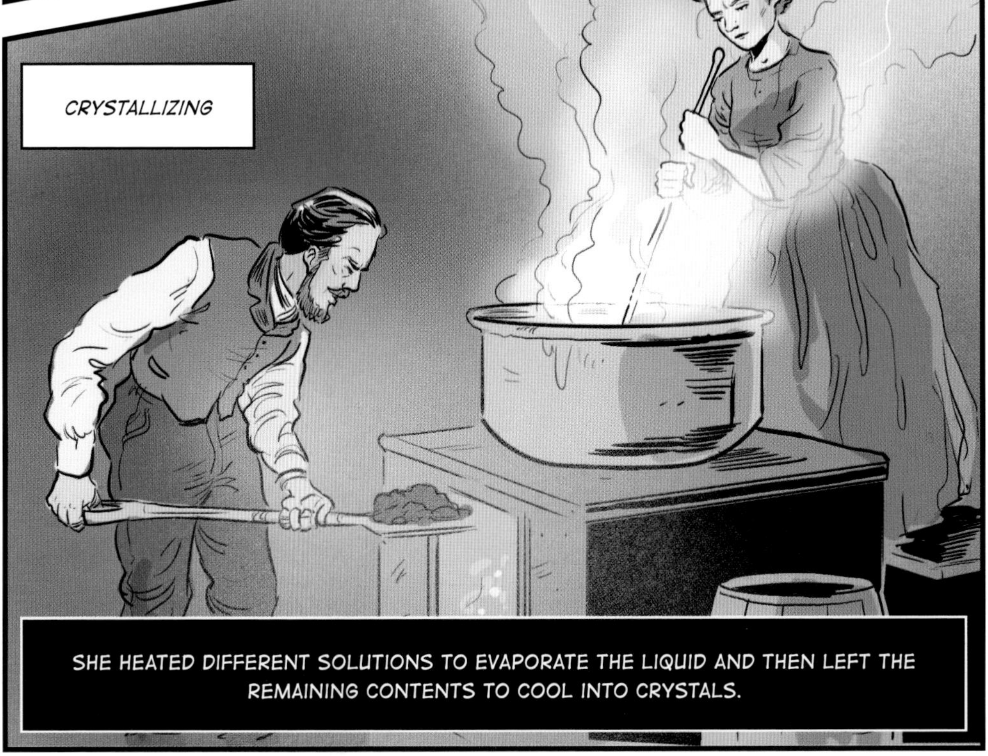
CRYSTALLIZING
SHE HEATED DIFFERENT SOLUTIONS TO EVAPORATE THE LIQUID AND THEN LEFT THE REMAINING CONTENTS TO COOL INTO CRYSTALS.

TO TEST IF ANY OF HER PITCHBLENDE EXPERIMENTS HAD ISOLATED URANIUM, MARIE USED A SPECIAL ELECTROMETER THAT HAD BEEN INVENTED BY PIERRE AND HIS BROTHER IN 1888. THIS INSTRUMENT WAS THE FIRST TO MEASURE RADIOACTIVITY

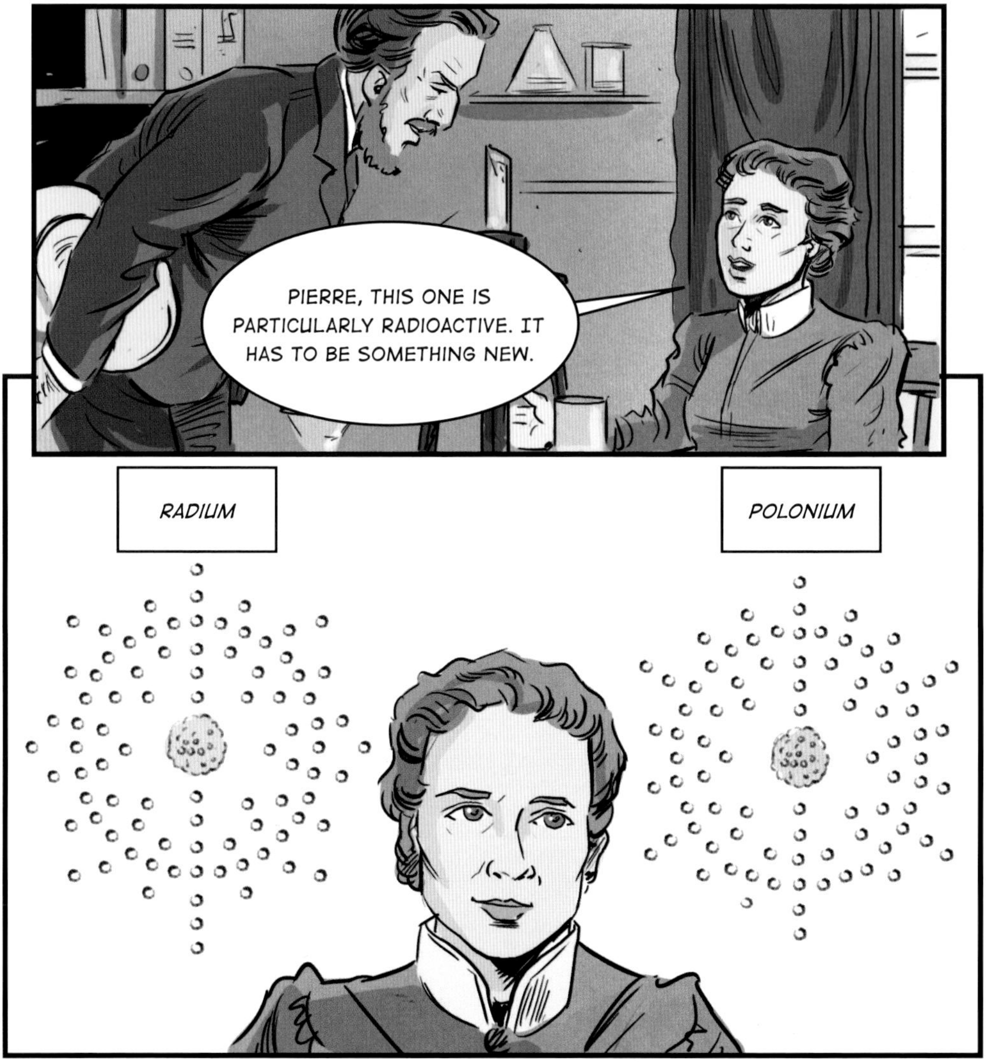
PIERRE, THIS ONE IS PARTICULARLY RADIOACTIVE. IT HAS TO BE SOMETHING NEW.
RADIUM
POLONIUM

FROM HER WORK WITH RADIOACTIVITY, MARIE DISCOVERED TWO NEW ELEMENTS. SHE NAMED POLONIUM AFTER HER HOMELAND POLAND. SHE NAMED RADIUM FOR THE ELEMENT THAT GAVE OFF SUCH STRONG RADIOACTIVE RAYS. IN 1906, PIERRE WAS TRAGICALLY KILLED IN A TRAFFIC ACCIDENT.

IN 1911, MARIE WON THE NOBEL PRIZE IN CHEMISTRY FOR THE DISCOVERY OF POLONIUM AND RADIUM. SHE WAS THE FIRST PERSON TO BE AWARDED TWO NOBEL PRIZES—ONE OF ONLY FOUR PEOPLE TO HAVE EVER ACHIEVED THIS.

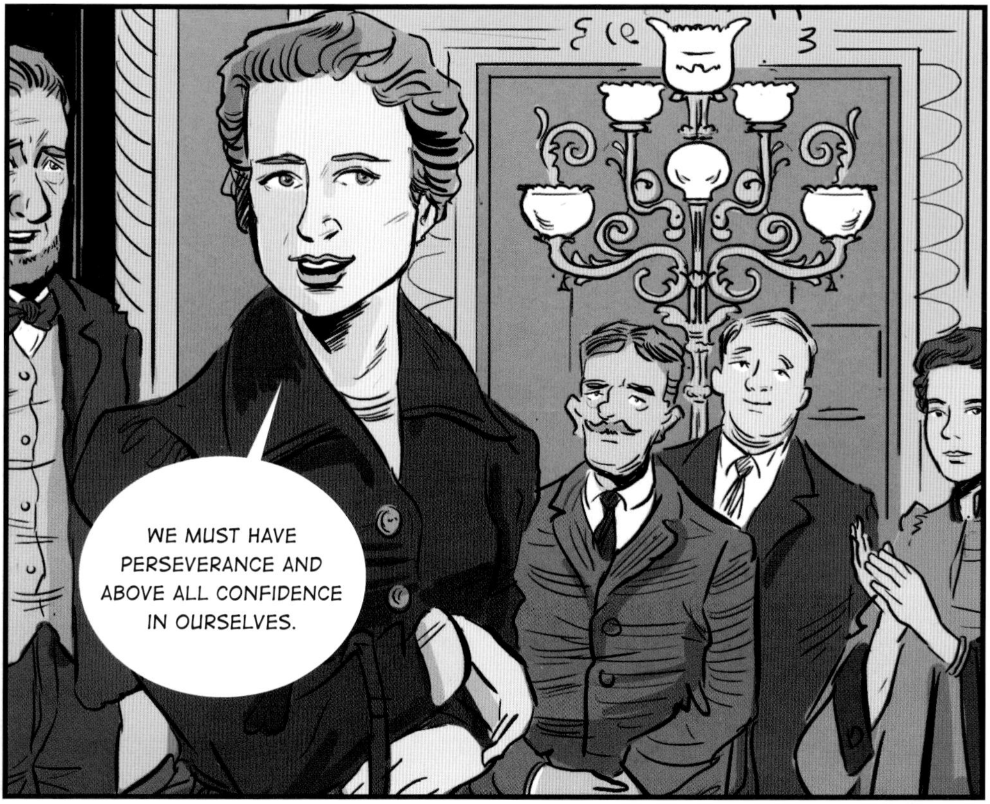
WE MUST HAVE PERSEVERANCE AND ABOVE ALL CONFIDENCE IN OURSELVES.

RADIOACTIVITY IS DANGEROUS. IT DAMAGES HUMAN CELLS. BUT THE CURIES DIDN'T KNOW OF THE RISKS. AFTER PIERRE'S DEATH, MARIE CONTINUED HER INVESTIGATIONS. HER HANDS WERE RAW AND INFLAMED FROM HANDLING HIGHLY RADIOACTIVE MATERIALS.

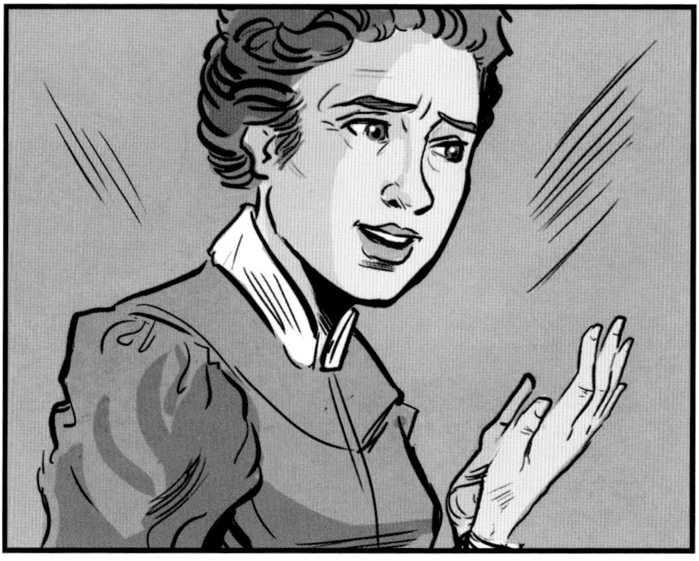

HER WORK INSPIRED OTHER SCIENTISTS TO USE RADIATION TO DEVELOP BETTER X-RAY MACHINES, WHICH COULD LOOK INSIDE THE BODY AND DISPLAY IMAGES OF BROKEN BONES, CHEST INFECTIONS LIKE TUBERCULOSIS, AND OTHER DETAILS.

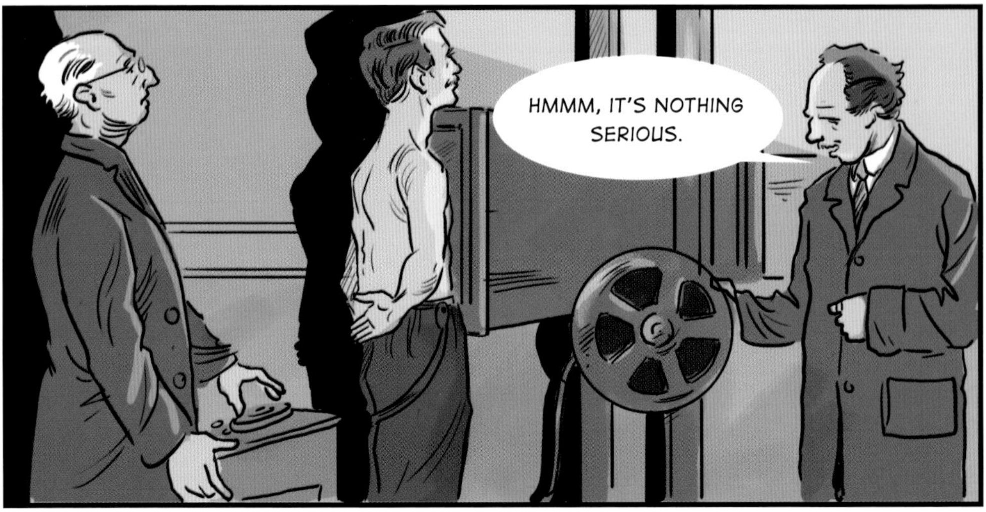
HMMM, IT'S NOTHING SERIOUS.

DURING WORLD WAR I, THERE WERE NOT ENOUGH X-RAY MACHINES FOR EVERY MILITARY HOSPITAL TO HAVE ONE. CURIE DEVISED A MOBILE X-RAY MACHINE, WHICH COULD TRAVEL FROM HOSPITAL TO HOSPITAL IN THE BACK OF A TRUCK.

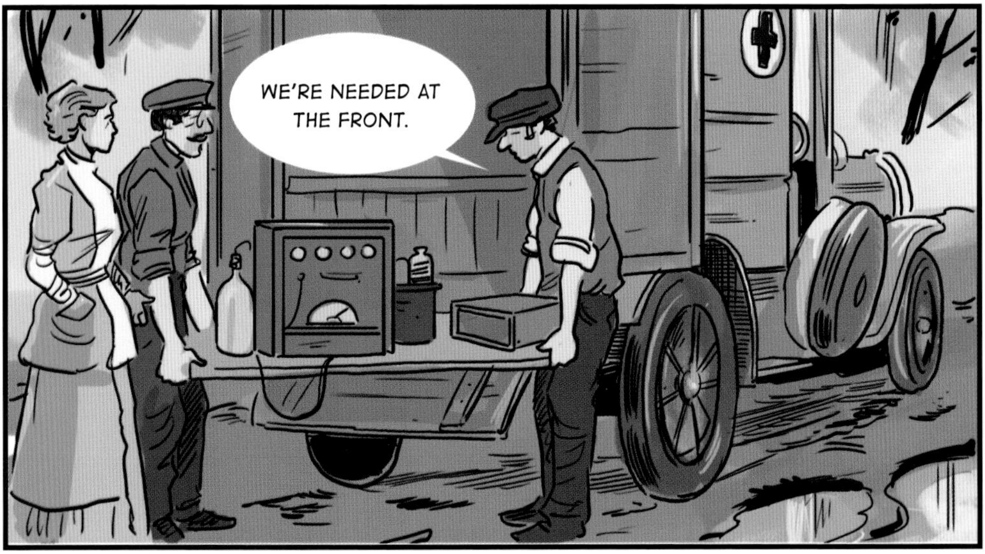
WE'RE NEEDED AT THE FRONT.

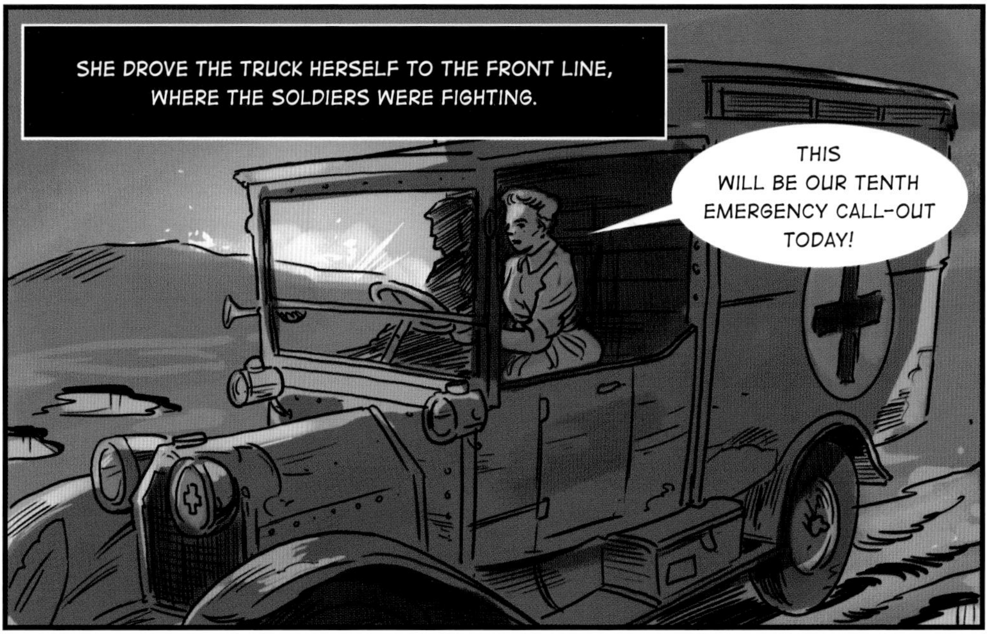
SHE DROVE THE TRUCK HERSELF TO THE FRONT LINE, WHERE THE SOLDIERS WERE FIGHTING.
THIS WILL BE OUR TENTH EMERGENCY CALL-OUT TODAY!

THE TRUCKS BECAME KNOWN AS "LITTLE CURIES," FOR THE MINI X-RAY MACHINES THEY CARRIED. MARIE ALSO CAME UP WITH THE IDEA TO POWER THE MACHINES WITH A DYNAMO, WHICH WAS IN TURN POWERED BY THE TRUCK'S ENGINE. THESE TRUCKS DELIVERED HELP TO OVER A MILLION SOLDIERS DURING THE WAR.

THE INTERNATIONAL RED CROSS MADE MARIE HEAD OF THE RADIOLOGICAL SERVICE. SHE RAN TRAINING SESSIONS FOR DOCTORS AND NURSES ON HOW TO USE THE MACHINES.

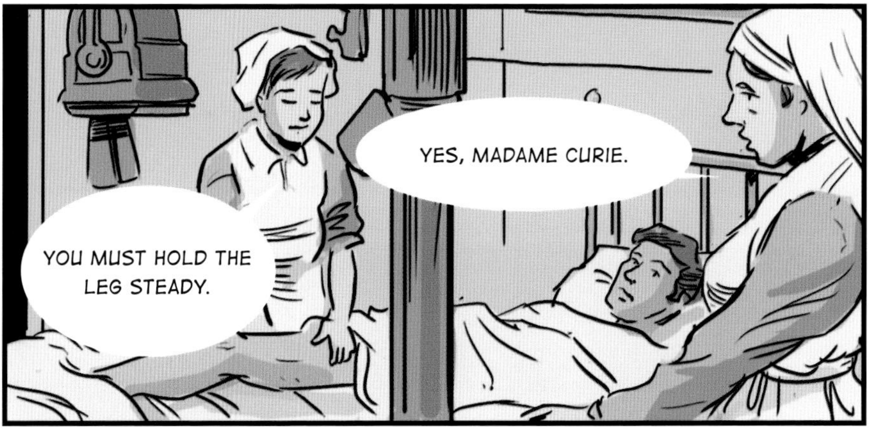
YOU MUST HOLD THE LEG STEADY.
YES, MADAME CURIE.

DOCTORS DISCOVERED THAT RADIOLOGY COULD HELP DIAGNOSE CANCER BY SHOWING DARK SHADOWS WITHIN THE BODY. THE DOCTORS WERE THEN ABLE TO TEST TISSUE REMOVED FROM THE DARK PATCHES TO CHECK IF THEY WERE CANCEROUS TUMORS.

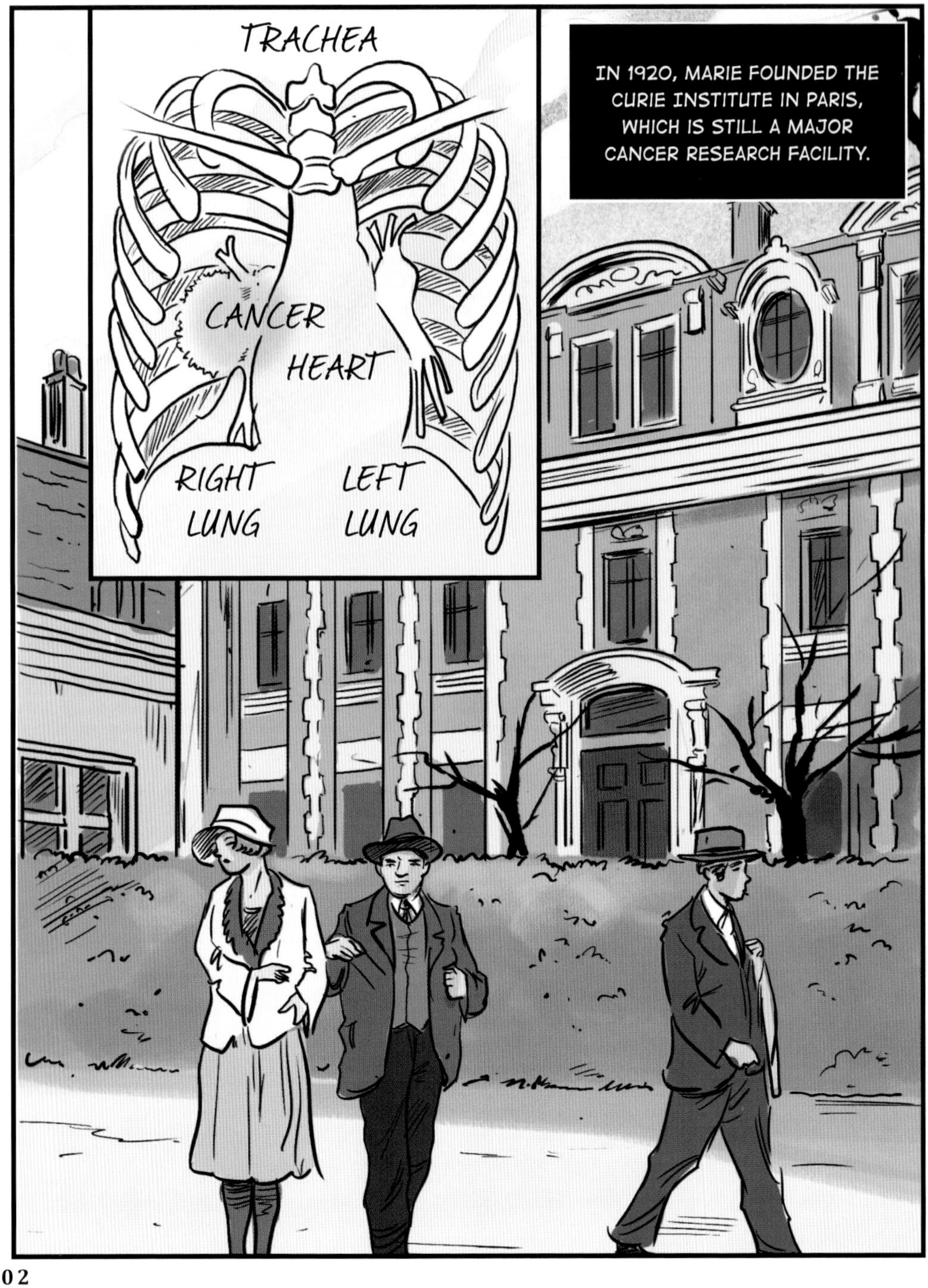
TRACHEA
CANCER
HEART
RIGHT LUNG
LEFT LUNG
IN 1920, MARIE FOUNDED THE CURIE INSTITUTE IN PARIS, WHICH IS STILL A MAJOR CANCER RESEARCH FACILITY.

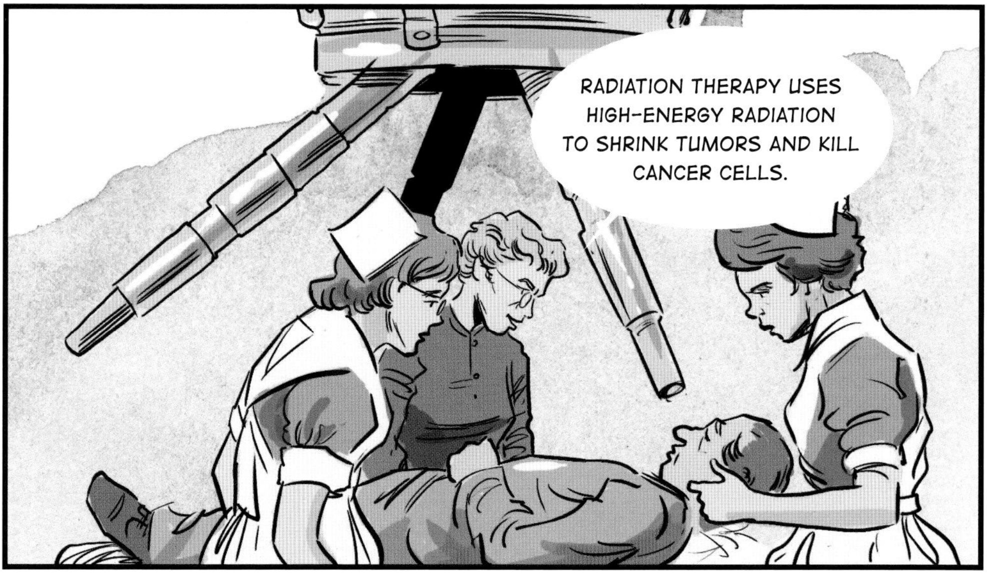
RADIATION THERAPY USES HIGH-ENERGY RADIATION TO SHRINK TUMORS AND KILL CANCER CELLS.

TOO MUCH RADIATION CAN BE HARMFUL, HOWEVER. MARIE DIED IN 1934, FROM DAMAGE TO HER CELLS. YEARS OF EXPOSURE TO RADIATION FROM HER EXPERIMENTS AND X-RAY MACHINES MAY HAVE CAUSED THE PROBLEM.

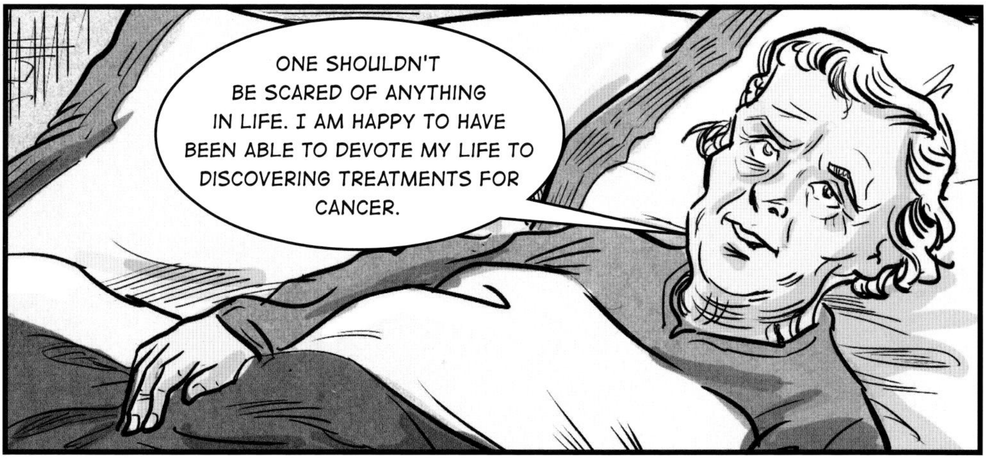
ONE SHOULDN'T BE SCARED OF ANYTHING IN LIFE. I AM HAPPY TO HAVE BEEN ABLE TO DEVOTE MY LIFE TO DISCOVERING TREATMENTS FOR CANCER.

MARIE CURIE DEMONSTRATED THAT RADIATION DOES NOT JUST DESTROY LIVING CELLS, IT CAN ALSO CURE CANCER AND SKIN ULCERS. MARIE WAS THE FIRST WOMAN OF SCIENCE, TECHNOLOGY, ENGINEERING, AND MATH. HER RESEARCH ALSO LED TO A GREATER UNDERSTANDING OF THE STRUCTURE OF ATOMS.

WATSON, CRICK & FRANKLIN

(1928–present, 1916–2004 & 1920–1958)

UNRAVELING THE DOUBLE HELIX

THERE WERE TWO TEAMS INTERESTED IN THE STRUCTURE OF DEOXYRIBONUCLEIC ACID, MORE COMMONLY KNOWN AS THE DNA MOLECULE. THE TEAMS WERE FRANCIS CRICK AND JAMES WATSON IN CAMBRIDGE, ENGLAND, AND JOHN RANDALL, MAURICE WILKINS, AND RAYMOND GOSLING IN LONDON, ENGLAND. FRANCIS AND JAMES MET AT CAVENDISH LABORATORY IN CAMBRIDGE. FRANCIS WAS LOUD AND OFTEN OVERENTHUSIASTIC. JAMES WAS SHY, BUT BIG-HEADED. EVEN THOUGH THEY HAD DIFFERENT PERSONALITIES, THEY BECAME GOOD FRIENDS.

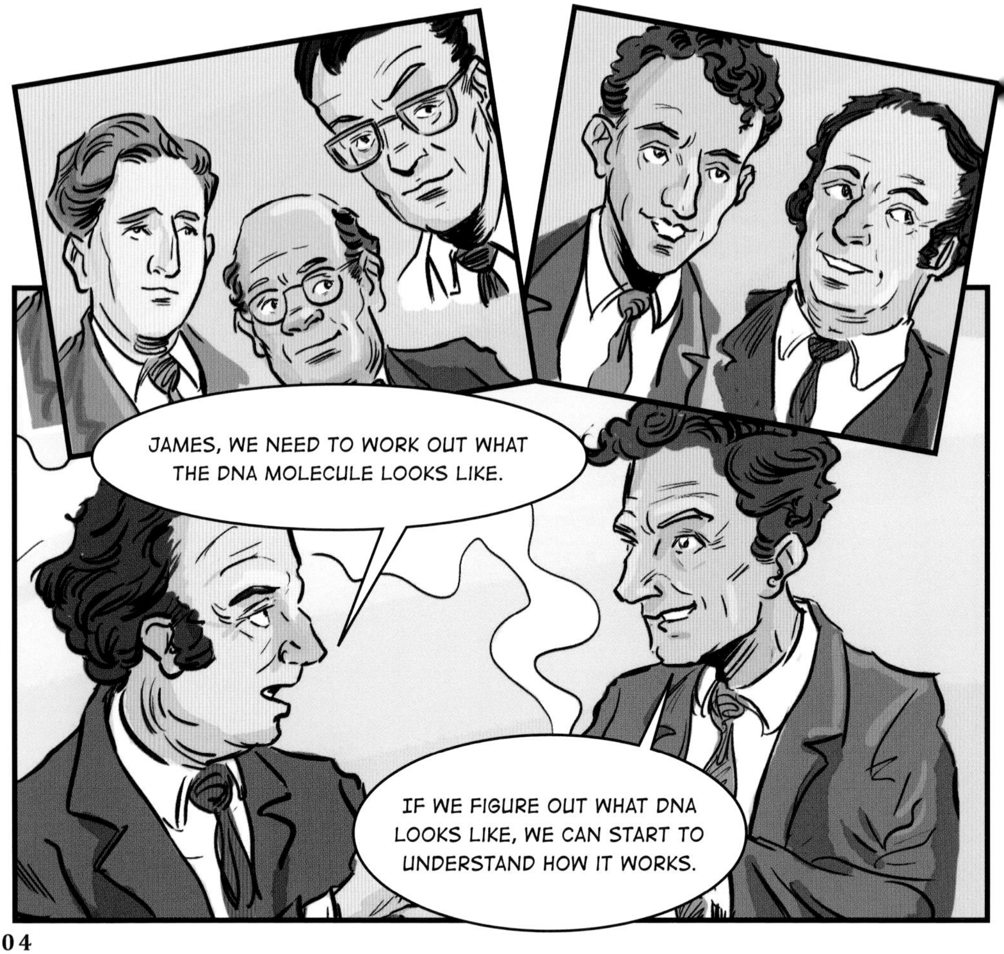
JAMES, WE NEED TO WORK OUT WHAT THE DNA MOLECULE LOOKS LIKE.
IF WE FIGURE OUT WHAT DNA LOOKS LIKE, WE CAN START TO UNDERSTAND HOW IT WORKS.

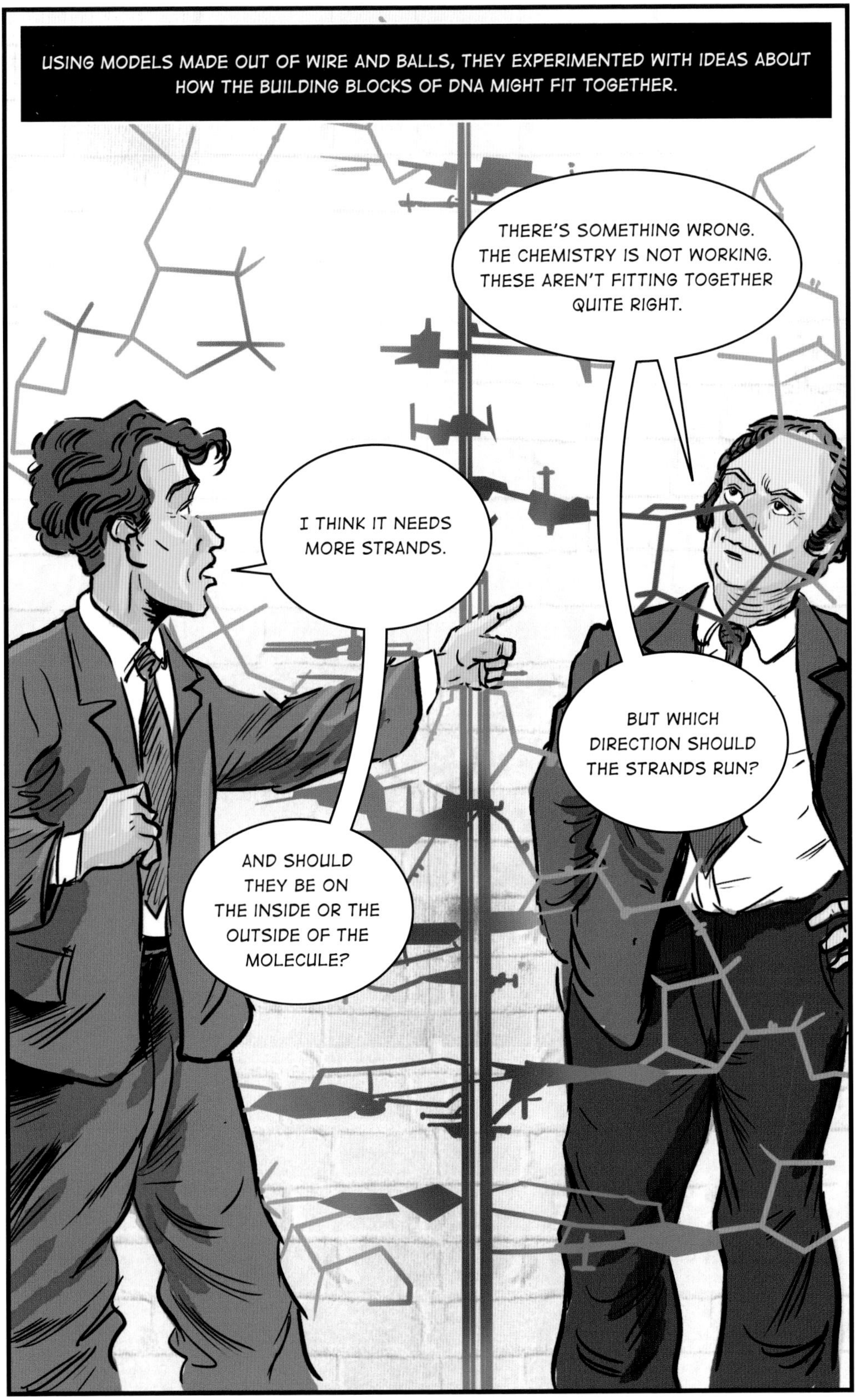
USING MODELS MADE OUT OF WIRE AND BALLS, THEY EXPERIMENTED WITH IDEAS ABOUT HOW THE BUILDING BLOCKS OF DNA MIGHT FIT TOGETHER.
THERE'S SOMETHING WRONG. THE CHEMISTRY IS NOT WORKING. THESE AREN'T FITTING TOGETHER QUITE RIGHT.
I THINK IT NEEDS MORE STRANDS.
BUT WHICH DIRECTION SHOULD THE STRANDS RUN?
AND SHOULD THEY BE ON THE INSIDE OR THE OUTSIDE OF THE MOLECULE?

MEANWHILE, AT KING'S COLLEGE UNIVERSITY IN LONDON, SENIOR SCIENTIST MAURICE WILKINS AND HIS PHD STUDENT RAYMOND GOSLING HAD MADE A DISCOVERY.

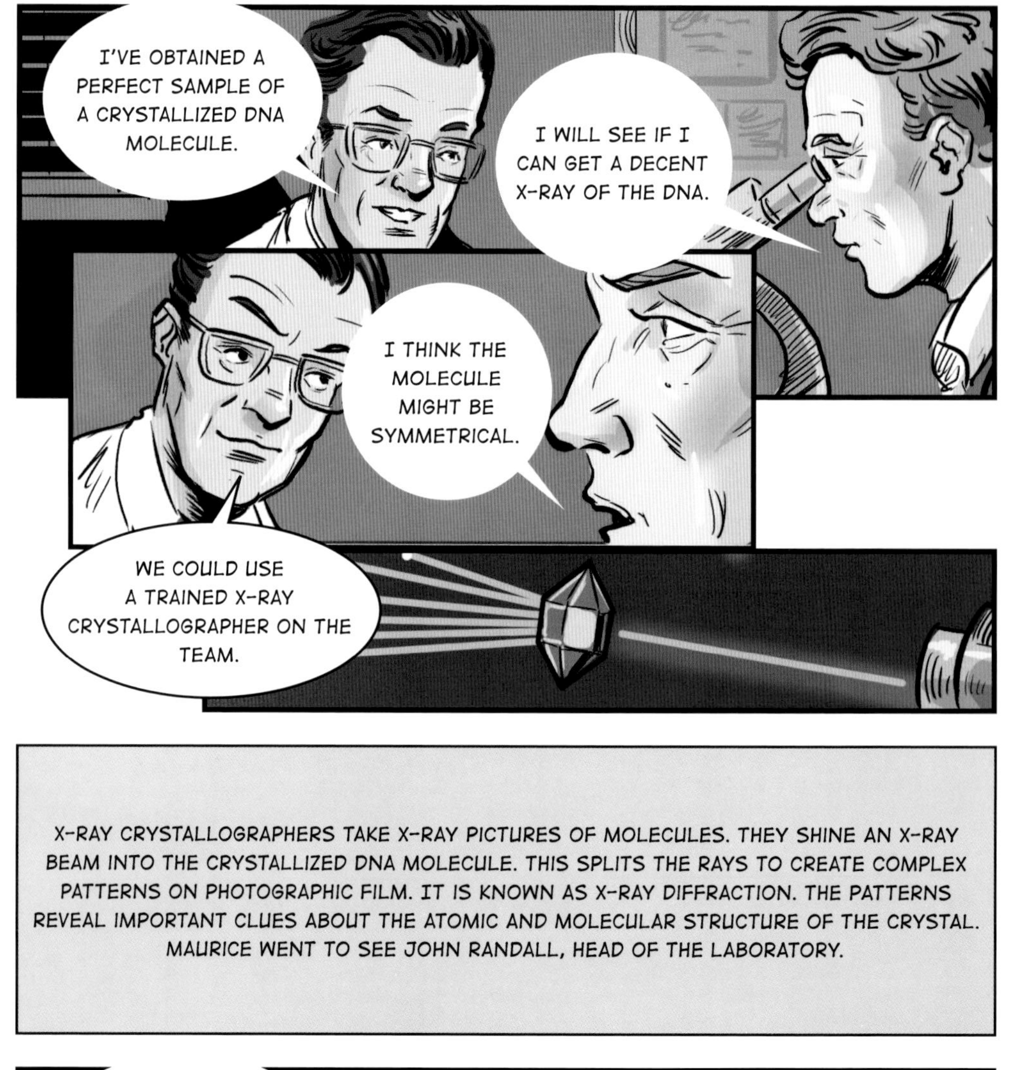
I'VE OBTAINED A PERFECT SAMPLE OF A CRYSTALLIZED DNA MOLECULE.
I WILL SEE IF I CAN GET A DECENT X-RAY OF THE DNA.
I THINK THE MOLECULE MIGHT BE SYMMETRICAL.
WE COULD USE A TRAINED X-RAY CRYSTALLOGRAPHER ON THE TEAM.

X-RAY CRYSTALLOGRAPHERS TAKE X-RAY PICTURES OF MOLECULES. THEY SHINE AN X-RAY BEAM INTO THE CRYSTALLIZED DNA MOLECULE. THIS SPLITS THE RAYS TO CREATE COMPLEX PATTERNS ON PHOTOGRAPHIC FILM. IT IS KNOWN AS X-RAY DIFFRACTION. THE PATTERNS REVEAL IMPORTANT CLUES ABOUT THE ATOMIC AND MOLECULAR STRUCTURE OF THE CRYSTAL. MAURICE WENT TO SEE JOHN RANDALL, HEAD OF THE LABORATORY.

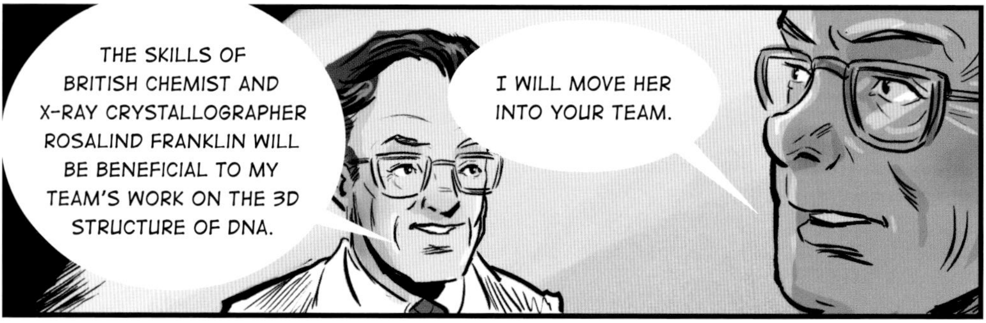
THE SKILLS OF BRITISH CHEMIST AND X-RAY CRYSTALLOGRAPHER ROSALIND FRANKLIN WILL BE BENEFICIAL TO MY TEAM'S WORK ON THE 3D STRUCTURE OF DNA.
I WILL MOVE HER INTO YOUR TEAM.

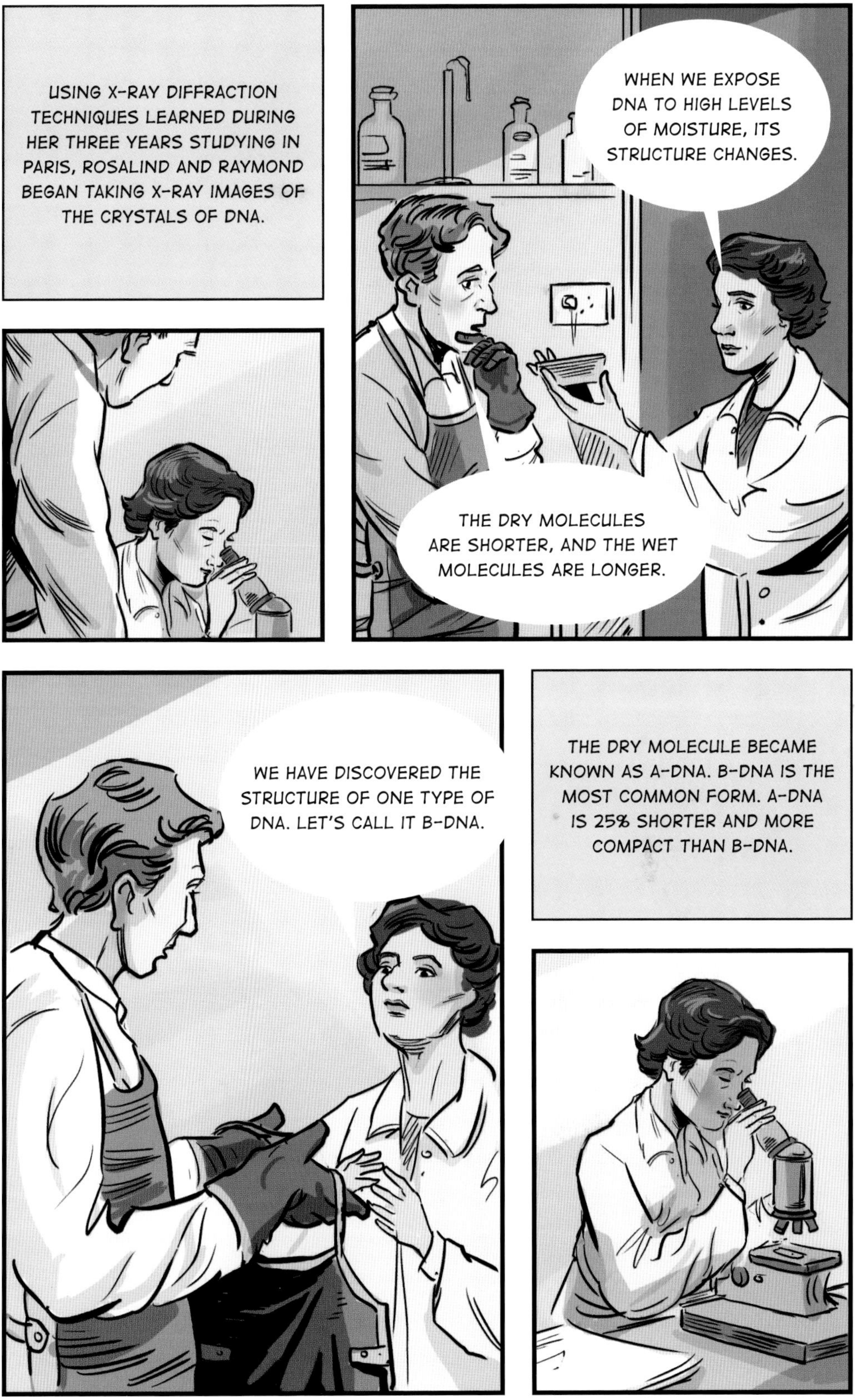
USING X-RAY DIFFRACTION TECHNIQUES LEARNED DURING HER THREE YEARS STUDYING IN PARIS, ROSALIND AND RAYMOND BEGAN TAKING X-RAY IMAGES OF THE CRYSTALS OF DNA.
WHEN WE EXPOSE DNA TO HIGH LEVELS OF MOISTURE, ITS STRUCTURE CHANGES.
THE DRY MOLECULES ARE SHORTER, AND THE WET MOLECULES ARE LONGER.
WE HAVE DISCOVERED THE STRUCTURE OF ONE TYPE OF DNA. LET'S CALL IT B-DNA.
THE DRY MOLECULE BECAME KNOWN AS A-DNA. B-DNA IS THE MOST COMMON FORM. A-DNA IS 25% SHORTER AND MORE COMPACT THAN B-DNA.

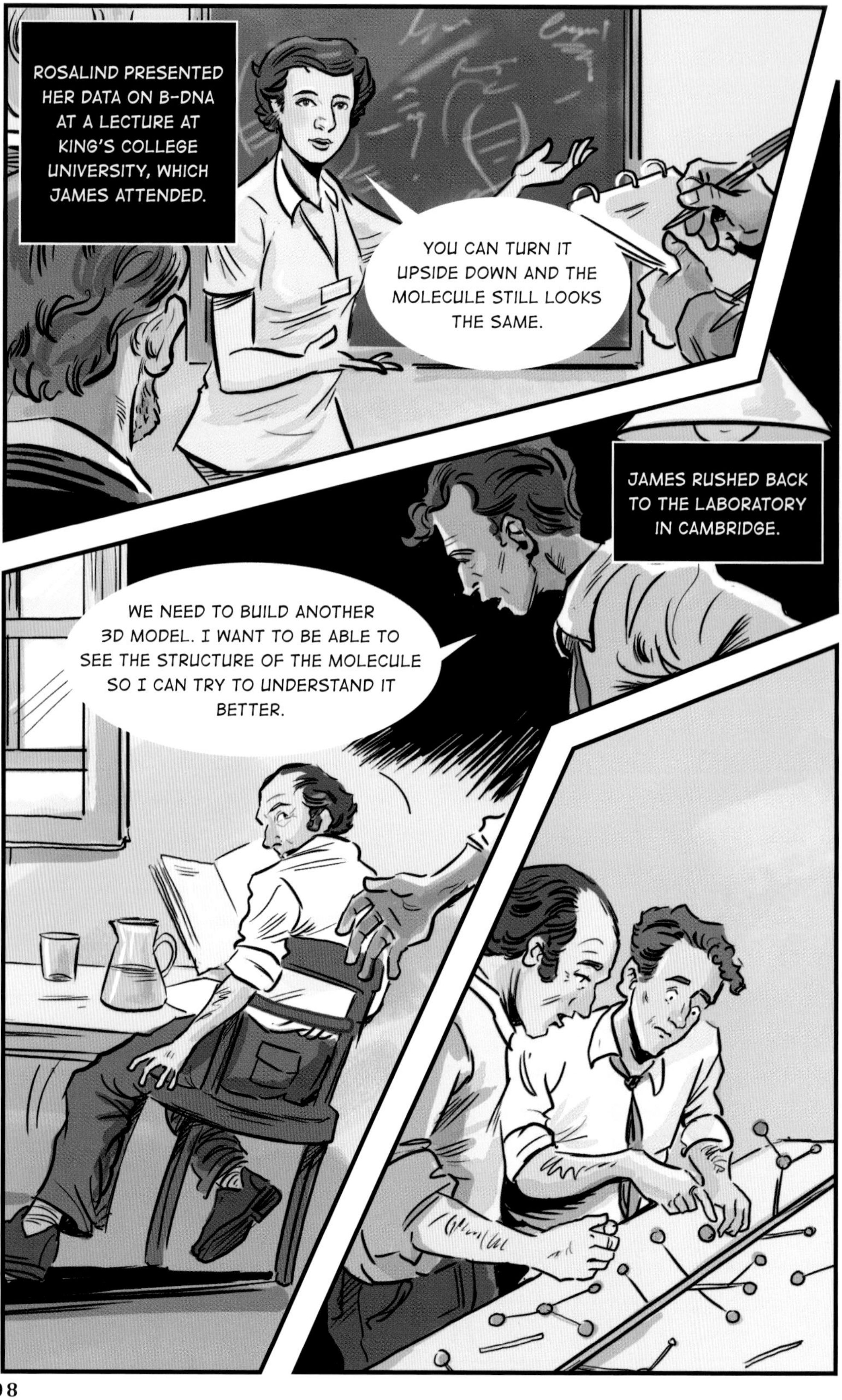
ROSALIND PRESENTED HER DATA ON B-DNA AT A LECTURE AT KING'S COLLEGE UNIVERSITY, WHICH JAMES ATTENDED.
YOU CAN TURN IT UPSIDE DOWN AND THE MOLECULE STILL LOOKS THE SAME.
JAMES RUSHED BACK TO THE LABORATORY IN CAMBRIDGE.
WE NEED TO BUILD ANOTHER 3D MODEL. I WANT TO BE ABLE TO SEE THE STRUCTURE OF THE MOLECULE SO I CAN TRY TO UNDERSTAND IT BETTER.

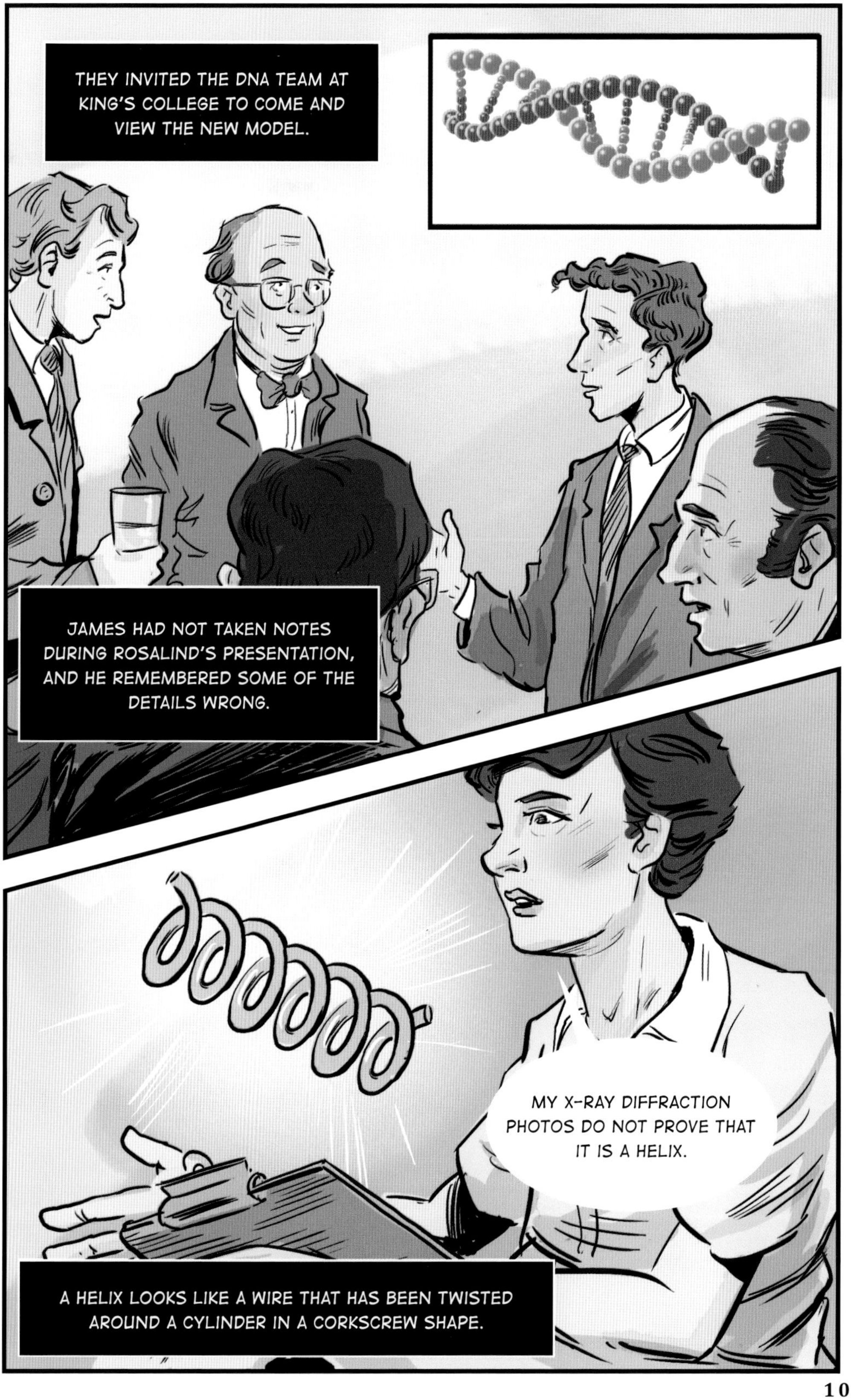
THEY INVITED THE DNA TEAM AT KING'S COLLEGE TO COME AND VIEW THE NEW MODEL.
JAMES HAD NOT TAKEN NOTES DURING ROSALIND'S PRESENTATION, AND HE REMEMBERED SOME OF THE DETAILS WRONG.
MY X-RAY DIFFRACTION PHOTOS DO NOT PROVE THAT IT IS A HELIX.
A HELIX LOOKS LIKE A WIRE THAT HAS BEEN TWISTED AROUND A CYLINDER IN A CORKSCREW SHAPE.

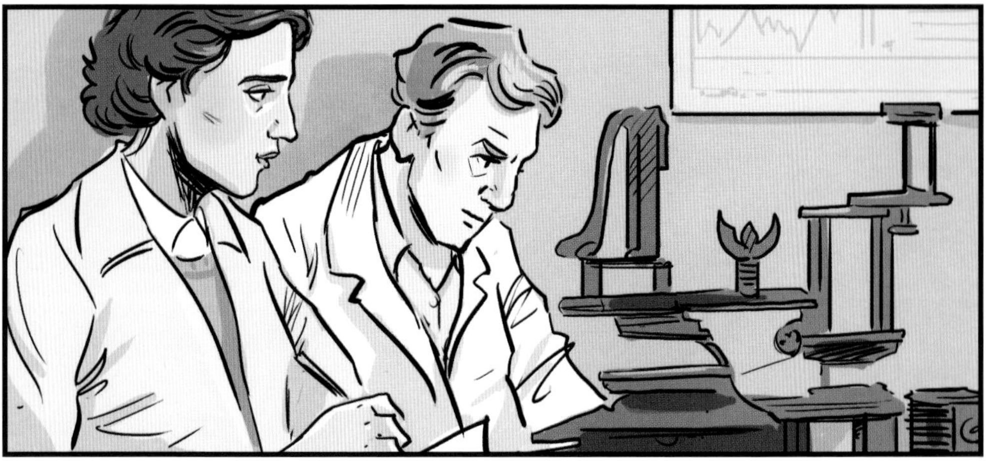

BACK AT KING'S COLLEGE, ON MAY 2, 1952, RAYMOND TOOK AN X-RAY DIFFRACTION PHOTO LABELED PHOTO 51, UNDER ROSALIND'S SUPERVISION. THIS PHOTO PROVED TO BE VERY IMPORTANT.

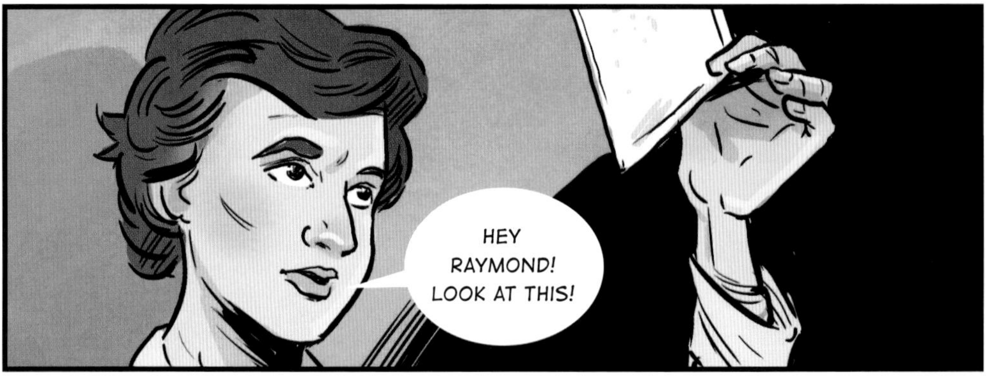
HEY RAYMOND! LOOK AT THIS!

PHOTO 51 WAS CLEAR AND SHARP. IT CONFIRMED ROSALIND'S PREVIOUS DATA SUGGESTING THAT B-DNA WAS SYMMETRICAL. SHE HAD SENT THIS DATA IN A REPORT TO THE MEDICAL RESEARCH COUNCIL. THIS WAS A BRITISH FUNDING AGENCY DEDICATED TO SUPPORTING MEDICAL RESEARCH THAT WOULD IMPROVE PEOPLE'S HEALTH. THE MEDICAL RESEARCH COUNCIL PUBLISHED HER REPORT.

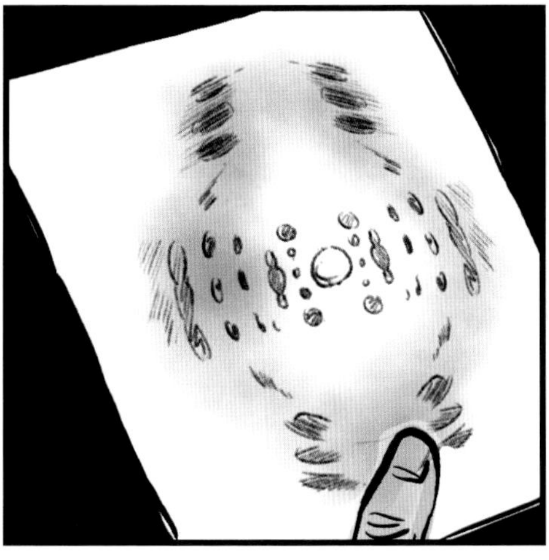

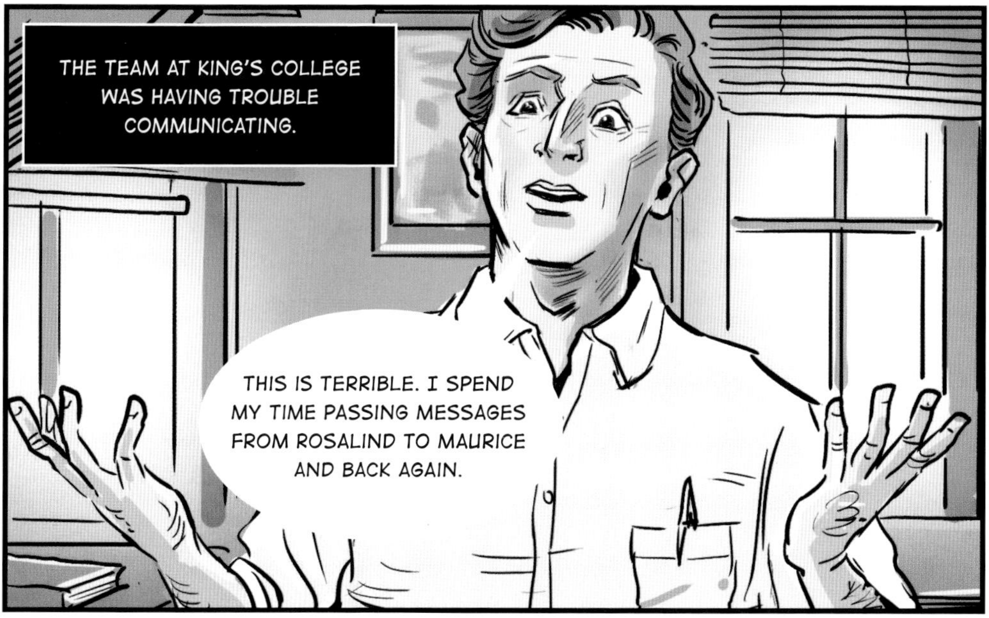
THE TEAM AT KING'S COLLEGE WAS HAVING TROUBLE COMMUNICATING.
THIS IS TERRIBLE. I SPEND MY TIME PASSING MESSAGES FROM ROSALIND TO MAURICE AND BACK AGAIN.

ROSALIND WAS SO UNHAPPY WITH THE COMMUNICATION PROBLEMS, SHE TOOK A NEW JOB AT BIRKBECK COLLEGE UNIVERSITY IN LONDON. RAYMOND CONTINUED WORKING TOWARD HIS PHD UNDER THE SUPERVISION OF MAURICE. HE SHOWED PHOTO 51 TO MAURICE.

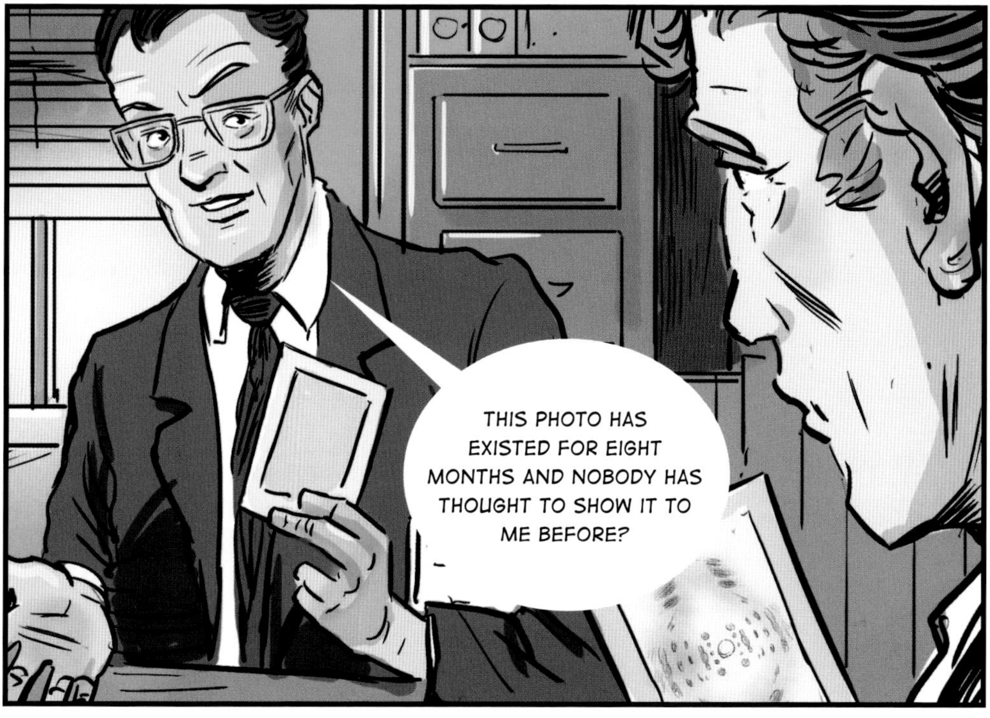
THIS PHOTO HAS EXISTED FOR EIGHT MONTHS AND NOBODY HAS THOUGHT TO SHOW IT TO ME BEFORE?

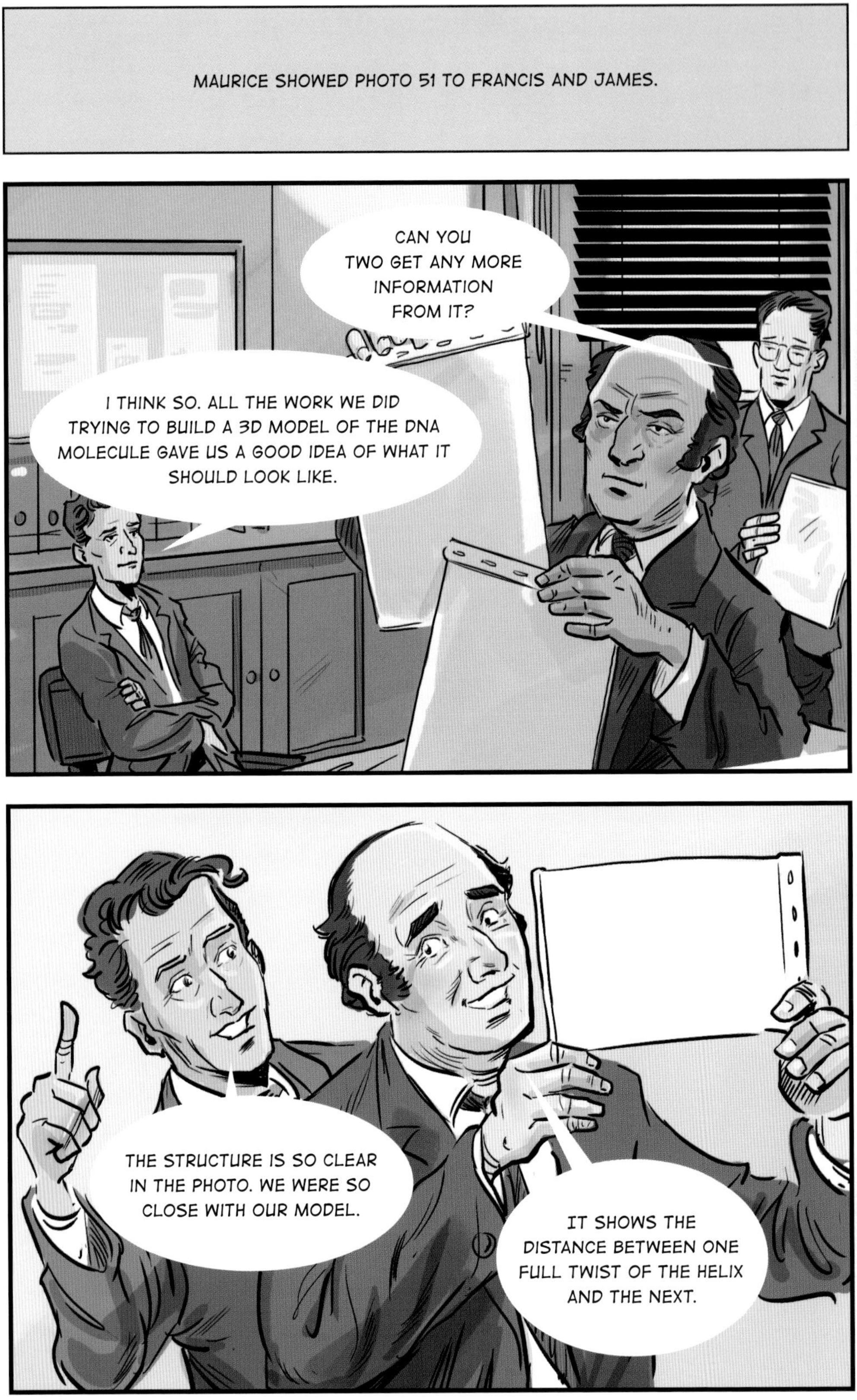
MAURICE SHOWED PHOTO 51 TO FRANCIS AND JAMES.
CAN YOU TWO GET ANY MORE INFORMATION FROM IT?
I THINK SO. ALL THE WORK WE DID TRYING TO BUILD A 3D MODEL OF THE DNA MOLECULE GAVE US A GOOD IDEA OF WHAT IT SHOULD LOOK LIKE.
THE STRUCTURE IS SO CLEAR IN THE PHOTO. WE WERE SO CLOSE WITH OUR MODEL.
IT SHOWS THE DISTANCE BETWEEN ONE FULL TWIST OF THE HELIX AND THE NEXT.

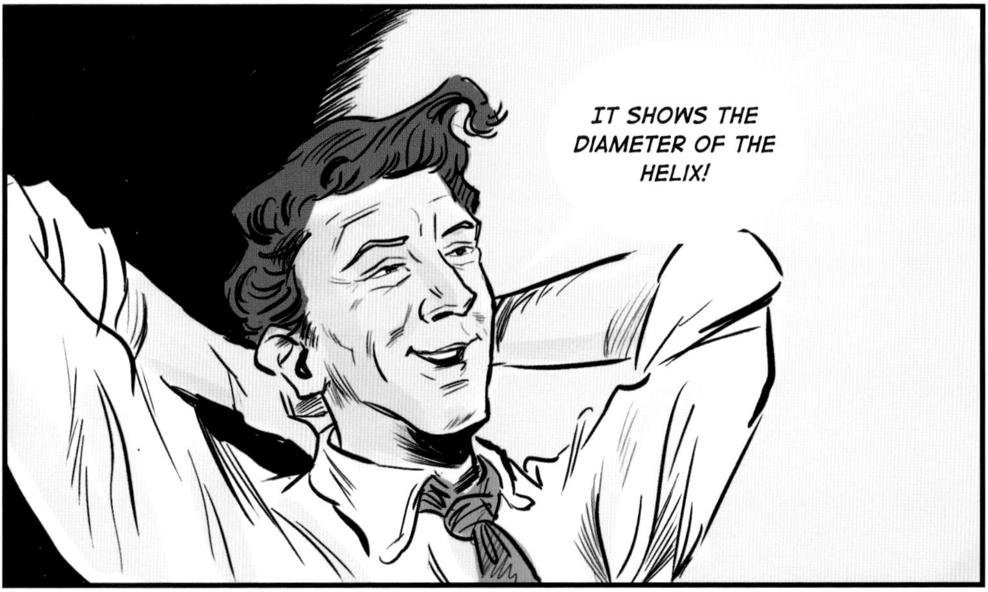
IT SHOWS THE DIAMETER OF THE HELIX!

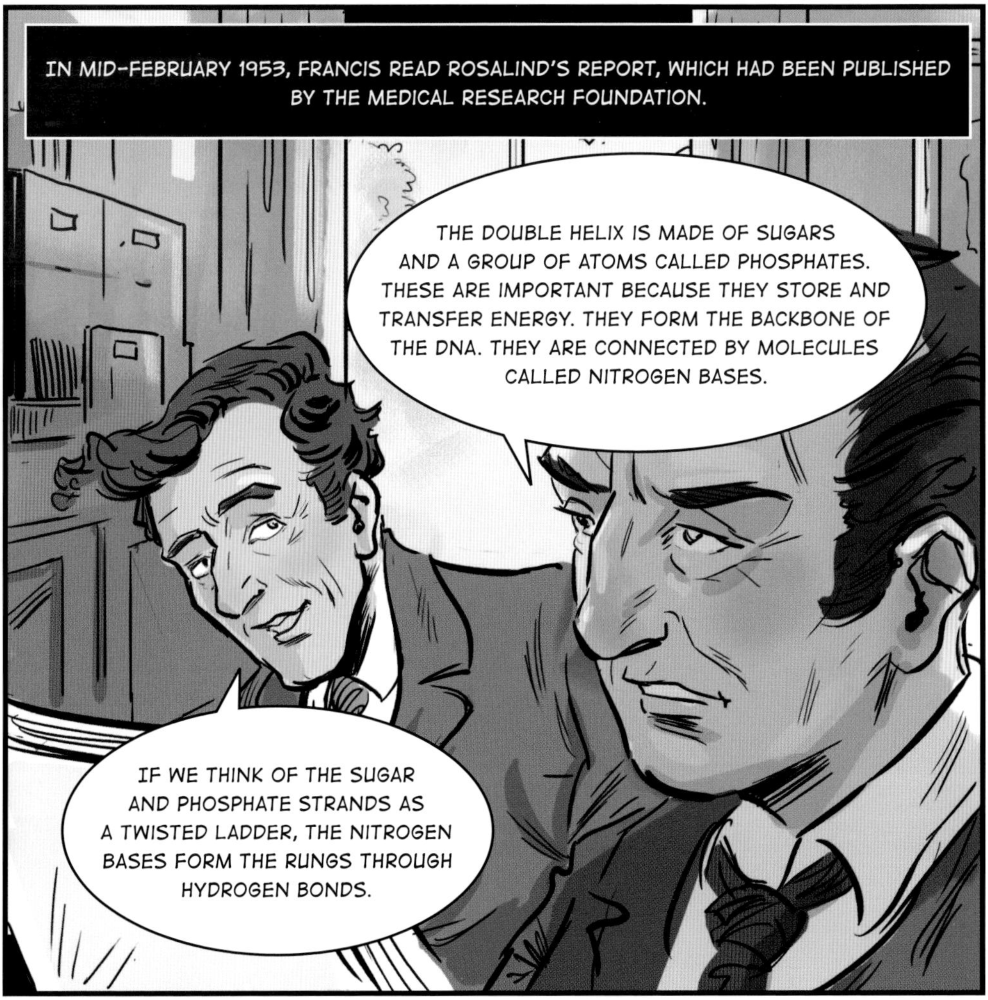
IN MID-FEBRUARY 1953, FRANCIS READ ROSALIND'S REPORT, WHICH HAD BEEN PUBLISHED BY THE MEDICAL RESEARCH FOUNDATION.
THE DOUBLE HELIX IS MADE OF SUGARS AND A GROUP OF ATOMS CALLED PHOSPHATES. THESE ARE IMPORTANT BECAUSE THEY STORE AND TRANSFER ENERGY. THEY FORM THE BACKBONE OF THE DNA. THEY ARE CONNECTED BY MOLECULES CALLED NITROGEN BASES.
IF WE THINK OF THE SUGAR AND PHOSPHATE STRANDS AS A TWISTED LADDER, THE NITROGEN BASES FORM THE RUNGS THROUGH HYDROGEN BONDS.

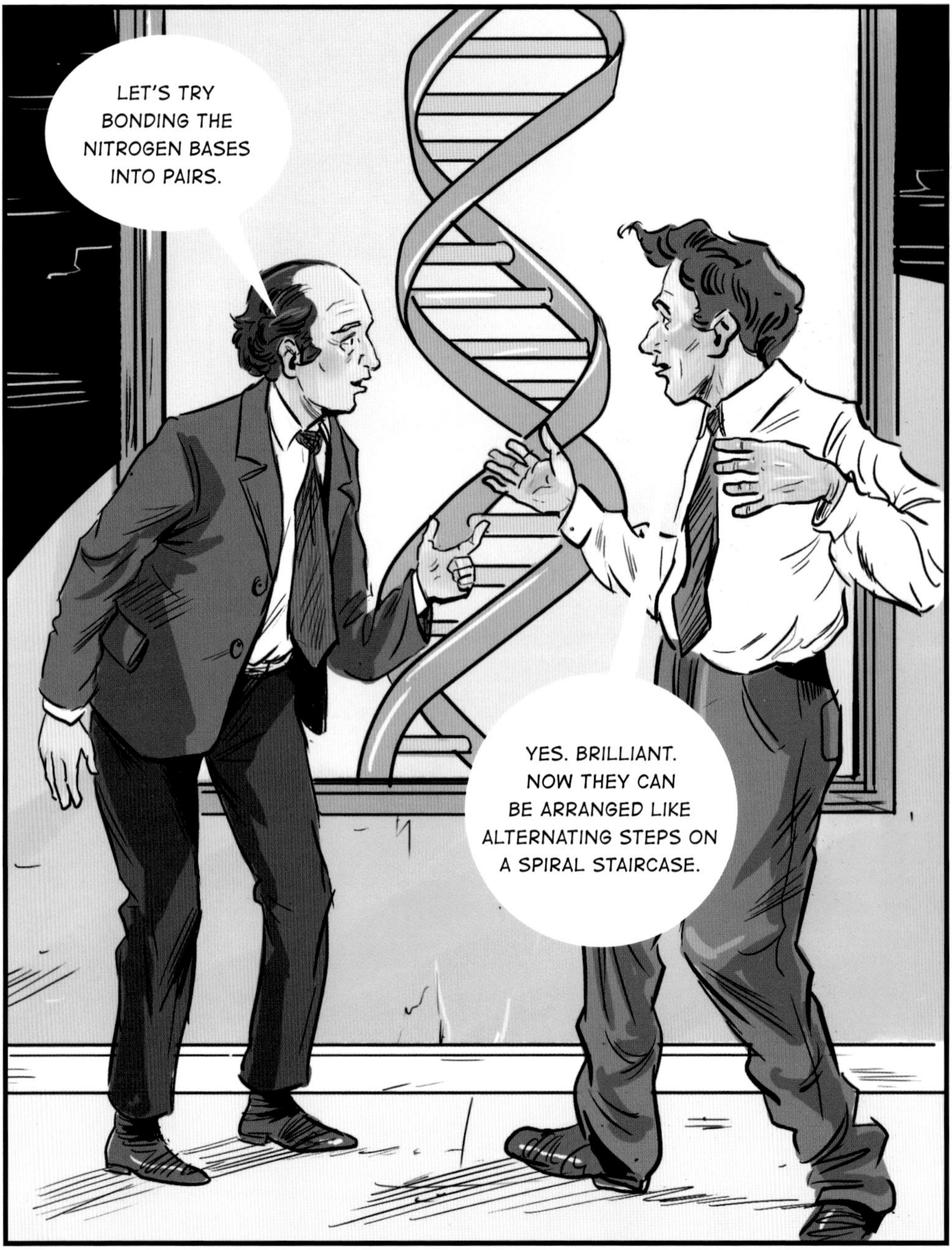
LET'S TRY BONDING THE NITROGEN BASES INTO PAIRS.
YES. BRILLIANT. NOW THEY CAN BE ARRANGED LIKE ALTERNATING STEPS ON A SPIRAL STAIRCASE.

GENES ARE SHORT SECTIONS OF DNA (DEOXYRIBONUCLEIC ACID). CHROMOSOMES ARE MADE FROM DNA MOLECULES. DIFFERENT SPECIES HAVE A DIFFERENT NUMBER OF CHROMOSOME PAIRS. HUMANS HAVE 23 PAIRS.

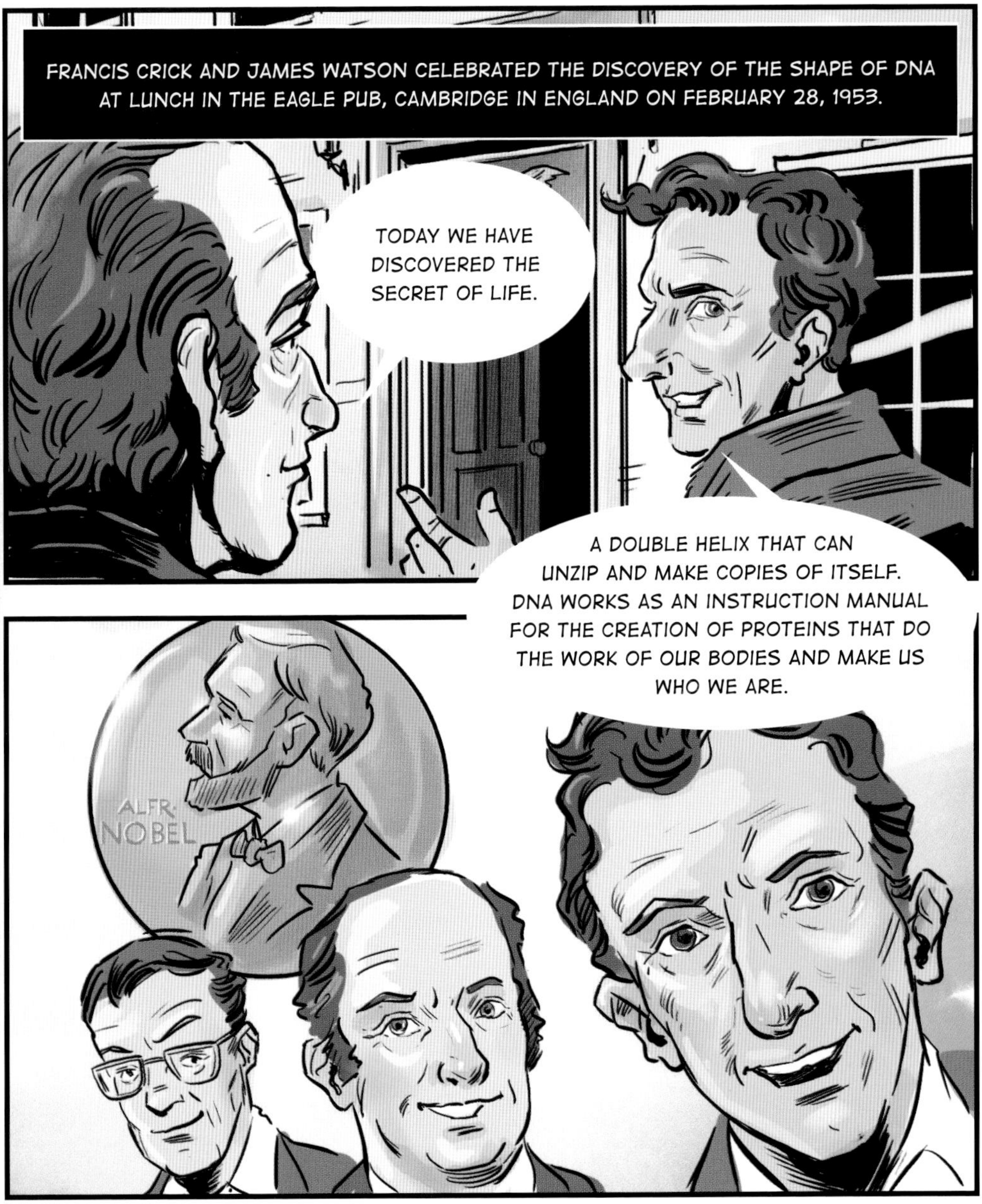
FRANCIS CRICK AND JAMES WATSON CELEBRATED THE DISCOVERY OF THE SHAPE OF DNA AT LUNCH IN THE EAGLE PUB, CAMBRIDGE IN ENGLAND ON FEBRUARY 28, 1953.
TODAY WE HAVE DISCOVERED THE SECRET OF LIFE.
A DOUBLE HELIX THAT CAN UNZIP AND MAKE COPIES OF ITSELF. DNA WORKS AS AN INSTRUCTION MANUAL FOR THE CREATION OF PROTEINS THAT DO THE WORK OF OUR BODIES AND MAKE US WHO WE ARE.
ALFR. NOBEL

IN 1962, MAURICE WILKINS, JAMES WATSON, AND FRANCIS CRICK RECEIVED THE NOBEL PRIZE IN PHYSIOLOGY FOR THEIR WORK. ROSALIND FRANKLIN WOULD HAVE BEEN NAMED ON THE AWARD, TOO, BUT SHE HAD DIED A FEW YEARS EARLIER OF OVARIAN CANCER. SHE WAS 37. DOCTORS SUSPECT THAT YEARS OF WORK WITH X-RAYS MAY HAVE BEEN TO BLAME. THE WORK OF WILKINS, WATSON, CRICK, AND FRANKLIN HAS HELPED OTHER SCIENTISTS STUDY CHROMOSOMES, DNA, AND GENES. RESEARCHERS AROUND THE WORLD HAVE BEEN LOOKING AT DNA'S ROLE IN PASSING ON GENES FROM PARENT TO CHILD. THIS DETERMINES WHAT A PERSON LOOKS LIKE, HOW THEIR VOICE SOUNDS, AND EVEN WHETHER THEY WILL INHERIT CERTAIN ILLNESSES.

VERA RUBIN
(1928–2016)
SEEING THE INVISIBLE

WHEN VERA RUBIN WAS ABOUT TEN, SHE BECAME INTRIGUED BY THE STARS AND THE WAY THEY REVOLVED AROUND POLARIS, THE NORTH STAR. SHE WOULD STAY AWAKE AT HOME IN WASHINGTON D.C. UNTIL THE EARLY HOURS WATCHING THE TWINKLING LIGHTS.

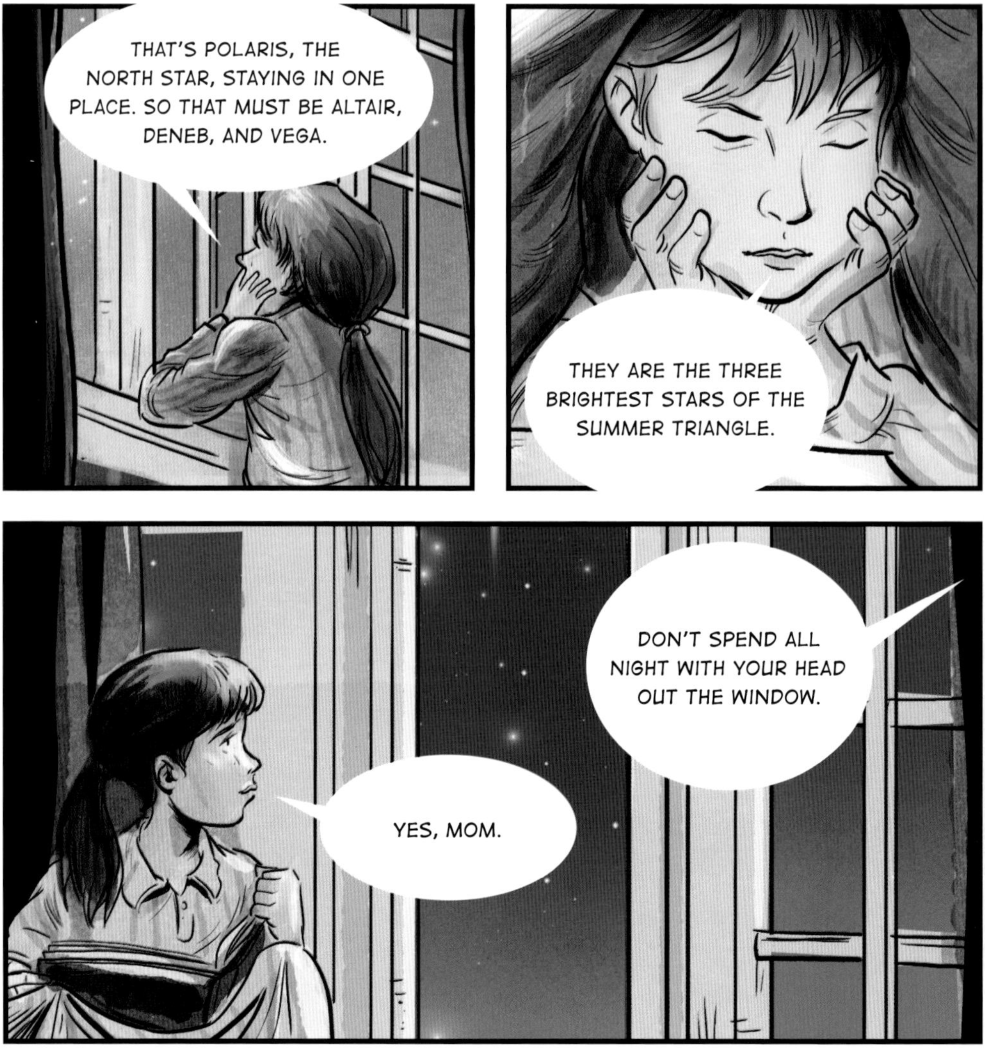
THAT'S POLARIS, THE NORTH STAR, STAYING IN ONE PLACE. SO THAT MUST BE ALTAIR, DENEB, AND VEGA.
THEY ARE THE THREE BRIGHTEST STARS OF THE SUMMER TRIANGLE.
DON'T SPEND ALL NIGHT WITH YOUR HEAD OUT THE WINDOW.
YES, MOM.

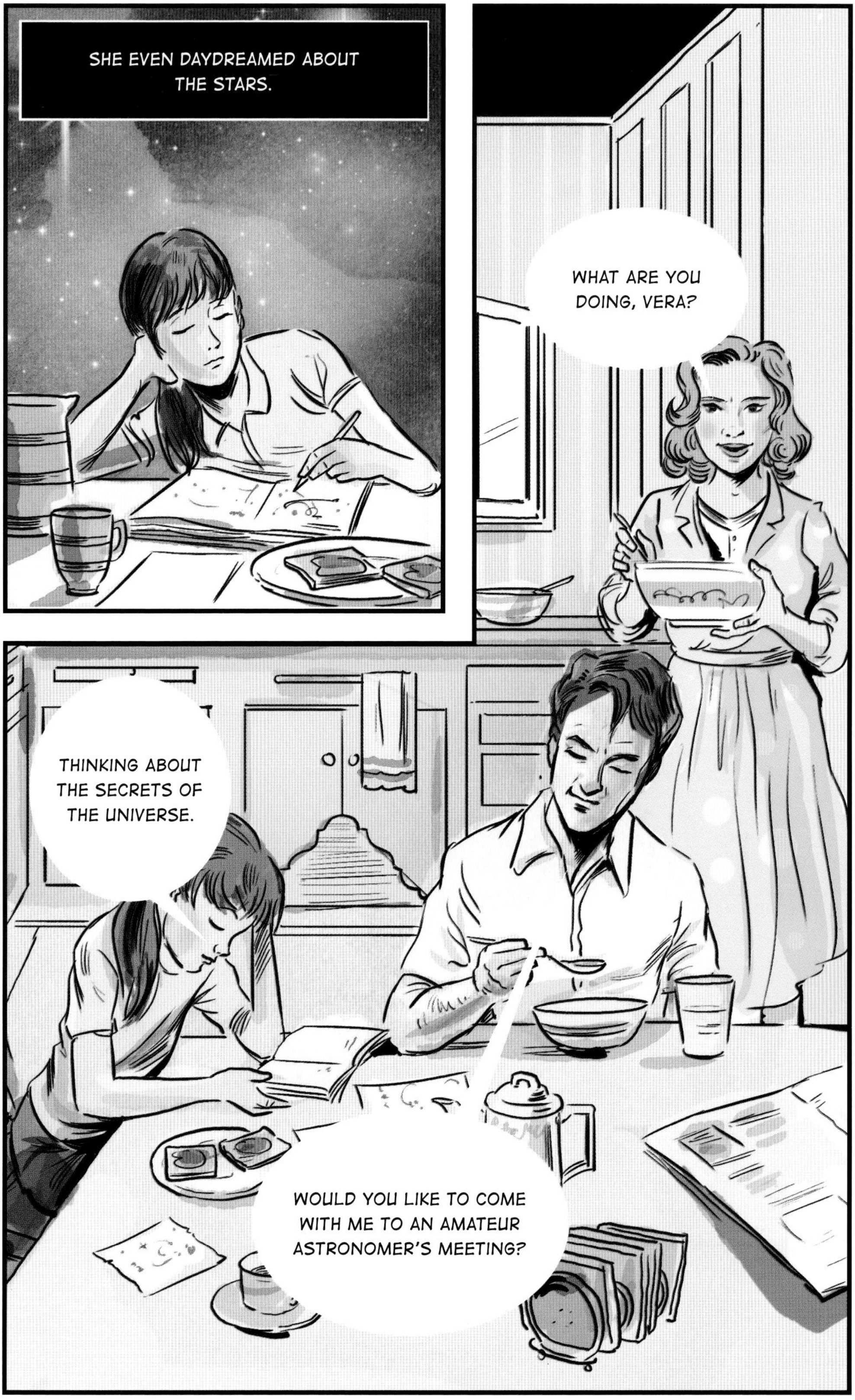
SHE EVEN DAYDREAMED ABOUT THE STARS.
WHAT ARE YOU DOING, VERA?
THINKING ABOUT THE SECRETS OF THE UNIVERSE.
WOULD YOU LIKE TO COME WITH ME TO AN AMATEUR ASTRONOMER'S MEETING?

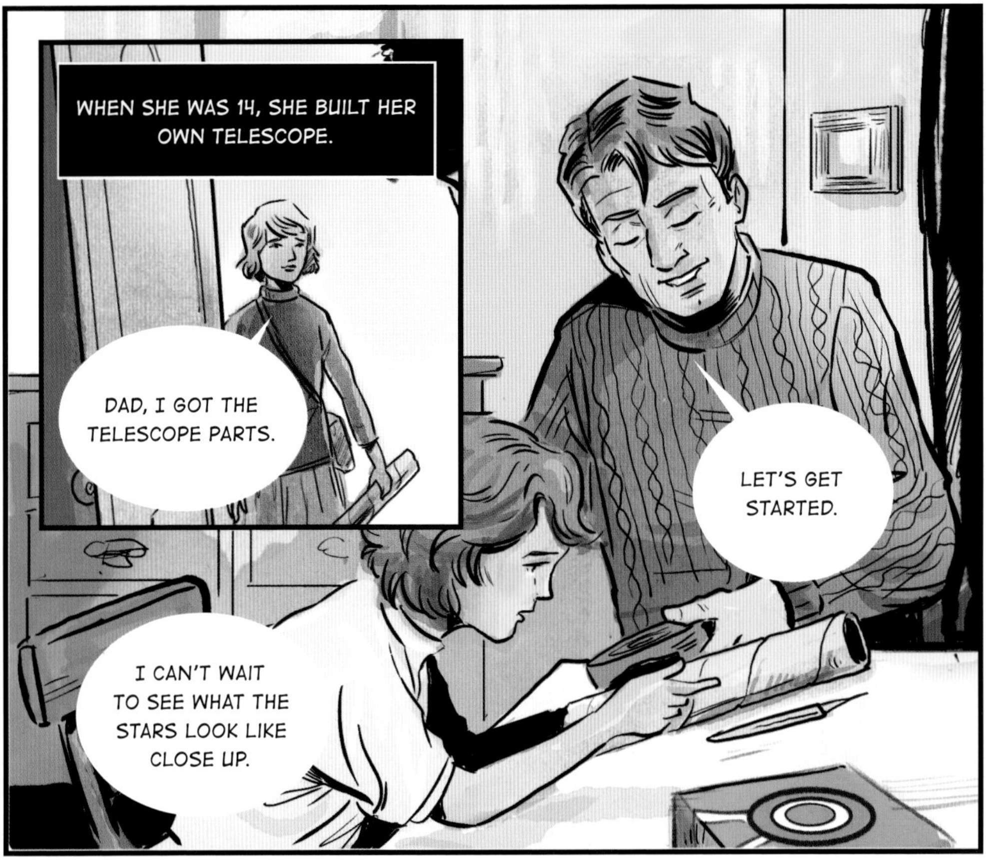
WHEN SHE WAS 14, SHE BUILT HER OWN TELESCOPE.
DAD, I GOT THE TELESCOPE PARTS.
LET'S GET STARTED.
I CAN'T WAIT TO SEE WHAT THE STARS LOOK LIKE CLOSE UP.

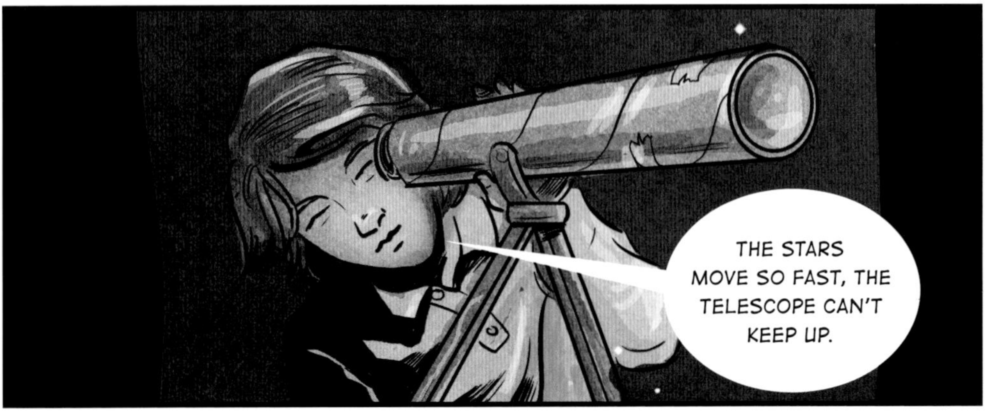
THE STARS MOVE SO FAST, THE TELESCOPE CAN'T KEEP UP.

VERA WAS ONE OF THE FIRST WOMEN TO GET A BACHELOR'S DEGREE IN ASTRONOMY. SHE WENT ON TO GET A MASTER'S DEGREE AT CORNELL UNIVERSITY IN NEW YORK, WHERE SHE WAS TUTORED BY ASTRONOMER MARTHA STAHR CARPENTER.

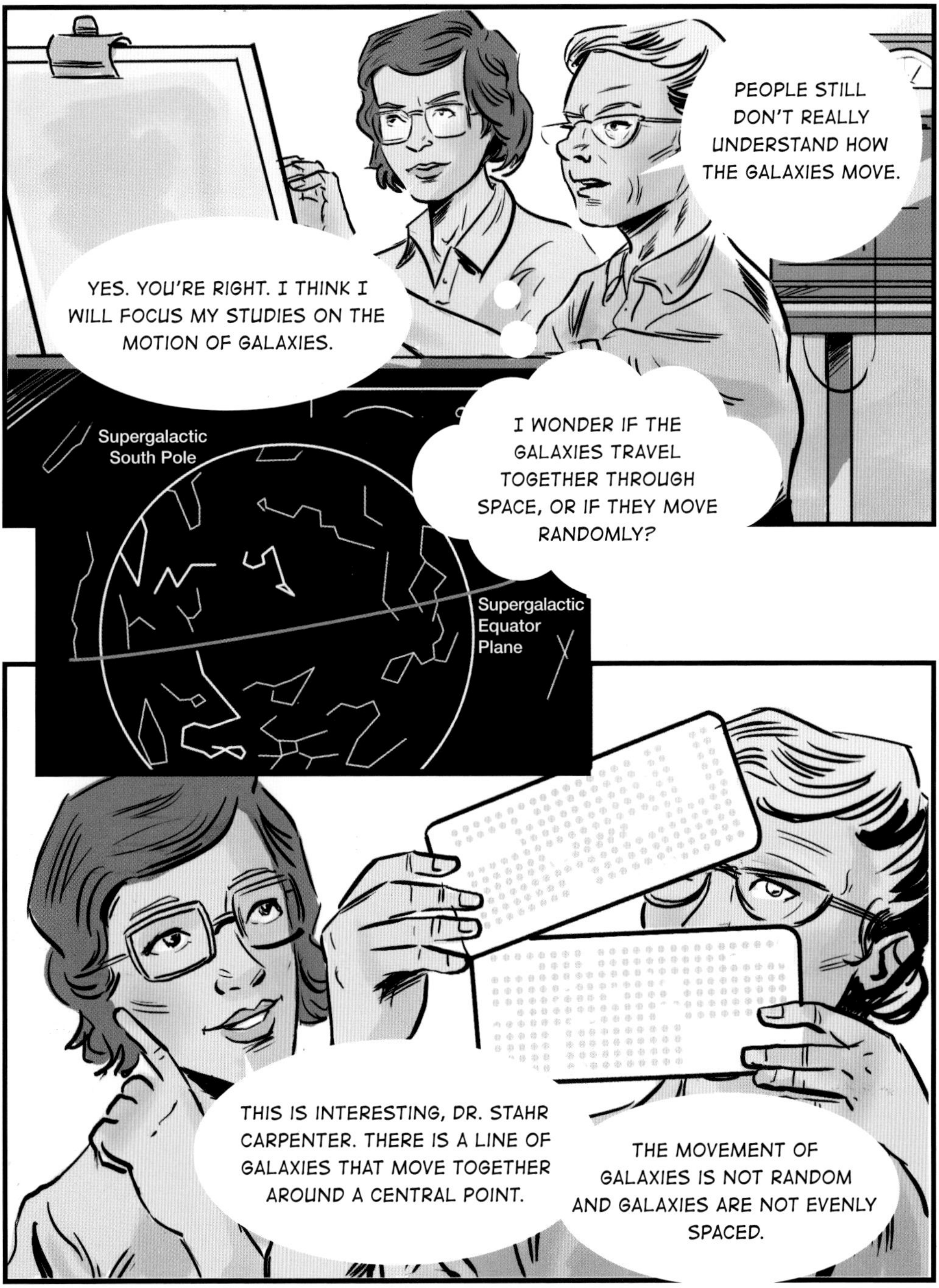
PEOPLE STILL DON'T REALLY UNDERSTAND HOW THE GALAXIES MOVE.
YES. YOU'RE RIGHT. I THINK I WILL FOCUS MY STUDIES ON THE MOTION OF GALAXIES.
I WONDER IF THE GALAXIES TRAVEL TOGETHER THROUGH SPACE, OR IF THEY MOVE RANDOMLY?
Supergalactic South Pole
Supergalactic Equator Plane
THIS IS INTERESTING, DR. STAHR CARPENTER. THERE IS A LINE OF GALAXIES THAT MOVE TOGETHER AROUND A CENTRAL POINT.
THE MOVEMENT OF GALAXIES IS NOT RANDOM AND GALAXIES ARE NOT EVENLY SPACED.

VERA HAD IDENTIFIED THE SUPERGALACTIC PLANE. THIS IS THE EQUATOR OF THE UNIVERSE. HER DISCOVERY HELPED ASTRONOMERS PRODUCE MORE ACCURATE MAPS OF OUR CLUSTER OF GALAXIES. NOBODY HAD PROVED THIS BEFORE. UNFORTUNATELY, VERA WAS NEVER ABLE TO PUBLISH HER FINDINGS. AT THE TIME, IT WAS HARD FOR WOMEN TO GET RESPECT FOR THEIR WORK.

IN 1965, VERA MOVED TO WASHINGTON, D.C., AND CONTINUED HER WORK ON THE MOVEMENT OF GALAXIES. AT THE DEPARTMENT OF TERRESTRIAL MAGNETISM (DTM) AT THE CARNEGIE INSTITUTION FOR SCIENCE IN WASHINGTON, D.C., SHE MET ASTRONOMER KENT FORD, WHO HAD DEVELOPED A VERY SENSITIVE SPECTROMETER. THIS TOOL SPLITS LIGHT COMING FROM STARS INTO ITS DIFFERENT WAVELENGTHS. VERA AND KENT USED IT TO MEASURE THE MOVEMENTS OF STARS INSIDE SPIRAL GALAXIES, SUCH AS ANDROMEDA.

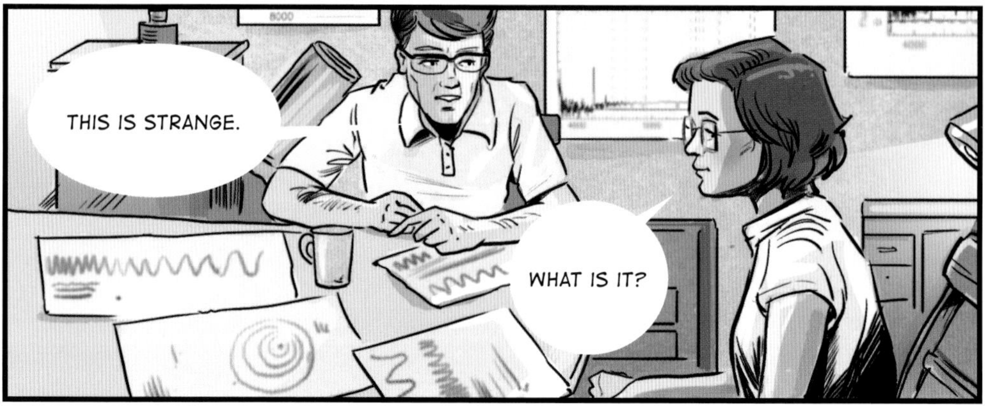
THIS IS STRANGE.
WHAT IS IT?

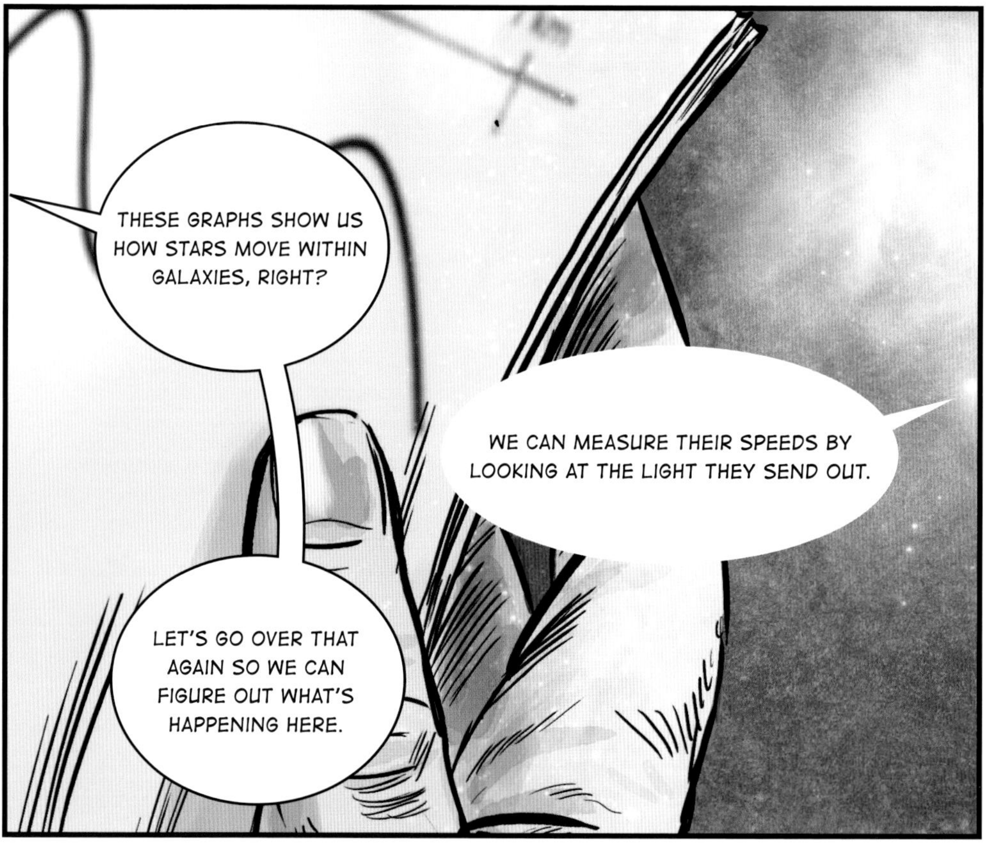
THESE GRAPHS SHOW US HOW STARS MOVE WITHIN GALAXIES, RIGHT?
WE CAN MEASURE THEIR SPEEDS BY LOOKING AT THE LIGHT THEY SEND OUT.
LET'S GO OVER THAT AGAIN SO WE CAN FIGURE OUT WHAT'S HAPPENING HERE.

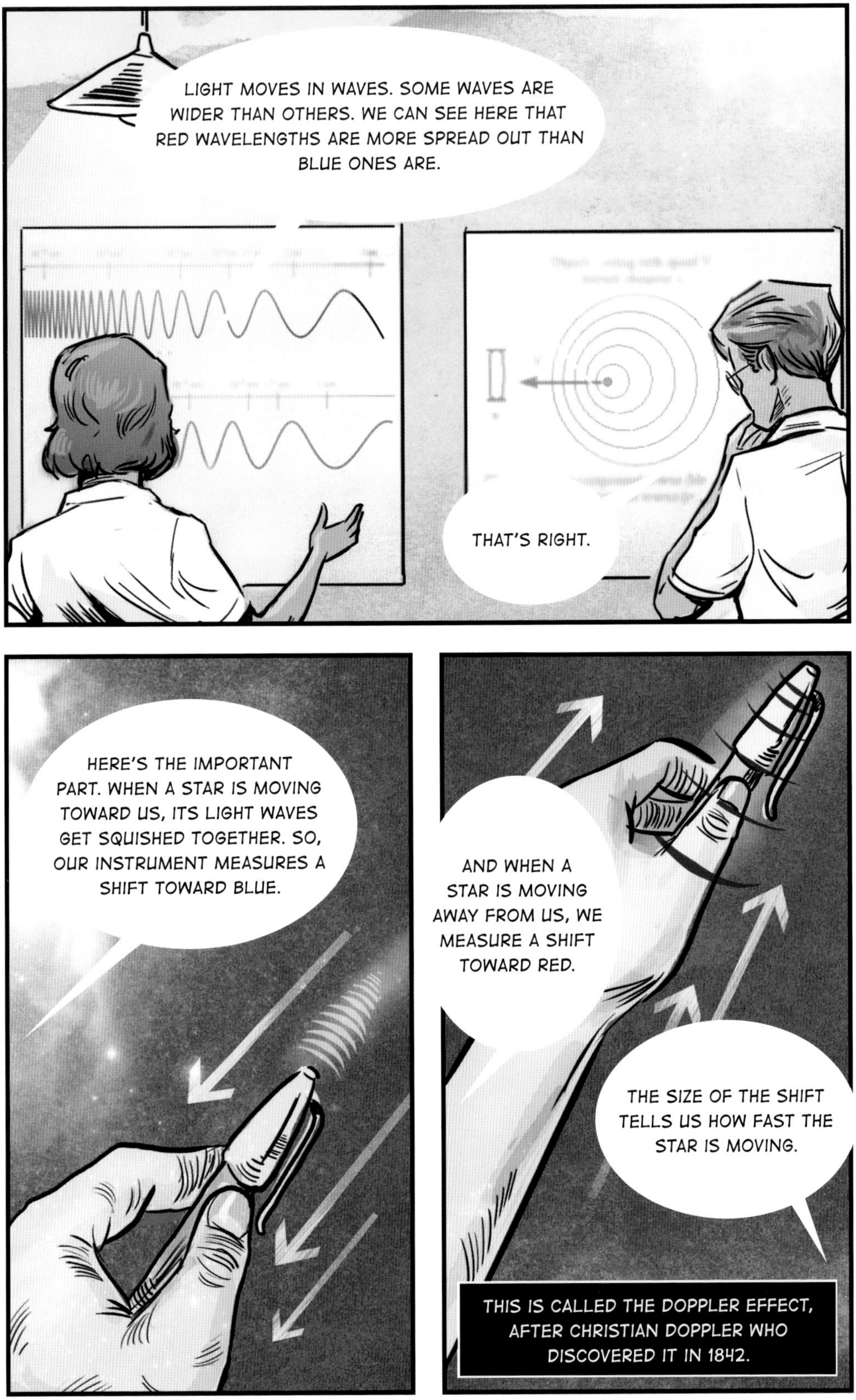
LIGHT MOVES IN WAVES. SOME WAVES ARE WIDER THAN OTHERS. WE CAN SEE HERE THAT RED WAVELENGTHS ARE MORE SPREAD OUT THAN BLUE ONES ARE.
THAT'S RIGHT.
HERE'S THE IMPORTANT PART. WHEN A STAR IS MOVING TOWARD US, ITS LIGHT WAVES GET SQUISHED TOGETHER. SO, OUR INSTRUMENT MEASURES A SHIFT TOWARD BLUE.
AND WHEN A STAR IS MOVING AWAY FROM US, WE MEASURE A SHIFT TOWARD RED.
THE SIZE OF THE SHIFT TELLS US HOW FAST THE STAR IS MOVING.
THIS IS CALLED THE DOPPLER EFFECT, AFTER CHRISTIAN DOPPLER WHO DISCOVERED IT IN 1842.

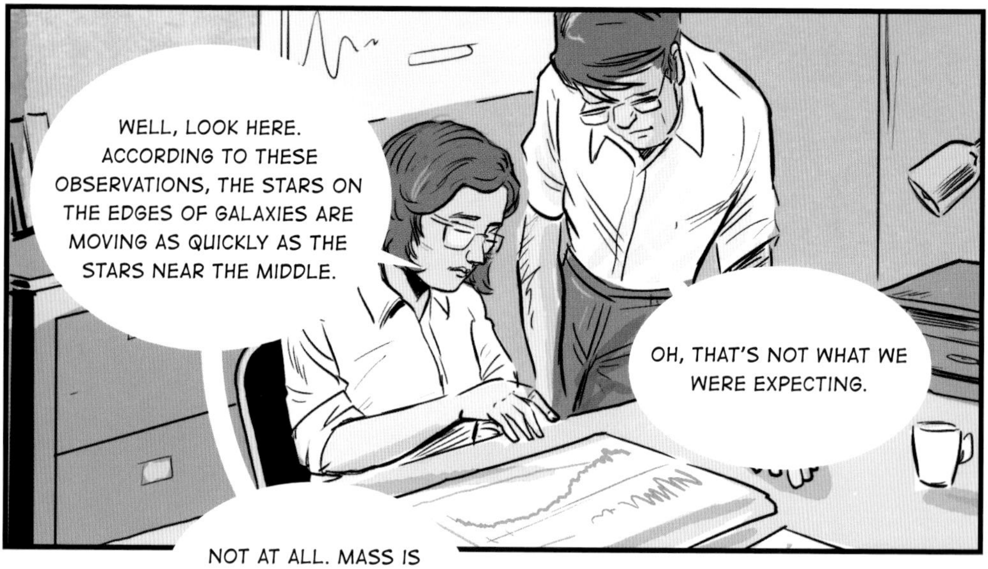
WELL, LOOK HERE. ACCORDING TO THESE OBSERVATIONS, THE STARS ON THE EDGES OF GALAXIES ARE MOVING AS QUICKLY AS THE STARS NEAR THE MIDDLE.
OH, THAT'S NOT WHAT WE WERE EXPECTING.
NOT AT ALL. MASS IS WHAT MAKES STUFF MOVE IN THE UNIVERSE.

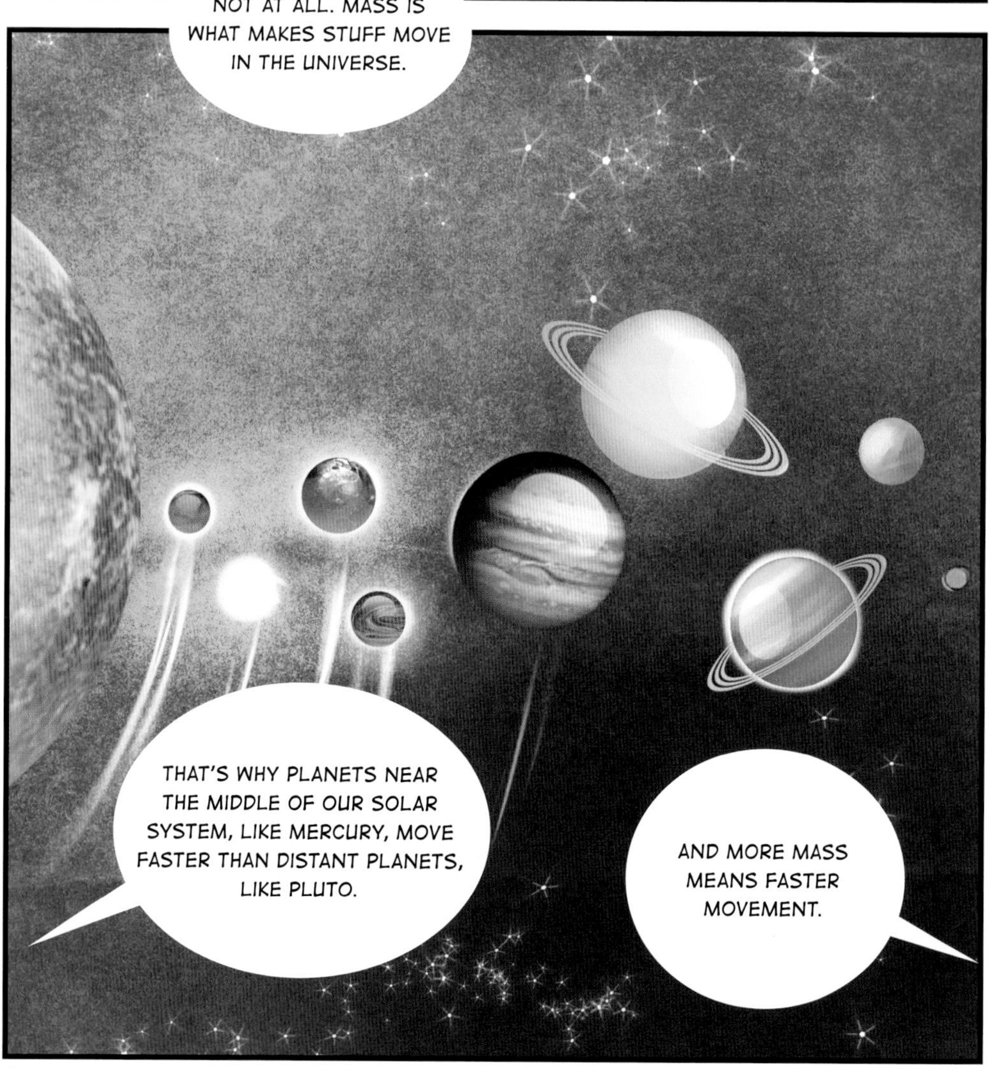
THAT'S WHY PLANETS NEAR THE MIDDLE OF OUR SOLAR SYSTEM, LIKE MERCURY, MOVE FASTER THAN DISTANT PLANETS, LIKE PLUTO.
AND MORE MASS MEANS FASTER MOVEMENT.

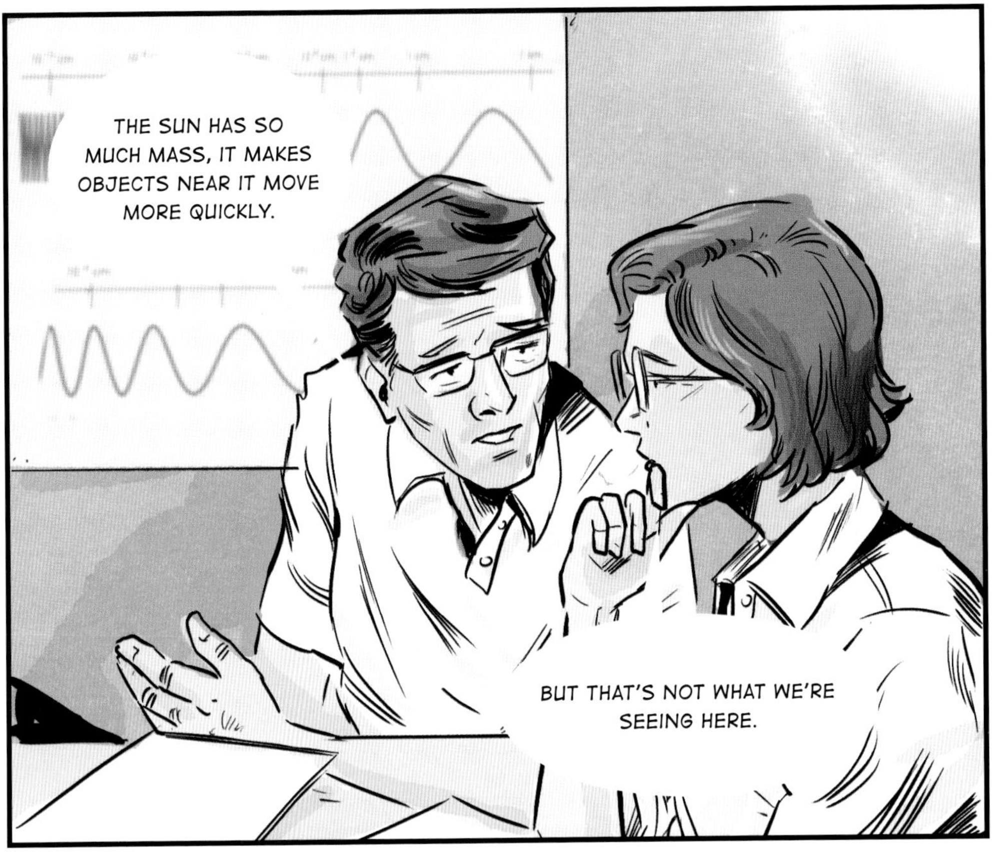
THE SUN HAS SO MUCH MASS, IT MAKES OBJECTS NEAR IT MOVE MORE QUICKLY.
BUT THAT'S NOT WHAT WE'RE SEEING HERE.

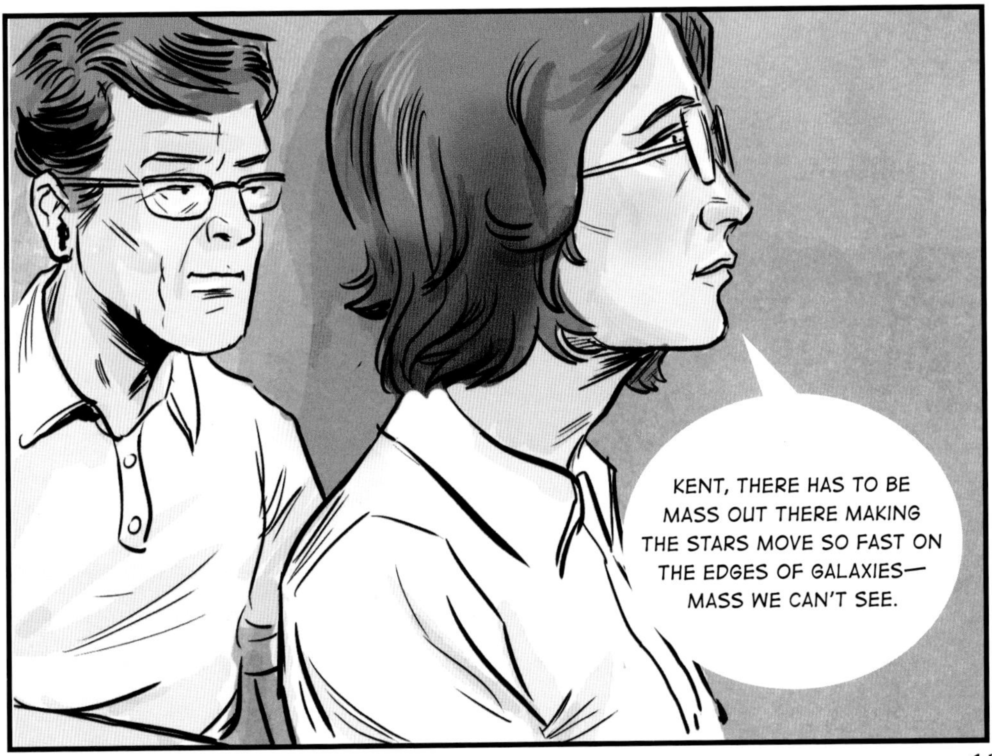
KENT, THERE HAS TO BE MASS OUT THERE MAKING THE STARS MOVE SO FAST ON THE EDGES OF GALAXIES—MASS WE CAN'T SEE.

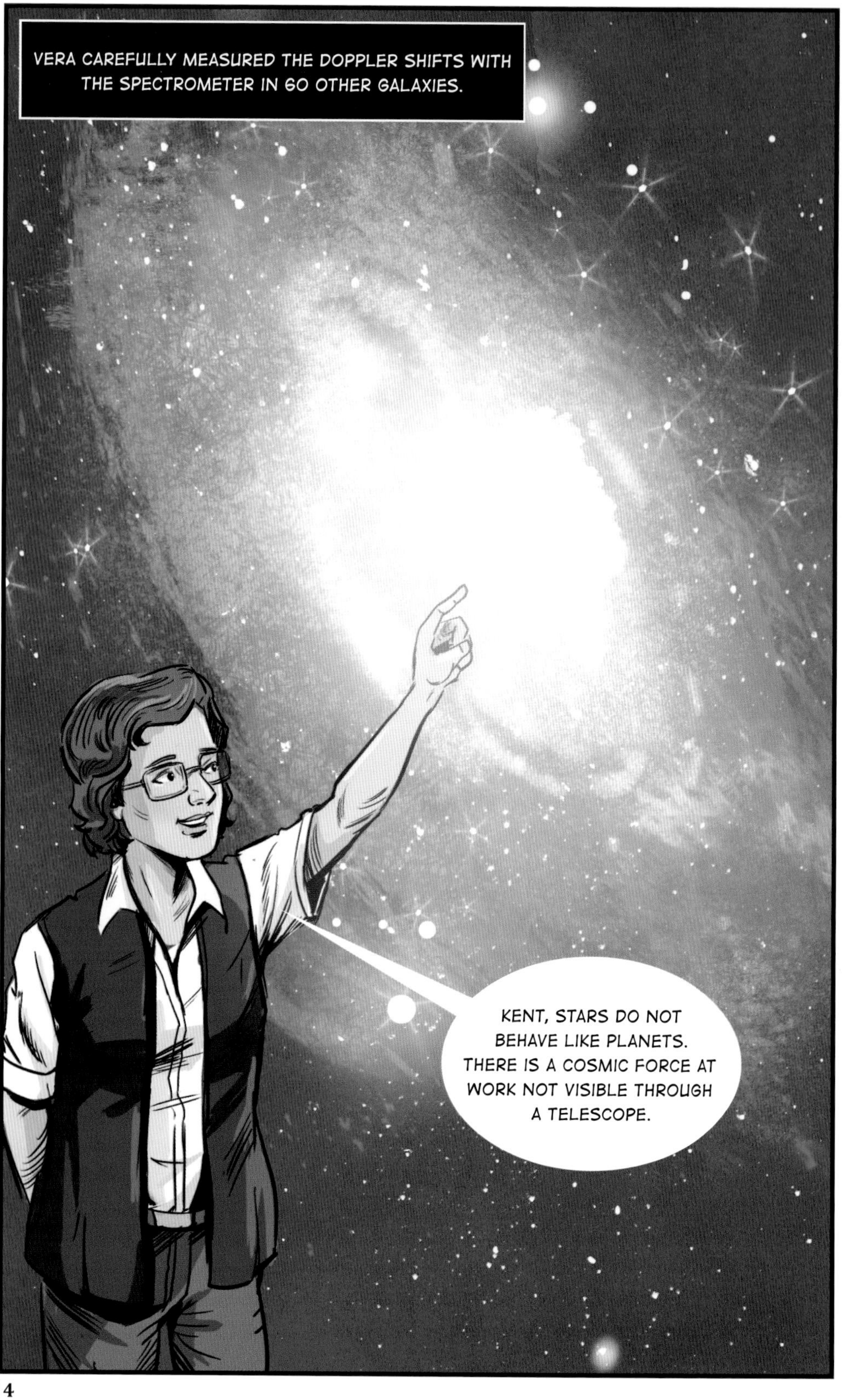
VERA CAREFULLY MEASURED THE DOPPLER SHIFTS WITH THE SPECTROMETER IN 60 OTHER GALAXIES.
KENT, STARS DO NOT BEHAVE LIKE PLANETS. THERE IS A COSMIC FORCE AT WORK NOT VISIBLE THROUGH A TELESCOPE.

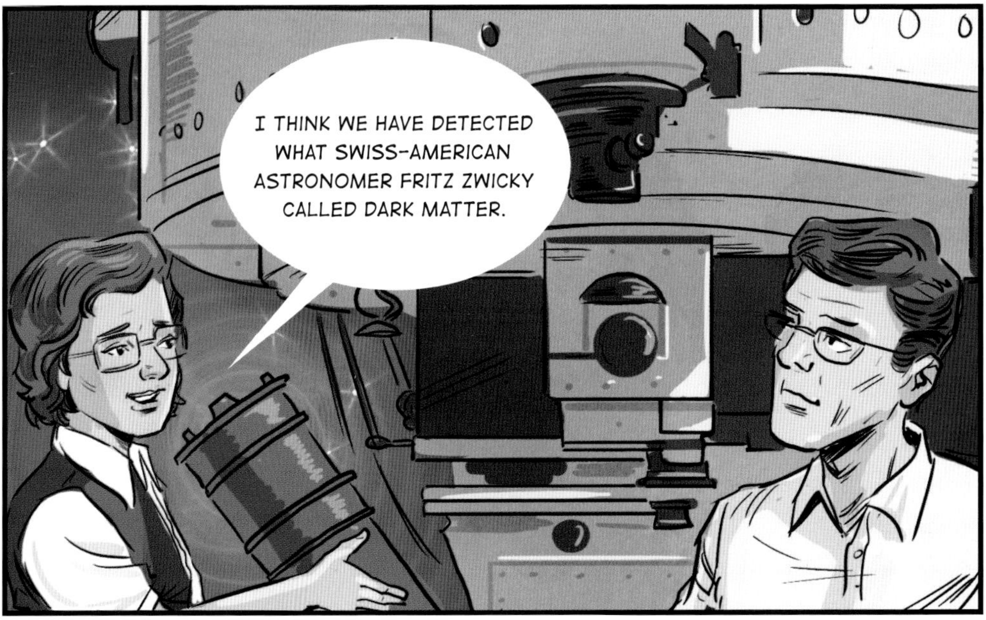
I THINK WE HAVE DETECTED WHAT SWISS-AMERICAN ASTRONOMER FRITZ ZWICKY CALLED DARK MATTER.

VERA AND KENT ATTACHED SPECTROGRAPHS TO POWERFUL TELESCOPES ALL OVER THE WORLD. THEY MEASURED MOVEMENT OF THE STARS AT DIFFERENT DISTANCES FROM THE CENTERS OF GALAXIES. EACH TIME, THEY CAME TO EXACTLY THE SAME CONCLUSION: THE EDGES OF THE GALAXIES MOVED AT THE SAME SPEED AS THE CENTERS OF THE GALAXIES. THIS CONTRADICTED SIR ISAAC NEWTON'S LAWS OF MOTION, WHICH PREDICTED THAT THE INNER STARS WOULD MOVE MORE QUICKLY AND THAT THE OUTER STARS WOULD MOVE MORE SLOWLY.

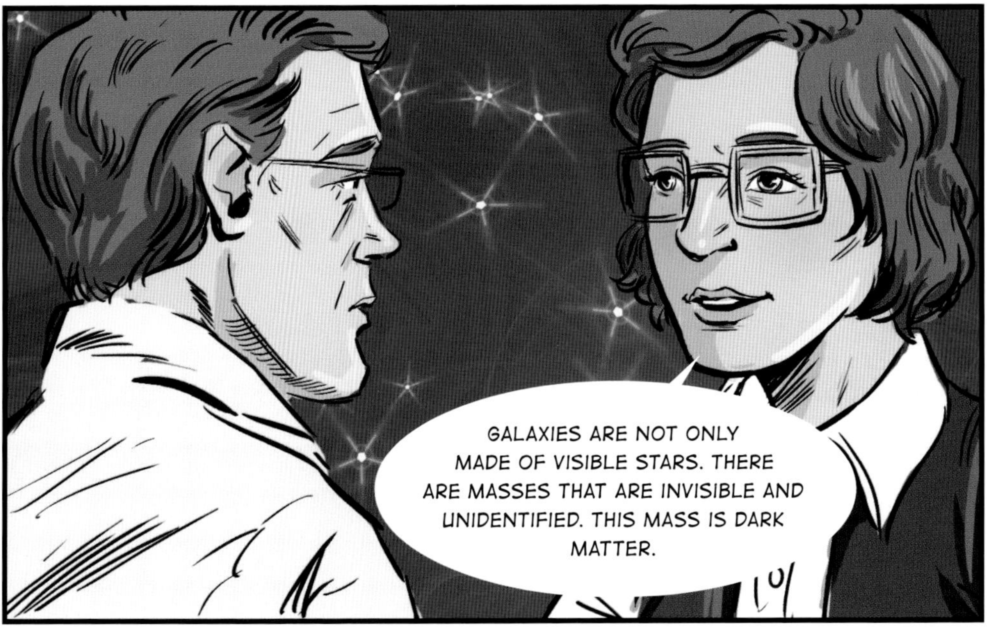
GALAXIES ARE NOT ONLY MADE OF VISIBLE STARS. THERE ARE MASSES THAT ARE INVISIBLE AND UNIDENTIFIED. THIS MASS IS DARK MATTER.

VERA CONTINUED TO STUDY GALAXIES. IN 1992, SHE DISCOVERED A GALAXY IN WHICH HALF THE STARS ORBITED IN ONE DIRECTION AND THE OTHER HALF ORBITED IN THE OPPOSITE DIRECTION. SHE CALLED IT AN INTERMINGLED GALAXY.

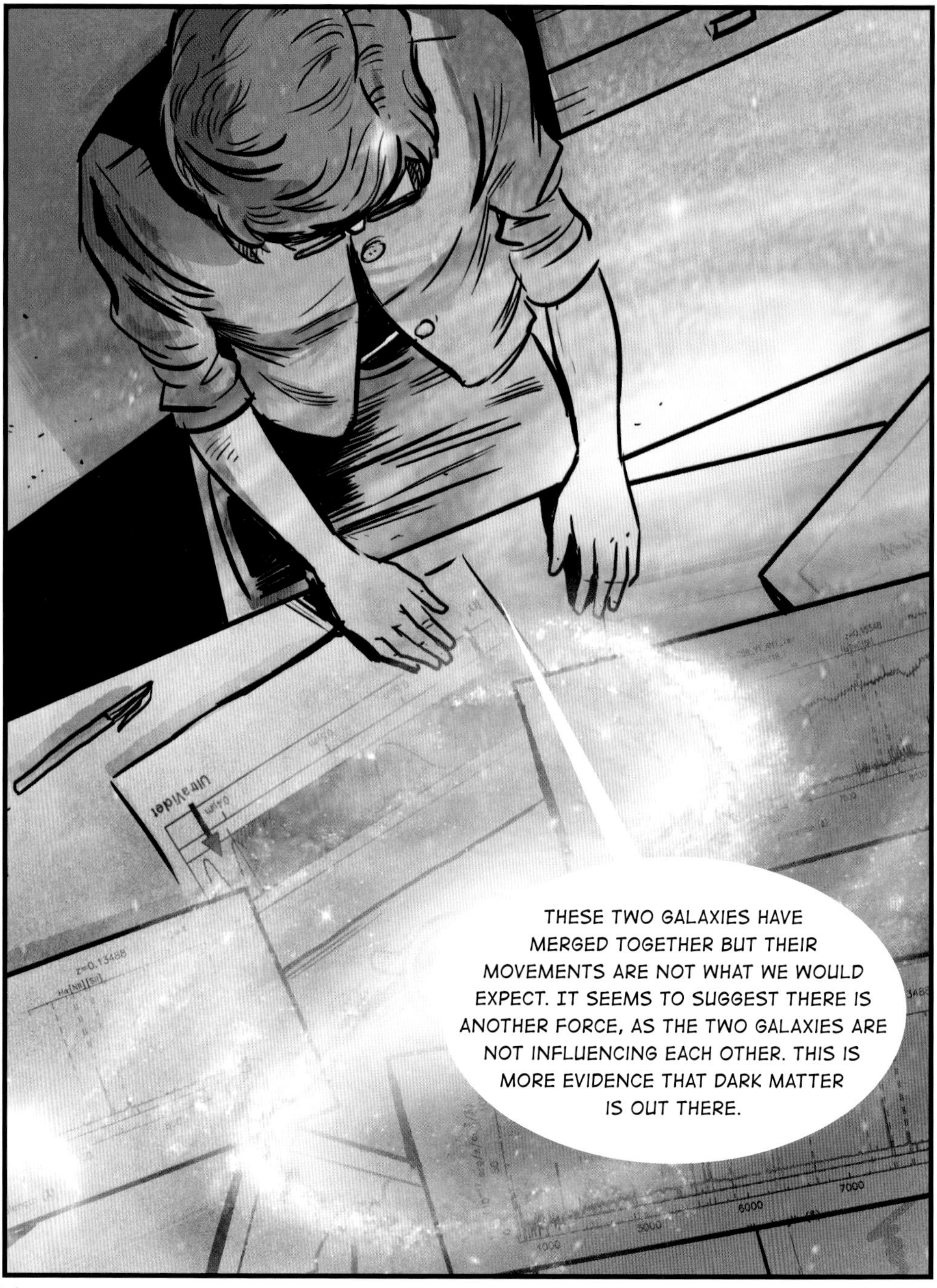
THESE TWO GALAXIES HAVE MERGED TOGETHER BUT THEIR MOVEMENTS ARE NOT WHAT WE WOULD EXPECT. IT SEEMS TO SUGGEST THERE IS ANOTHER FORCE, AS THE TWO GALAXIES ARE NOT INFLUENCING EACH OTHER. THIS IS MORE EVIDENCE THAT DARK MATTER IS OUT THERE.

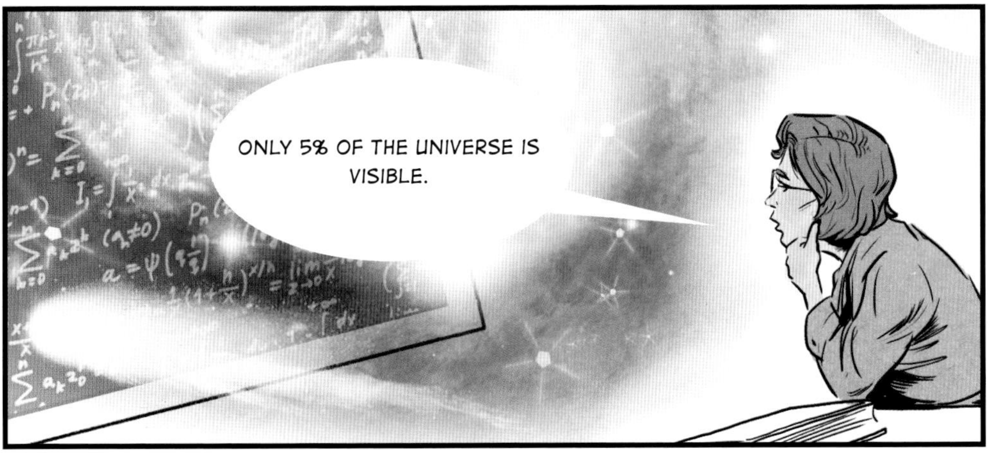
ONLY 5% OF THE UNIVERSE IS VISIBLE.

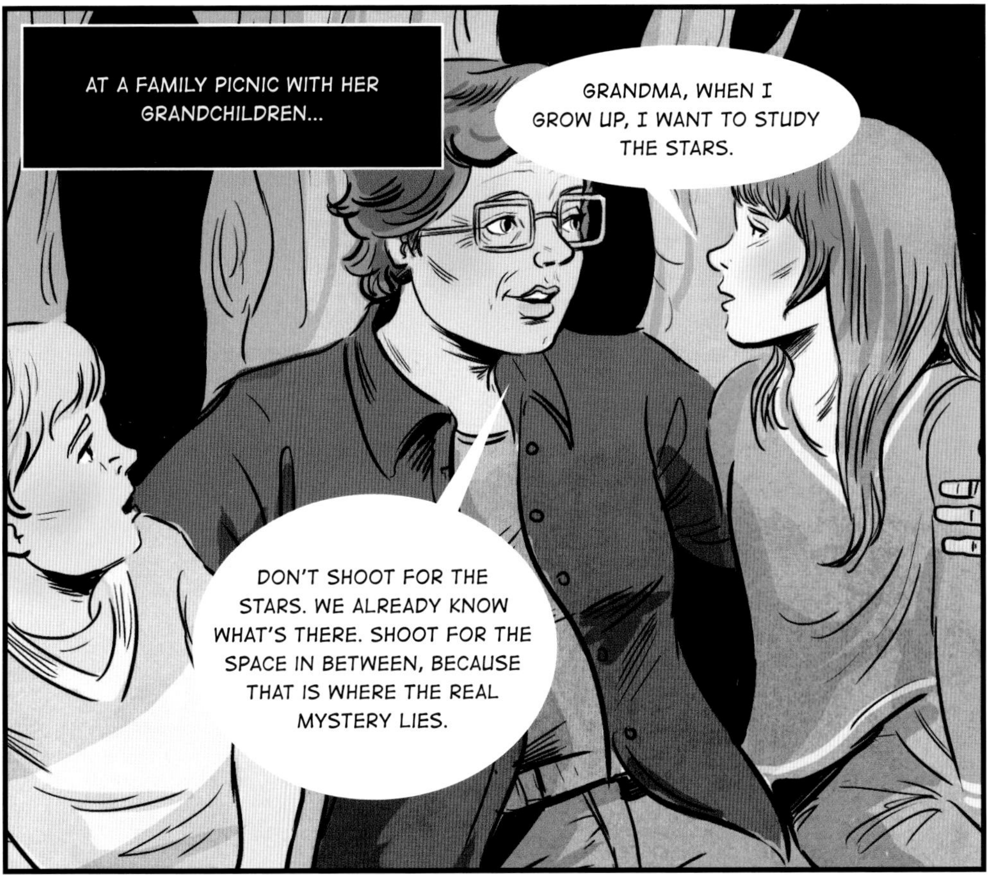
AT A FAMILY PICNIC WITH HER GRANDCHILDREN...
GRANDMA, WHEN I GROW UP, I WANT TO STUDY THE STARS.
DON'T SHOOT FOR THE STARS. WE ALREADY KNOW WHAT'S THERE. SHOOT FOR THE SPACE IN BETWEEN, BECAUSE THAT IS WHERE THE REAL MYSTERY LIES.

VERA'S WORK IS IMPORTANT BECAUSE SHE DISCOVERED THAT GALAXIES DO NOT ROTATE THE WAY SCIENTISTS PREDICTED. THIS SUPPORTS THE THEORY THAT SOME OTHER FORCE IS AT WORK. THIS FORCE IS DARK MATTER.

INDEX

A
Aristarchus of Samos 21, 25
Aristotle   9, 35
atomic bombs   86

B
Becquerel, Henri   94
Brownian motion   82

C
cancer   102–103
Carpenter, Martha Stahr
                      118–119
Cline, Dr. Henry   53
color wheel   40
Copernicus, Nicolaus 20–31
Covington, Syms   60–62
Crick, Francis   104–115
Curie, Marie   92–103
Curie, Pierre   93, 95, 98

D
dark matter   125, 126–127
Darwin, Charles   56–67
Descartes, René   35
DNA   104–115
Doppler effect   121

E
Earth
    circumference   9–17
    tilt   18, 25, 26–27
Einstein, Albert   80–91
electrometer   98
E=MC^2 86
equivalence principle 86–89
Eratosthenes   8–19, 25

F
fermentation   68–70
Fitzroy, Captain Robert 58
Ford, Kent   120–125
Franklin, Rosalind
          106–111, 113, 115

G
galaxies, motion of 119–127
Galileo   31
general relativity   90–91

Gosling, Raymond
104, 106, 107, 110–111
Grossman, Marcel   86–87

H
Habicht, Conrad   84–85
heliocentric theory   20–31
Henderson, Dr. Donald A.
                           55
Henslow, John   58
Hooke, Robert
             36, 40, 42, 43

J
Jenner, Edward   44–55, 79
Jenner, Robert   51

K
Kepler, Johannes   31

L
light
    particle theory of 34–43
    speed of   83
Line, Francis   41
Lucas, Father Anthony   41

M
map of world, first   19
Mariotte, Édme   43
mass-energy
equivalence theory   86
Meister, Joseph   79
moon, the   25

N
Napoleon III, Emperor   78
natural selection   60–67
Nelmes, Sarah   46–47
Newton, Isaac   32–43, 125

O
Osiander, Andreas   29–30

P
particle theory of light
                        34–43
Pasteur, Louis   68–79
Pasteur, Marie

69–72, 73, 74–75
Phipps, James   48–49
photoelectric effect   82
polonium   98
Pouchet, Felix   76
Ptolemy   20, 21, 28

R
radioactivity   94–103
radium   98
rainbows   38–39
Randall, John   104, 106
reflective telescope   39
Rheticus, Georg Joachim
                     29–30, 31
Röntgen, Wilhelm   94
Rubin, Vera   116–127

S
Schöner, Johannes   31
seasons   26–27
smallpox vaccine   44–55
Solovine, Maurice   84–85
special relativity   84–85
spectrum   38
Spencer, Herbert   67
supergalactic plane   119
survival of the fittest   67

T
Talmey, Max   80
telescopes   31, 39
thought experiments 81–82

W
Wallace, Alfred Russell
                        65–66
Watson, James   104–115
Wilkins, Maurice   104, 106,
                     111–112

X
X-ray diffraction
          106–107, 109, 110
X-rays   100–102

Z
Zwicky, Fritz   125